X

SUDDENLY
PSYCHIC

Other Books by Maureen Caudill

In Our Own Image: Building an Artificial Person (Oxford
University Press, 1992)

Understanding Neural Networks: Computer Explorations (MIT
Press, 1992)

Naturally Intelligent Systems (MIT Press, 1989)

SUDDENLY
PSYCHIC

A SKEPTIC'S JOURNEY

MAUREEN CAUDILL

HAMPTON ROADS
PUBLISHING COMPANY, INC.

Cover design by Frame25 Productions
Cover art by Erick N. c/o Shutterstock

"The Journey." Dream Work copyright ©1986 by Mary Oliver.
Used by permission of Grove/Atlantic, Inc.

Hampton Roads Publishing Company, Inc.
1125 Stoney Ridge Road
Charlottesville, VA 22902

434-296-2772
fax: 434-296-5096
e-mail: hrpc@hrpub.com
www.hrpub.com

If you are unable to order this book from your local
bookseller, you may order directly from the publisher.
Call 1-800-766-8009, toll-free.

Library of Congress Cataloging-in-Publication Data

Caudill, Maureen.
  Suddenly psychic : a skeptic's journey / Maureen Caudill.
      p. cm.
  Summary: "A firsthand account by a scientist who began to experience scientifically
impossible psychic phenomena, such as spoon-bending, remote viewing, and channeling.
Offers evidence that "paranormal" abilities are a normal part of human consciousness and
anyone can learn them"--Provided by publisher.
  Includes bibliographical references and index.
  ISBN 1-57174-501-7 (6 x 9 tp : alk. paper)
  1. Parapsychology and science. 2. Psychic ability. 3. Caudill, Maureen. I. Title.
BF1045.S33C38 2006
133.8--dc22
                                2006026169

ISBN 1-57174-501-7
10 9 8 7 6 5 4 3 2 1
Printed on acid-free paper in the United States

Dedication

For David,
with love.

In Memory of
Charles Butler

The Journey

by Mary Oliver

One day you finally knew
what you had to do, and began,
though the voices around you
kept shouting
their bad advice—
though the whole house
began to tremble
and you felt the old tug
at your ankles.
"Mend my life!"
each voice cried.
But you didn't stop.
You knew what you had to do,
though the wind pried
with its stiff fingers
at the very foundations,
though their melancholy
was terrible.

It was already late
enough, and a wild night,
and the road full of fallen
branches and stones.
But little by little,
as you left their voices behind,
the stars began to burn
through the sheets of clouds,
and there was a new voice
which you slowly
recognized as your own,
that kept you company
as you strode deeper and deeper
into the world,
determined to do
the only thing you could do—
determined to save
the only life that you could save.

Table of Contents

Acknowledgments

I admit it. This book wasn't my idea originally. I had to be dragged into this project, kicking and screaming and complaining all the way, by my friend, Frank DeMarco, who clearly knew what was best for me better than I did. (See, Frank? I admit it!) He is the best of friends and a brilliant editor too, and his faith in me and in my writing humbles me—none of which will in any way diminish my determination to convince him to pay off on lunch bets, real or imaginary.

I am twice-blessed with an incredibly brave agent, Bill Gladstone of Waterside Productions, Inc. Bill agreed to represent me based on absolutely nothing except Frank's confidence in me and a synchronistic coincidence. Thank you, Bill!

My deepest thanks also go to Deb Aaron, roommate par excellence, and an incredibly powerful energy worker. Her skills elevated mine, her attention and companionship proved to be a steady rudder on a shifting ocean of exploration. I would never have gotten so far without her.

Another word of thanks goes to a super friend of many years, Caro Dosé Birchfield. She provided a willing read and wonderful comments, as she always does. We've seen each other through a great deal in the past 20 years, and her friendship is very dear to me.

I also must certainly mention the wonderful people at The Monroe Institute (TMI). Everyone there, starting with the housekeeping staff and going all the way to Laurie Monroe herself, is incredibly supportive to all who pass through the TMI doors. I have little family remaining, but the TMI folks are the family of my heart. Laurie Monroe, Skip Atwater, Dar Miller, Shirley Bliley, Karen Viar, all the trainers and staff, I adore each and every one of them. If you haven't had the chance to go to one of TMI's programs, I heartily recommend that you do so as soon as possible. If you have been to a program there, you know what I'm talking about.

Robert Bruce is also deserving of my thanks. (Yet another thing I have to thank Frank for is providing me with the opportunity to meet Robert Bruce.) The work Robert has done in developing simple, easy to learn methods to increase and control subtle energies is phenomenal. I found his knowledge stellar and his charm boundless. I learned some great jokes from him too; one or two are even repeatable in polite company.

Last, but far from least, I thank David Elam for more than I can possibly say; for hours and hours of mind-stretching, enthralling conversation; for brilliant ideas and superb creative suggestions; for introducing me to the joys of both Wilber and wine tasting. And when I occasionally came back from TMI still just a teensy bit "out there" in the metaphysical realms, for spending endless hours talking me down until I no longer required *Babel fish* (see glossary) translations between me and the rest of the world. I'm sure somewhere there exists a bartender or wine steward who actually believes David's explanations that the process of pouring wine down my throat was really a method of "sobering me up." Thanks, love. I needed that.

1

Gateway to Strangeness

This is the story of a journey of the mind, of the spirit, of the heart. It is also a story of how I have tried to reconcile the places I've seen and the experiences I've had—all of which are far stranger than the Orient must have seemed to Marco Polo—with what I thought I knew before I began. The result of my journey, which I am still taking, is that I now know that everything I thought I understood about the world, life, and the universe is in question. The beliefs that I built my life around have crumbled under my feet as I walked this path. I have questioned everything about my life, beginning with the "facts" of the world and ending with my philosophy and theology.

Christopher Vogler in *The Writer's Journey* outlined a mythic structure for storytelling that's based on Joseph Campbell's study of world mythology. Good stories of all kinds, Vogler contends, have the same basic structure throughout the world, across all cultures. They start with a sense of the Hero's ordinary world—what is his (or her) life like just before things start to happen? Then comes the call to adventure—a call to step outside the realm of the ordinary to do extraordinary, even heroic, things. Our Hero generally initially refuses the call and can only be persuaded to answer it by increasingly dire circumstances, or the advice from a mentor. And so on.

My life has been like that. I was an ordinary person who received a call to adventure—and refused it. Years later, that call was repeated, under more dire circumstances. And this time . . . I accepted. I set out on a journey to go somewhere—I didn't know where—and to do something—I didn't know what. It was, in fact, my own personal Hero's quest. I haven't yet reached the end of my story, so I don't yet know if I will be able to return the elixir—the goal of the Hero's quest—to my ordinary world. Perhaps I'll succeed; perhaps I won't. Either way, the journey itself is the story—and the journey is what matters, not the result.

So how did my journey finally begin? With a call to adventure, a call to walk through a gateway to a special world. . . .

I am more than my physical body. Because I am more than physical matter, I can perceive that which is greater than the physical world.

—the beginning of the Gateway Affirmation

I first encountered these words several years ago when I attended a six-day residential program conducted at The Monroe Institute in Faber, Virginia. I felt more than a little uncomfortable with them on that first hearing. I didn't honestly know what I was doing attending a spiritual retreat as my first true vacation in many years.

At the time, I was a senior scientist and project manager for a major Department of Defense contractor, doing research and development in artificial intelligence and neural networks—computing systems that mimic the brain. My training in college and graduate school was in physics and mathematics; my career since then had been exclusively in computer science, with a foray or two into the structure of the brain deriving from my specialization in neural networks. I'd never had a psychic experience, and didn't believe in such things.

My advisor and mentor in college wasn't just a physicist, but an experimental physicist who thought theoreticians were way too "out there" to be trusted. If you couldn't measure a phenomenon, pick it up, weigh it, put a voltmeter on it, or do some such thing, it simply didn't exist in his worldview—and he had the lectures and examples to prove it. By the time I graduated as a University Scholar and *summa cum laude* in physics with the obligatory math minor, I too was convinced that physical reality was all there was. Psychics and their claimed capabilities might well be entertaining, in the way a stage magician's act is entertaining, but they mostly were hoaxes perpetrated on a gullible public. Or so I thought.

I'd never had anything even approximating a psychic experience. I'd never seen a UFO. I didn't believe in alien abductions—sleep paralysis and a desperate need for attention was my considered opinion as the cause of those incidents. Near death experiences? The last dying gasps of a brain shutting down. The mind itself? Merely an emergent behavioral property of the collection of a hundred billion or so electrochemically connected neurons, easily explained as soon as we had the biological detail and mathematics to describe it in the appropriate level of complexity. The mind was strictly biochemical and electrochemical. As for an afterlife, there simply wasn't one. As I'd opined to a co-worker in a discussion, when you're dead, you're dead, and that was that.

So what *was* I doing attending what could best be described as a "woo-woo" program? How did I come to be there at all?

The truth is, I didn't quite know. I'd gone through a deeply traumatic period a few years before. Taking a break from my career to look after my mother in her last months had left me financially ruined, traumatized, and grief-stricken—especially because in the space of four months, I suffered through three deaths of those very dear to me and discovered that a fourth was mortally ill. I had two sets of medical bills and funeral costs to pay, and I'd gone completely through my savings. I was broke, in despair, and had no idea how I'd recoup financially or personally. I was sure any light I perceived at the end of this dreary tunnel was only an oncoming train.

But somewhere in those bleak months, I'd accidentally run across a Buddhist saying that states, "with our minds we create our world." And I realized that my insistence on hanging onto a positive attitude with my mother and in doing what I felt was the right thing for her, no matter what the immediate cost to myself, had indeed reshaped the experience of becoming a de facto nurse—the last task I would *ever* have voluntarily undertaken—from a horrible experience to one that transformed me in a positive way. I realized I was a better person than when I started looking after her, more patient and more willing to help others. My own attitude had created that new reality.

It wasn't much of a personal revelation, but it was a start. From there I dabbled a bit in Buddhism, but was turned off by the reincarnation aspects. (Me? Live previous lives? Impossible! When you're dead, you're dead, remember?) I tried meditation, but couldn't turn off the "monkey chatter" in my head long enough to get anywhere.

But somewhere along the way a couple years later, I ran across a website for The Monroe Institute (TMI) and decided to order a set of their Gateway Experience CDs.[1] After trying them for a few weeks, I'd accomplished just enough to sense that they were important—very important. And so one early spring day I signed up for a Gateway Voyage residential program on the TMI campus in Faber, Virginia. I couldn't get away until August, but that was fine with me. It would take me a while to get up the nerve to attend such a program anyway. I'd never met or talked to anyone who'd ever been to a Gateway retreat and didn't have any real idea what the program was about.

Two days before I left, I found myself in the middle of a huge career crisis and in conflict with my immediate boss over, among other things, some ethical violations I'd reported on the project I was managing. By then my airfare was paid for—nonrefundable ticket of course—and the Gateway tuition was similarly paid for—nonrefundable also at that late stage. If I stayed home, I'd lose the money I'd already paid for the trip and program. If I went, I didn't have any idea if I'd have a job when I got back.

After thinking about it, I decided I badly needed the vacation, my first in a very long time. Even though I was sure the program itself would be a complete bust because I expected to spend the week obsessing about my work situation, at least I'd have a quiet time to gain some perspective and work out a plan for what to do next.

That's not quite the way things worked out. Almost from the moment I set foot on the TMI campus, it never occurred to me to wonder about what was happening back in California. And though the first day or so felt really peculiar—I'd never uttered an *Om* in my life, except perhaps when discussing Ohm's Law in electricity—by Monday of that week, strange things were happening . . . very strange things indeed.

The Strangeness Begins

The weirdness started right up front. While waiting for the program to begin, each of the 24 participants had a private intake interview with one of the two trainers. Things careened a little off-the-wall in that interview because the trainer interviewing me made a point of assuring me

---

[1]The website is www.monroeinstitute.org.

that only about 15 percent or so of Gateway participants go out-of-body during the program itself, and that I shouldn't set my expectations on doing so, or feel disappointed if that didn't happen for me.

Going out of my body? Oh, no! I obviously had wandered down the wrong rabbit hole! Anyway, what was an out-of-body experience, commonly referred to as an OBE, and why would anyone voluntarily want to do that?

Although I'd read Robert Monroe's books on his OBEs, it had never occurred to me to connect the strange, almost hallucinatory experiences he described with anything that would be in the program I'd signed up for.[2] The week hadn't even started, and already I clearly was in way over my head.

At the first session right after dinner Saturday night, we gathered in a large room and introduced ourselves. Here again, I could see I'd chosen the wrong venue for a vacation. Nearly everyone else was a bona fide New Ager, with years of meditation experience, healing, shamanic or Reiki background, leaving me as virtually the only "techie nerd" in the group.

Definitely I was in the wrong place.

I started wondering if I could leave and get any of my money back. Surely I'd do better fretting over my career issues at home, or even in a nice, innocuous motel room in Charlottesville, than here, surrounded by a bunch of strangers who took their *Oms* seriously.

Every skeptical bone in my body was convinced I was surrounded by a bunch of crazies—sincere crazies, maybe, and very *nice* crazies, but folks who definitely belonged in the lunatic fringe. No question about it. None of this stuff was real. None of it was true. And no one could make me believe that *resonant tuning* or playing with imaginary *energy bars* would do me or anyone else any good at all.[3]

And yet . . . by the end of that week—even as little as 48 hours into the program—everything looked very different. I could no longer count myself a skeptic of anything. Nor could I insist that psychics were all tricksters and hoaxers. You see, when you personally do magical things, you *know* that no trickery is involved.

---

[2]*Journeys Out of the Body, Far Journeys,* and *Ultimate Journey.* See the suggested reading at the back of the book for publication details.

[3]Check the glossary for definitions of terms that are unfamiliar.

And that was the essence of the program. No one told me what to believe. No one insisted I take anything on faith. They merely gave me the opportunity to experience altered states of consciousness in a safe, controlled fashion under the guidance of compassionate and caring facilitators, then let me draw my own conclusions from my own experiences.

♥

So what did I experience in that life-changing week?

I found myself taking messages from my best friend's dead mother, whom I never met, that meant nothing whatsoever to me but that were deeply meaningful and specific to my friend.

I discovered I could remote view—describing in perfect detail two separate blind targets. The first target was presented to us only with its latitude and longitude coordinates. I'm not a pilot, so latitude and longitude don't mean much to me. Besides, the target in that case was a specific structure, which I not only identified correctly—even naming it—but I also drew two sketches of it which corresponded precisely to the perspectives of the two images we were shown when it was time to check our work. For the second target, the trainers couldn't remember the longitude and latitude coordinates, so they just told us to describe the intended target, which was "somewhere in North America." Well, that certainly narrowed it down a lot, didn't it? It didn't matter; I described that one perfectly too, sketching it as if I had the picture directly in front of me. Again my sketches matched the exact perspectives of the images of the target we were later shown. Spooky. Downright spooky.

I did psychic healing on my desperately ill cat from 2500 miles away, literally feeling my kidneys acting as dialysis machines for him and had the success of that effort confirmed—to the astonishment of the vet—when I took him in for his previously scheduled checkup the day after I returned from the program.

I received precognitive flashes throughout the entire week, constantly knowing exactly what would happen next even though the trainers specifically made a point of not "front loading" the participants with information about upcoming exercises.

I connected with my own deceased family members—human and pets—and got unexpected but consistent messages from them.

I was, in fact, psychic that week in a big way, demonstrating a wide variety of psychic skills. Somehow, in the course of six days, I'd gone from Psychic Zero to Psychic in one astounding leap.

And what about my job? The night before returning home, after the program was officially over, I sat out at the picnic table at TMI, looking up at the stars and wondering vaguely what had happened to my career during the week I'd been gone. Even as I asked the question, I was filled with a deep confidence that somehow, things would work out in my favor and all would be well.

In that one last, meaningful step, I was connected to the spiritual guidance that has remained with me ever since.

And things did work out just fine. Within two months of my return, I was transferred to a much happier division in a different group. I had a new project to work on, and best of all, my new office was only five minutes from my house instead of an hour's drive away.

But the changes in me were longer lasting and far more meaningful than a new work assignment. Shortly after my return, my best friend only half-jokingly asked if I were a "pod person" because my personality had changed so much. I no longer obsessed about my work. I was calmer, more serene about everything. I was happier, more loving, more patient, more forgiving, and an overall nicer person than before—all because of six days spent learning how to release the psychic that apparently lurked inside me.

It sounds crazy, doesn't it? In fact, it sounds so completely nuts, that you no doubt are wondering what kind of *Looney Toon* wrote this book. But scientific evidence is beginning to mount that such claims perhaps are not so crazy after all. There is evidence that the underlying structure of the physical universe isn't exactly as physicists have been claiming for the past few centuries. Maybe, just maybe, mystics and seers and psychics have actually had a better understanding of truth than science has given them credit for.

What Next?

My experiences learning how to access altered states of consciousness have totally changed the course of my life. I realized I could no longer view the world or the universe in the simplistic scientific terms I was used to. In fact, my faith in scientific views of the world had been shaken at its very foundations. I recognized that some serious retrenching of my entire belief structure about how the universe works was needed, to align what I was experiencing with what I had believed true.

I'd always been skeptical of magical claims, though with a moderately open mind that insisted I should at least listen to such claims and try to find the flaws in their logic. That's how I was trained to think, and I found this ultralogical, rational viewpoint worked well for my experience with the world. The problem I now had was that such a viewpoint no longer described the world I was experiencing. In fact, my direct personal observations about the outside world completely contradicted several fundamental laws of physics. Nor could I claim that the events were hoaxes—*I was the one doing these things!*

If I did something impossible, could I claim that it was a hoax? I *knew* I hadn't fudged anything at all on any of these experiences, even if they might not stand up to the ultrarigor that the scientific establishment demands of all paranormal evidence. I hadn't, after all, *intended* to conduct a scientifically rigorous experiment in the first place!

Each of these experiences, and many others, happened. I somehow had to explain them to myself, if no one else, despite the fact that they individually and collectively contravened quite a number of fundamental laws of physics, biology, and chemistry. How could I possibly resolve such conflicts?

Worse, in the months following that first residential program, as I continued to explore these new areas, the apparent violations of physical laws worsened and spread. More and more often I found myself doing things that by any rational measure were simply impossible.

I continued to explore those altered states, and as I learned to go into deeper and deeper meditative modes, I also began reading deeply in subjects ranging from theology to psychology, from quantum physics to New Age energy systems, in an attempt to understand what I was experiencing and how my experiences could correlate to the rational, scientific world I used to inhabit.

As I read more, and as I experienced deeper phenomena, I realized I had to make a choice. One option was to believe that I suddenly had become psychotic and totally out of touch with the real world. In that case I should immediately start psychotherapy and likely brace myself for an ultraquick admission to a psychiatric ward.

A second option was to believe that the experiential data I'd accumulated were either fake or incorrect. But the data were generated in a wide variety of locations and circumstances, both public and private, and with varying numbers of others present. Furthermore, my experiences seemed to be similar to those of many other people using similar technologies to access altered states. If my data were incorrect, so were everyone else's. Could we all be wrong?

The third option was to find a way to explain these phenomena in terms at least somewhat compatible with my hard science background.

I rejected the first option. I believe I am not psychotic. I am still perfectly functional in society at large, and I have generally dealt with the peculiar events I've experienced with reasonable aplomb. Occasionally my mind has been stretched beyond its previous borders, but I consider that a *good* thing because it makes me reconsider my philosophy and understanding of the world I live in and forces me to think deeply about issues that matter in fundamental ways. For these reasons I rejected the possibility that I am in any way psychotic or mentally disturbed.

I also do not believe that I have hoaxed myself. Most of the experiences I will describe were quite unexpected—often happening when I planned or anticipated doing something else entirely. And while an outside observer might list half a dozen ways the effects *could* have been simulated or faked, I *know* I did neither. I can't prove it to others, of course, but I have satisfied myself that I have in no way faked *anything* described in this book. Furthermore, the testimony of many other people describes very similar events they have independently experienced. These are honorable, trustworthy people, the vast majority of whom *do not talk about their experiences to most others* lest they be labeled charlatans and hoaxers. Like the little child who runs with scissors, I'm willing to take the chance of being pilloried for describing my experiences as truthfully as I can.

That leaves me with only a final option: I need to find a way to reconcile my strange experiences with the science I was trained to believe in and respect. Fifty years ago, I would either have had to label myself a psychotic or I'd have had to turn my back completely on science. Today, however, things aren't quite so grim, though admitting publicly to having psychic skills and experiences still takes a significant amount of courage. I can only trust that society—and science—has advanced to the point where at least some acceptance of psychic events is present without labeling the people who experience them as psychotic or deranged.

While no commonly accepted scientific theories *explain* any psychic skill, mounds of data validate the *existence* of those skills. As I began reading the scientific literature of paranormal phenomena, I realized that in spite of the debunkers' claims to the contrary, a *ton* of scientific, peer-reviewed, highly respectable evidence exists to support the reality of paranormal and psychic phenomena.[4]

Learning about all that data acted almost as a "permission slip" to my scientific self to let me begin to believe that I truly might be psychic. And I discovered that courageous researchers in fields from physics to psychology are beginning to build some notions of how those skills might possibly be supported by a new, deeper understanding of the universe and our minds.

But no matter what, I had taken an unalterable step in my own life. I could no more turn my back on my new psychic self than I could transform myself into a toad—or a superstar. (Darn!) I have continued to deepen my own spiritual growth and development and have watched my own skills and sensitivities blossom. I'm now an accredited non-residential trainer in the TMI technology and offer weekend workshops to introduce others to the richness that awaits them within their own minds. I serve as a poster child for those who did not have (or do not recall) early childhood psychic experiences, but who may still discover their skills later in life.

What This Book Is About

This book is both the story of my personal journey into psychic and spiritual realms and an invitation to you to begin a journey of your own. As Mary Oliver's wonderful poem "The Journey" expresses, *One day you finally knew / what you had to do, and began . . .* One day several years ago, some half-buried part of me knew what I had to do. From somewhere, I found the courage to begin doing it. And in so doing, I began my journey into a new world, a new way of sensing, a new way of being. Part of this book details some of the key steps I've taken and a handful of the impor-

---

[4]See Dean Radin's meticulous study of the scientific evidence for various psychic phenomena, *The Conscious Universe*, listed in the suggested reading list. He also includes a fascinating chapter outlining the reasons "professional skeptics" and "debunkers" of the field flatly refuse to acknowledge the existence of the copious scientific evidence supporting psychic phenomena. Although a bit dry and heavy with statistics and probability analyses, it nonetheless makes fascinating reading and is definitely worth the effort.

tant experiences I've encountered. Most of all, I've encountered myself on this journey, but quite a different self than I ever imagined myself to be.

Thus, one purpose of this book is to let you understand what it's like to be psychic. It's an attempt to convey to you exactly what it feels like, after half a lifetime denying that psychic powers are real, to have experiences that are labeled "psychic" if you're lucky and "psychotic" if you're not. I want to share with you what a remote viewing session feels like when you're doing it, or what communicating with spirit guides feels like, or what it's like to use your intentionality to funnel energy and cause a perfectly normal spoon or fork to become pliable and bend.

I'm going to review key milestones I've experienced in my journey from skeptic to psychic. It's important to understand why these specific events stand out in my mind. Typically, these are events that blew holes in my standard scientific belief system, and I'll point out those holes as we go. In other words, these are events I have to reconcile with scientific theories and thoughts if I am to bring those two opposing world views into any kind of alignment.

Despite my new psychic persona, the scientist in me hasn't been eliminated. I also will explore a number of scientific theories that may help explain how such psychic events occur. It's entirely possible that science eventually will accept these phenomena—and possibly sooner than you think.

I've tried to ease the scientific path as much as I can by keeping the explanations as clear and simple as possible while still being reasonably precise. I'll dip into a variety of scientific disciplines along the way, ranging from psychology to neurobiology and from cosmology to quantum physics. Don't let those throw you. None of what is presented here should be difficult to grasp for anyone who has a lively curiosity and an interest in the subject. My goal is to make it comprehensible—to bring phenomena that are at the moment mysterious, esoteric, and perhaps even a little scary into the outer fringes of what we either may already understand or could possibly understand with some additional research.

Thus, by presenting you with a credible outline of a possible scientific basis for these phenomena, I hope to give your logical, rational self "permission" to believe in them too.

I am neither a theologian nor a philosopher, but these experiences have forced me to address such topics. I want to reconcile my new psychic self not only with science, but also with my own humanity. As you'll see, profound psychic experiences open a boatload of fundamental questions: Who am I? Why am I here? What purpose does my life serve to myself, or to humanity at large? Where did I come from? And, most of all, where am I going?

These are questions humanity has asked since time immemorial. They echo throughout our greatest literature and resonate in philosophical treatises. But now, my answers to at least some of them are becoming clear. Those answers are personal to me, of course, but I believe the insights I've gained may help others in defining their own answers for their own lives. I hope this is the case.

So take a step or two into my mind and learn what becoming suddenly psychic really means. Discover what it feels like to find yourself doing unexpected and amazing things every day. Understand what open-minded scientists think may be the underlying theories that support those near-magical events. Perhaps then you'll grant yourself permission to do similarly incredible, astonishing, and miraculous things, too.

Now that we know what we have to do, let's begin.

2

Beyond Here There Be Dragons

Before I begin reviewing the anomalous and just plain weird experiences that have studded my life the past several years, I need to revisit one
key question. What on earth happened to me at that Gateway program to
spark the revolution that occurred—and is still occurring—within me?
What did the program at TMI do to me? What influence is so powerful that in a mere six days the scientific attitudes of a lifetime could be
upended like so many Lego blocks, and a whole new person constructed
out of the rubble?

I'm sure most of the other participants in the program did not experience the complete life-changing impact I did. As I mentioned before,
they already had a strong core set of beliefs and knowledge of the metaphysical realms. So to a large extent, the powerful effect Gateway had on
me no doubt was largely because I attended it at the exact moment when
I was ready for a change of attitude.

But there's more to it than that. The basis of the Gateway program
(and the TMI CDs and other products) is a technology developed and

refined over the past forty or so years, called Hemi-Sync.[5] Using Hemi-Sync, you learn to enter altered states of consciousness at will. Once in those altered states, you have access to information, talents, and guidance that simply aren't easily accessible to you otherwise. What you do with those is up to you. You can ignore them, or you can make them an integral part of your life.

So what is an "altered state of consciousness"? And isn't it dangerous?

No, it's not normally dangerous. In fact, we enter most altered states naturally and sometimes accidentally, at various times during the day. For example, transitioning between sleeping and waking, getting lost in a daydream or reverie, or dreaming during sleep are all examples of being conscious in a different way than our usual awake-alert state. Generally, we transition to these other types of consciousness in an uncontrolled way, but we can use a variety of techniques—for example, meditation, chanting, singing, dancing, drumming, and many other techniques—to *control* when we change our conscious awareness. The natural, uncontrolled changes in consciousness are trivial to do but often are unpredictable. Learning how to go into altered states of consciousness at will takes some practice and effort—or the assistance of a technology like TMI's Hemi-Sync.

Please realize also that although I learned to access altered states of consciousness using Hemi-Sync, any of the other methods can accomplish much the same thing. Yet Hemi-Sync and TMI are so much a part of my personal journey that they figure powerfully in this narrative, so it's important to understand how Hemi-Sync works.

I'm sure you've had the experience of listening to music that has a powerful beat and finding yourself tapping your toe in time to it or your fingers drumming to the same rhythm. Perhaps, if you were really drawn into the sound, you were even breathing or walking or chewing in time to that rhythm. We all have a tendency to synchronize to compelling rhythms.

The brain does the same thing. It will tend to synchronize the brainwaves it produces to any rhythmic beat it perceives that matches the frequency pattern of a natural brainwave state. You can use this characteristic to guide your brain into altered states of consciousness. The trick is to make sure the perceived pattern corresponds to a natural brainwave pattern for the altered state of consciousness you're trying to enter.

---

[5]Hemi-Sync is a registered trademark of Monroe Products, Lovingston, Virginia.

Scientists generally group natural brainwave frequencies into four major bands, labeled Beta, Alpha, Theta, and Delta. A fifth band, Gamma refers to extremely high-frequency brainwaves, and its existence and function are somewhat controversial.

The Beta state corresponds to the awake-alert state that we usually are in when we're walking around in the daytime. In this state, the primary frequencies produced by the brain are in the range of 14 to about 35 Hertz (abbreviated Hz, where one Hertz is the same as one cycle every second).

The Alpha state is a day-dreamy or light trance type of state, such as when you're sitting, staring out the window, just enjoying the moment and not thinking much about anything at all. That state corresponds to frequencies primarily in the 7 Hz to 14 Hz range.

The Theta state is a light sleep state or a meditative or trance state that corresponds to dominant brainwave frequencies of about 4 Hz to about 7 Hz.

Finally, the deepest state is the Delta state, which is a deep sleep state, or a very deep meditative state. When in Delta, your dominant brainwaves have slowed down so their primary frequencies are between 0.5 Hz and about 4 Hz.

So, going into a meditative or altered state of consciousness typically means that you're slowing down your brainwaves from the active-alert Beta frequencies to slower, more meditative frequencies.

Obviously, then, if the brain synchronizes its brainwaves to frequencies it hears and you want to induce a meditative or trance-like state, for example, to go into Theta state, all you have to do is listen to a Theta-frequency tone, right?

Well, not quite. Human hearing can't perceive Theta frequency tones. The audible range for human hearing is about 20 Hz to 20,000 Hz. Trying to listen to, say, a 5 Hz Theta tone won't work—your ears can't hear it. In fact, the only brainwave frequencies you can directly hear are in the Beta awake-alert state, which isn't very useful for meditative exercises.

That's where the technology of binaural beats comes in. Binaural beats were discovered about 100 years ago. They work very simply. If you're listening to sounds on headphones, and in one ear you hear a 100 Hz tone—well within the human audible range—and in the other ear you hear a 105 Hz tone—also within the human audible range—what your brain actually perceives isn't the 100 Hz or the 105 Hz tones. Instead, the brain picks up the *beat* frequency—the *difference* between the two tones.

In other words, your brain "hears" a 5 Hz signal, a pure Theta tone. You have literally heard the unhearable.

So using binaural beats, you can hear any natural brainwave frequencies you want—and that's what Hemi-Sync offers. The actual implementation is more complicated than this, of course. The various Hemi-Sync CDs and tapes include not single brainwave frequencies, but complex mixtures of frequencies—typically 15 to 20 or more frequencies to construct truly natural brainwave patterns that correspond to specific altered states of consciousness. But no matter how complex the frequency patterns are, they still are constructed using that simple binaural beat concept. And by changing the patterns of signals you listen to—i.e., changing to a different CD or tape exercise—you can preselect the specific altered state of consciousness you want to enter.

TMI numbers the various altered states as Focus levels. Focus 10 or F-10, the first state you're taught to access, is the state where your mind is awake and alert while your body is deeply asleep. Sounds contradictory, doesn't it? Yet we all go in and out of that state at least twice every day. For example, when you're dropping off to sleep and your body begins to feel very tired and heavy but you're still mentally awake, you've just entered F-10. Similarly, in the morning there's a brief period where your mind has awakened, yet your body is still heavy and immobile. Sometimes this is called "sleep paralysis" because it feels as if you literally can't move. That's also F-10.

If you sustain F-10 for a while, instead of passing through the state briefly as part of the falling-asleep or waking-up cycle, sometimes you may hear yourself snore! I've seen people absolutely convinced that they couldn't possibly have been in any altered state at all because the person next to them was snoring and distracting them. What they don't realize is that *they* were the ones snoring up a storm. And they can't accept that because if they were snoring, they'd have to be asleep, and they couldn't possibly have been asleep because the snoring was keeping them awake. Sometimes, it literally takes a tape recorder or video camera to convince these people that they truly were in F-10—snoring away!

For many meditators using conventional methods, this is the key trance state, and most meditators never learn to go beyond this state. With Hemi-Sync, however, F-10 barely scratches the surface of what you can experience.

Focus 12 or F-12 is the next important altered state. In F-12, you're in a state of expanded awareness, where you have access to information and understanding from far beyond your five physical senses.

An example from a workshop I led a few years ago will clarify what I mean. One couple in that workshop was deeply skeptical of everything about altered states. At the end of the Introduction to F-12 exercise, they both came out of it complaining bitterly that they hadn't been able to get into the meditation at all because there was so much noise from a car radio installation company nearby. The music was blaring from that company, they complained, and it distracted them so much they couldn't concentrate on the exercise. They suggested that I should never again hold this workshop in that particular location (a rented hotel suite) because it clearly was far too noisy for participants to gain anything from the program.

I listened to this and smiled. There was indeed a car radio installation business nearby—but it was well over a quarter-mile away. There were three buildings between the ground-floor suite where the workshop was being held and where they were installing radios. The windows of the suite we were in were closed tightly. And my cotrainer and I were fully awake and alert the entire time of the exercise, monitoring how people were doing—and we never heard a thing. This couple's hearing had been so enhanced by their access to F-12 that they didn't even realize they were hearing the unhearable.

Focus 15 or F-15, the next state presented in Gateway, is the state of no time. While F-12 allows you to access information that is from any place—far beyond what you can directly sense with your five physical senses, F-15 allows you to access any *time*. You can get information about the past—or the future. You can go anywhere and, even more astonishingly, any *when*.

As one example, in one excursion I took in F-15, I visited the cockpit of Amelia Earhart's airplane during her final, fatal ride over the Pacific. I might have chalked up the experience to mere fantasy and imagination—except I came out of the session having explicitly, and correctly, cited the name of her navigator and the name of the island she was headed for at the time her plane disappeared. Yes, it *could* have been a coincidence, and skeptics no doubt will label it so. But I have no conscious memory of knowing that information prior to that session. Nor is Amelia Earhart a special interest of mine; I couldn't remember any particular mention of her or exposure to her sad fate for years prior to that particular session. It's not scientifically valid proof of anything, but it makes you wonder—it certainly made *me* wonder.

The final altered state presented in the Gateway Voyage program is Focus 21 or F-21, the bridge state. This one is hard to describe except that it's the bridge between physical reality states and nonphysical states. This state is often used to consult with inner guidance, or to communicate with those who have passed on. This is, for example, the state I was in when I got messages from my best friend's deceased mother.

The altered states of consciousness that I learned to enter while at the Gateway program are all natural states. Throughout history, nearly every culture has had some form of ritual designed to put people into such states: prayer, meditation, chanting, drumming, dancing, singing, or ingesting chemicals. Whatever the mechanism, the goal is to access states of being that are hard to access as part of our everyday reality.

The difference between those techniques and TMI's technology is that Hemi-Sync provides a safe, reliable, repeatable tool for entering any of these states. The technology has been independently scientifically validated in peer-reviewed studies—with results reported in major scientific journals—by organizations like St. Andrews Hospital in Scotland and Mount Sinai Hospital in New York.

In fact, the technological and scientifically validated aspects of Hemi-Sync are likely part of the reason it worked so well for me. They acted like *Good Housekeeping* seals of approval to my logical, rational brain, thus giving my conscious mind "permission" to let myself experience what I did.

You don't ingest anything with Hemi-Sync. You don't have to dance or smoke or chant or sing for hours. You simply put on a set of headphones, relax, and let the signals you hear guide you into an altered state of consciousness. The whole process usually takes only 10 or 15 minutes—and it can be confirmed with physiological monitoring.

Of course, the truth is, it doesn't matter how you access these altered states. Other tools accomplish much the same thing. And if you like, you can also use nontechnological mechanisms: You can pray, meditate, chant, etc. until you get there. But I don't like having to work that hard.

Furthermore, once you learn how to access these states reliably using Hemi-Sync, you can enter them at any time or place. You simply *choose* to go into, for example, F-12—and you're there. Once you know how to do it, it's simple and doesn't require any support from Hemi-Sync signals. All it takes is a little practice and an intention to do it.

These focus levels are the basic tools. I worked with them for months after that first residential program. Later I'll expand this repertoire to yet-higher realms of altered states. But for the moment, this is enough to help you understand the initial events that started me down my path through the psychic realms. The one thing to remember is that accessing altered states merely means changing the state of the brain by changing the frequency pattern of brainwaves it produces.

So . . . how *does* the brain work? The brain contains a special kind of cell called a neuron.[6] These cells are different from other cells in the body, just as a muscle cell is different from a blood cell. Neurons have one very special property: they form connections to each other. In fact, they form a *lot* of connections. Any given neuron may connect to between 10,000 and 100,000 other neurons. So while each of us may have a total of about 100 billion neurons, there are as many as *ten million billion* connections.

Connections are important in the brain because it is the *connections* that store information and memories, not the neurons themselves. The more connections you have, the more memories and information you can store. Furthermore, the neurons in the cerebral cortex are arranged as a crumpled flat sheet of a few layers of neurons—perhaps as few as six or eight layers in all.[7] Different perceptual functions are performed in different sections of that flat sheet. Let me give an example.

Suppose you see the word "table" on the printed page. To perceive it, light reflected from the page enters your eyes, where it strikes the retina at the back of the eyeball. The retina has light-sensitive cells—rods and cones—that get excited and send signals up the optic nerve to the brain where the visual system recognizes a known symbol: the word "table."

This recognition probably produces a mental image of a table—a kind of imaginary picture of what a typical table looks like to you. That image has a set of characteristics that you associate with tables

---

[6]There are several different kinds of neural cells, but for my purposes here, I'll consider only those in the cerebral cortex, the primary reasoning portion of the brain.

[7]The cerebral cortex is the thinking portion of the brain, as opposed to older (in an evolutionary sense) brain structures that handle functions like emotional responses, breathing, walking, and the like. The crumpled structure is a way of fitting the large flat sheet of the cerebral cortex into the relatively small space of the skull.

in general. For example, it's probably a piece of furniture with a flat top and one or more legs to raise it above the level of the floor. Those characteristics are stored in a set of feature detector connections in the brain. When that set of feature detectors is stimulated by the imaginary picture of a table you've associated with the word table, it in turn stimulates a set of neural connections associated with the general concept of "being a table."

Thus, when you see the word "table" you process it through a series of mental functions to produce, in turn, an image of a generic table, a set of features that correspond to general table-ness, and a generalized concept of being a table.

Once you've reached that point in your mental process, you then can construct an appropriate response to that word. One such response might be to utter the word "table" aloud—which in turn implies a series of processes to convert your intention to say the word into a series of muscular movements to force air through your vocal cords and shape your mouth, tongue, and lips in such a way to make the appropriate sounds come out. Another type of response might be to make a prediction about that object represented by the symbol, table: that you can lay objects on it, for example, or that you can sit at it to eat a meal.

In other words, the sequence of mental operations in this example is one of moving from the perception of an abstract symbol—the word "table" on the printed page—to having a mental image of the object the symbol represents, to a set of generalized features about that mental object, to a conception of the experience of what a table is like. It's a process of moving from "mental image" to "general features" to "concept." Each of these steps is itself a series of mental operations and each is performed by separate portions of the cerebral cortex. In a sense, the action moves from one area of the brain to the next in a form of spreading activation through the cerebral cortex as a whole.[8]

But people can also have the reverse experience in which a new experience or concept of something leads to the determination of a new

---

[8]If the object viewed has an emotional context for you, such as a photograph of a loved one, the spreading activation would also activate portions of the brain outside the cerebral cortex to generate an emotional response. If the senses perceive something that implies immediate danger, it might also activate instinctive fight-or-flight reflexes, which also lie outside the cerebral cortex. So this discussion of "table" is a highly simplified presentation.

set of fundamental, defining features of the concept, which in turn leads to a new image of this new idea. Sometimes, if this happens suddenly and unexpectedly, we call this an "aha!" experience. It also corresponds to learning new things.

For example, when we have a new experience that matches some of the general features we associate with a table, we are likely to be reminded of the concept of table. For example, the first explorers in the American southwest saw a new type of landscape of tall, steep-sided hills with very flat tops. Those hills reminded them of tables—they were flat on top, had a single "leg" to support the flat surface, and were raised above the surrounding area—so they called them *mesas*, which is the Spanish word for "tables." (The early explorers were, after all, Spanish.) Today these are also sometimes called "tablelands." Associating new experiences with existing patterns to create new symbols—in this case appending a new meaning onto an existing symbol, "mesa"—is something the brain does with remarkable ease.

Learning in the brain is the process of having the neurons grow new connections or modify connections they already have to represent new symbols—like the word "table," new mental images—of what a generic table looks like, new sets of features—that can be used to identify objects matching "table," or new concepts and experiences—such as a new geographical object that has similarities to the generic "table" concept.

An example might clarify this. Suppose you grew up in a very remote location where no such thing as television existed—or even was heard of. One day, some kindly (or not so kindly) person tells you that you've won the lottery and you're going to get to see an amazing new device called a "television." The set is turned on . . . and there are *little people talking to each other and having a meal right in front of you!*

When your brain tries to sort out what it perceives, it will first see if any parts of the perceptions match patterns and experiences it already knows. In this case, you've never seen a box like this, so that's all new. You've never seen anything electronic, so that's new too. But you have seen people talking with each other and eating a meal. So what conclusion is your brain likely to come to? Most likely that there are tiny people inside the box who are really there, talking and eating just as you see. Perhaps you'll want to open the box to look inside and meet these strange beings. Of course, if it's a flat panel TV, that's going to cause even more confusion.

As it turns out, perhaps the person showing you the television indeed opens the back side of the box to show you there are no people really inside. Now what? Well, this means your brain has to *learn something new.*

In fact, the brain is a superb learning machine, and generally can and does learn anything that it's presented with that meets certain criteria: 1) It's something the brain doesn't already know; 2) it's something that happens more than once—and the more it happens, the more likely it is the brain will learn it; or 3) it's something that may only happen once, but it happens for a long time—it's something that *persists.* In other words, after you've watched the television for a few hours, and noticed that the people never respond to anything you do, you'll likely conclude this magic box is just showing *pictures* of people. You don't have to know how a television works electronically to have learned that it only shows images, and is not itself real. You're also likely to come to that same conclusion if you don't get to see the television working for a long time, but you do see it every day for a number of days. Again, after enough exposures to the television, you'll figure out what it's really doing.

The brain's neural structure, one that uses connections to store information rather than individual cells, offers major advantages. These can be summed up as *adaptability, space efficiency, robustness to loss, and robustness to poor input.*

First, a living being must be *adaptable,* if nothing else. The environment around an animal constantly changes. A system that is preprogrammed is far less flexible than one that can learn and adapt. Neural networks easily learn and adapt. Although we don't grow neurons very well, we *do* grow new connections between neurons—and we do it all the time. That's how we learn new things. Which is a good thing, really, because neurons die off every day of our lives—and the replacement rate in which we grow new neurons is much less than the rate of die-off. We can compensate for that by growing more *connections* with the remaining neurons we have.

Second, the brain has highly *efficient storage* of data, particularly of patterns of information. In a computer, each piece of data is stored in an individual memory bin. To retrieve the data, all you need to know is the specific location of that bin. That works well for individual pieces of information—except, remember, the brain is constantly losing neurons. If individual memories were stored in individual cells, and those cells were to die as part of the natural aging process, the corresponding memories would be lost forever. A biological memory that has neural cells dying daily has to have a lot more redundancy than that.[9]

The space efficiency of memory storage in brains is particularly striking when you consider the type of data that must be stored. The world around us is rarely separated into neat bins of information, so the brain stores *patterns* of information and associates multiple patterns together. We also learn new things by determining the patterns or features that identify that object or experience.

The brain is also incredibly *robust in terms of damage to its physical structure.* We start off with about 100 billion neurons as infants and lose neurons virtually every day of our lives. The relatively small number of replacement neurons we may grow under normal circumstances doesn't come close to replacing the neurons we kill off every day. A single drink of alcohol, for example, may kill tens of thousands of neurons. Other drugs—prescription, over the counter, and illegal—can have similar effects.

With this kind of loss going on from birth to death, it's essential that the memory system be highly redundant and have the ability to suffer significant losses of "hardware," i.e., cells and connections. A neural network can do exactly that. Even a small network can sustain huge percentage losses—sometimes up to 50 percent or more of the total connections in the system—with astonishingly small impacts on the network's overall performance. Within a given memory section of the brain, it appears to store all information in all parts of the network. It has a limited ability to lose substantial pieces of its network structure and still retain almost total recall of the originally stored data.

One final key advantage of the brain's neural network structure is its *robustness in terms of dealing with incomplete, noisy, or even inaccurate input data.* If your sensory input is coming from an electrochemical system, as the brain's does, it's going to have a *lot* of noise and misfires and other inaccuracies buried in the input data. Brains actually learn *better* when the learning data is noisy and somewhat inconsistent. As a result, they

---

[9]Interestingly, certain types of memories *do* appear to be associated with individual cells of the brain. In recent research, scientists discovered that in young adult males, a *single neuron* appears to perform recognition tasks for faces (and bodies) of famous celebrities such as Halle Berry and Jennifer Lopez. Neuroscientists are still struggling to understand what this may imply about why those specific types of learning are stored in such a fragile way.

can take wildly incomplete or poor quality inputs and produce exactly the correct response anyway. Neural network simulations have astonishingly accurate performance at seemingly impossible tasks—reliably recognizing patterns of images that are so noisy even people have trouble finding the right answer.[10]

In a very real sense, the brain stores information similarly to how a hologram stores information. I'll talk much more about holograms later, but for now the key characteristics about them with respect to the brain is that holograms are extraordinarily robust with respect to damage to the memory, and they store massive amounts of data in highly compact memories.

One last point about the brain. It's intrinsically *electro-chemical* in its operation. And there are a lot of chemicals naturally produced in the brain that we're just beginning to understand. One of them, an exotic chemical named N, N-dimethyltryptamine, or DMT, is present in everyone's brain and appears to be associated with an obscure little brain structure called the pineal gland. This chemical has an amazing effect on people when it is available in the body in unusually large quantities—and those effects replicate, in many respects, the types of experiences psychics and mystics have. I'll talk much more about this amazing chemical later.

The key points to remember now are that the brain is similar to a hologram both in its abilities to store and recall information and its ability to sustain substantial physical damage and still retain memories, and that there may be at least one naturally occurring chemical in the brain that in some way is involved in attaining psychic states. For the moment, that's enough.

---

[10]One more aspect of the brain deserves mention because it has gotten a fair amount of press. Recent research has discovered that the brain has "mirror neurons" that seem to allow us to sense what other people are feeling. In the press, this has sometimes been portrayed as "reading other people's minds," but the reality is far from that. In essence, these neurons merely allow us to project what *we* might feel in a particular situation onto our mental model of what *other people* are actually experiencing. In other words, rather than being the seat of telepathy, the mirror neurons are more the seat of empathy, allowing us to mirror the plight of others in our own minds and thus treat them with greater cooperation, mercy, and sympathy. Scientists find this discovery highly important in large part because the assumption has been that individuals always act out of their own self interest, so the concepts of altruism and sympathy for others has been difficult to explain. But with the discovery of mirror neurons in people and animals, cooperative, altruistic behavior now has a scientific explanation.

But also remember that this is how the *brain* works. This functional, physiologically based description may or may not be how the *mind* works. Scientists generally believe today that the physical brain is the same thing as the mind—but that does not match with Eastern and other traditions that hold that the mind is somehow (at least partially) co-located with the brain, but is something more. We'll revisit this topic in a later chapter, but do be aware that *brain* and *mind* may (or may not) be the same thing.

Once started down my path of accessing meditative states using Hemi-Sync, I soon felt like an ancient seafarer staring at maps that end abruptly at the edge of the page. On the limits of the known world would appear a magical-looking beast, and the words: "Beyond here be dragons." I have yet to encounter any actual dragons, but from this point, the weirdness truly begins.

3

Seeing Is Believing

About five months after my Gateway program, I was back at TMI attending a program on remote viewing.[11] At Gateway I'd experienced something truly astonishing. In one evening program we'd been asked to try to remote view two targets, one identified only with latitude and longitude, and the other identified only as "someplace in North America."

In both cases I'd sketched the targets perfectly. In the first case, I'd actually named the specific structure of the target and sketched it from the two exact perspectives of the two photographs we were shown when the target was revealed. In the second case, I drew the target repeatedly, again echoing the perspectives of the specific target photos. I didn't name this second target, but it was certainly recognizable from my sketches.

To say my jaw dropped when the targets were shown to us would be to underestimate the effect of that exercise on me. I almost literally didn't

---

[11]I've been asked to point out that I had a phenomenal roommate at the remote viewing program. And it's true; I did. We've been close friends ever since, a not unusual circumstance for those who attend TMI programs.

believe what I'd done. I stared at my sketches, stared at the photographs of the target, and could only shake my head in stunned disbelief.

What had happened?

More importantly, *how* had I done it? When the trainers announced that a brand new week-long remote viewing program had been added to the TMI residential program schedule with two such programs offered before the end of the year, I knew instantly that I was going to attend one.

Remote viewing is the skill of describing locations that are inaccessible to your five physical senses. Essentially, you sit in a quiet place, as featureless a location as you can find, and concentrate your mind on a target which might be identified with only a randomly generated coordinate that references a specific photograph of the target photo site. Or you might be asked to describe the location an outbounder participant is seeing at that moment.[12] Or you might be asked to describe a place that is only outlined in words or by latitude and longitude—again in a sealed envelope that you are never allowed to open. Your task is to describe the location of interest accurately enough to enable a third party to choose the correct picture out of a set of four pictures.

In short, you have to describe a place you've never seen without even knowing what place it is you're describing. You go into an altered, relaxed state and note all sensory impressions of the target location. Is it hot or cold? Indoors or outdoors? Rough or smooth? Wet or dry? And so on. You sketch what you perceive in broad strokes: a green area here, a dark area there, something flashing red here and here.

The one thing you don't do as a remote viewer is try to name what you perceive. For example, if you try to say the target is the Sistine Chapel, you'll almost certainly be wrong. That's called analytical overlay or AOL for short. But if you say you perceive a place that feels holy or religious, that it's a structure with an arched ceiling and a lot of painted or flat figures of people around, you're describing rather than naming.

The other thing you don't do as a remote viewer is you don't allow anyone to "front load" you with information about the target. To my surprise, and no doubt the surprise of any skeptics reading this, it's much easier to remote view a target when you're completely blind to it than to remote view one when you know the general type or location of the

---

[12]An outbounder is one who physically travels to a specific, randomly chosen site. The remote viewer tries to view the site by connecting psychically to the outbounder's perceptions.

target you're trying to remote view. When you know what the target is or generally where it is, you tend to let your conscious, rational, logical mind insert extraneous information known as "guesses." It's also harder to tell whether the information you're receiving about the target are actual perceptions or only your imagination supplying made-up details. If you know nothing at all about the target, your imagination can't readily fill in details that aren't there.

During the week-long remote viewing program, I learned more about remote viewing than I could possibly ever want to know. And I had the chance to practice my new skills. One of the factoids I learned was that nearly everyone can be taught to remote view except for one small group of people. Apparently those who have an "eidetic" or photographic memory can't remote view. Something about how their memories are organized—no one knows quite what—appears to block the viewing skill.

While at that program, I participated in an ongoing double-blind remote viewing study that had begun in the first remote viewing program. Ours was the second.

On Wednesday, after only four days of practice, the 24 program participants were divided into eight teams of three. One person in each team acted as the remote viewer, and a second person acted as the viewer's "monitor"—the person who took notes, gave the viewer specific targeting instruction, asked questions such as "If you view the target from above, what do you perceive?" or "Turn around and look behind you. Describe what's there."—and generally monitored the viewing session. The third person didn't participate in or observe the viewing session, but used the notes from that session to try to identify which of four possible photo sites had been described.

We'd learned that there were some pitfalls in the remote viewing process. One was that the monitor had to precisely word the instructions to the viewer. For example, the viewer couldn't simply be told to "describe the photo site in the target envelope" because there were two dozen different target envelopes floating around TMI that day. Instead, the wording had to be very precise: "Describe the photo site in the target envelope coded C-3 *at the time the photo was taken.*"

The last part of that instruction was crucial: Remote viewers can perceive information about the target from any *time* as well as from any place. It's not all that unusual for poorly targeted viewers to describe the target site at some other time—perhaps 50 or 60 years before the desired day, for example.

Furthermore, you can't bury a target; remote viewers can view underground as easily as aboveground targets. You can't hide a target in a safe or vault or behind lead walls; remote viewers can perceive right through such barriers. In fact, there appear to be few or no reliable mechanisms that block a remote viewer from viewing anything anywhere at any time, something that has caused enormous consternation among military intelligence types for decades.

In the three viewing sessions we did that day, everyone had the opportunity to act in each of the three roles of viewer, monitor, and judge. Each viewer on each team had a different target and a different set of four photo sites from which the judge had to choose, and no one, not even the trainers, knew what the correct sites were.

Random chance would predict that each judge had a one-in-four probability of guessing the correct photo site from the four possible photos. So, with 24 total viewings (eight viewings in each of the three sessions), chance alone would predict that about six of the judges—about two in each of the three sessions—would choose the correct photo sites.

So what happened?

We were all nervous while we waited for Skip Atwater, Director of Research at TMI and the developer of the remote viewing program, to report the result from the day's testing. We wanted to do well, to demonstrate that our hard work all week had been worthwhile. We'd become a close-knit group over the course of the program, and each of us wanted everyone to succeed.

We weren't sure how things had gone because we'd been instructed not to discuss the results or the images from our individual trials with each other for fear of contaminating viewings later in the day. This was for much the same reason that the monitors had to be precise about exactly which envelope we were to target and that the surroundings where the viewers worked should be bland and unremarkable. So tension ran high as we waited for the final results. How well—or poorly—had we done?

Remote viewing is one of the most studied psychic functions. How can we perceive accurately locations and times that are far beyond what our physical senses can directly access?

Nearly 30 years of scientific research in remote viewing has produced some conclusions about what viewers can do and what they can't do. In

Miracles of Mind Russell Targ, physicist and cofounder of Stanford Research Institute's research into psychic phenomena (he is now retired from Lockheed Missile and Space), and coauthor Jane Katra, have written a thoughtful and provocative analysis of what we know about things the mind can do—even if conventional science says those things are impossible.

From his work on hundreds or thousands of remote viewing trials over two decades of investigations, Targ outlined certain characteristics of this skill:[13]

First, it's not necessary for anyone to be present at the site being viewed. In fact, it is not necessary for the target even to have been *chosen* at the time the viewing takes place! Early experiments used an outbounder protocol in which the remote viewer would try to view the site by connecting to the outbounder's perceptions. That's still sometimes used in training remote viewing because novice viewers often find it easier to connect with a known person than with an unknown location. But it's not at all necessary, even in training, to go to such elaborate lengths to set up a session.

Second, it is easier to get general physical properties of the target than anything else, especially for inexperienced viewers. So if trying to distinguish between two separate targets, it is easier to do so if such characteristics as shape, color, and form are distinctly different.

Third, shielding of any sort, including electrical shielding, makes no difference to a good remote viewer. If anything, putting a viewer inside a shielded room will *increase* accuracy and performance, not decrease it. Some experimental results have hinted that solar flares and galactic radiation from the Milky Way galaxy may interfere with viewers to some small degree, possibly by distracting them, so being shielded from that radiation apparently helps viewers connect with their targets.

Another surprising quality of remote viewing is that physical distance has *no bearing* on the difficulty or sharpness of the viewing results. Distances of up to 10,000 miles—the longest distance that has been scientifically verified—do not affect a viewer's accuracy or precision. This conclusion and the shielding result mentioned above almost totally preclude electromagnetic signals from having anything to do with what generates the viewer's perceptions. Electromagnetic signals diminish over distance due to the geometry of space-time and are blocked by

---

[13]The following points are summarized from Targ and Katra's highly recommended *Miracles of Mind*. See suggested reading for details.

appropriate shielding. Thus, remote viewing is not done with your eyes or your visual system in general.

Astonishingly, expert remote viewers are sometimes so accurate that they can literally draw blueprints and circuit diagrams of the target. Remote viewer Joe McMoneagle is especially noted for his skill at this particular level of detail. Furthermore, resolution by an expert viewer can be as small as one mm (about .04 of an inch).[14]

Nor do viewers' abilities decrease over time. In contrast, practice definitely makes perfect, and accuracy improves with experience. Expert viewers, like expert musicians, spend hours practicing their skills every day.

Certain viewing factors can improve results. These include everyone involved having a belief and faith in each other and in the reality of remote viewing, a sincere desire to succeed in the remote viewing task, and enough experience remote viewing to have learned to separate analysis (guesses) from perceptions.

It is very important, also, to try to sketch your perceptions. Sketching is a nonanalytical mechanism that directly accesses the remote viewing process. It's a right brain activity whereas verbal description, since it involves language, is more of a left brain activity.

While you are learning how to remote view it is important to get feedback, in large part to build your confidence in your skills. However, once you're a trained viewer, that feedback isn't essential at all.

Certain factors can inhibit a quality remote viewing session. One of the biggest is having knowledge about the intended target—ignorance of the target is remote viewing bliss!

---

[14]Some remote viewers use their skill to locate objects, animals, or people who are missing. This requires particular practice because the viewers have to obtain enough clues about the surroundings of the missing person or thing to enable that location to be identified clearly. They also need to get a sense of direction and physical distance, something that's inherently difficult to do in an altered state of consciousness where you're generally disconnected somewhat from physical reality. It's a difficult skill. Thus one exceptionally talented remote viewer, who has independently validated accuracy of well over 85 percent in straightforward remote viewing tasks, has a similarly validated accuracy of about 50 percent in locating people who have been missing for many years. Some of that loss of accuracy may be because some of the missing persons he was tested on may no longer be alive and their remains may not be identifiable. But since those missing persons are still missing, that's only speculation.

Where you work is also important—it should be as featureless and free of distractions as possible, with no pictures, television, radio, or any other audio or visual distractions. A plain table and chair, in a bare gray or beige or white room, with plain white paper and simple pencils is ideal. If there is a picture on the wall or a song playing on the radio, it will tend to show up in your report.

Surprisingly, viewing numbers is very hard, much harder than viewing locations or objects. Apparently, remote viewers look for novelty when searching for something to report—and numbers are simply not novel. We know everything there is to know about the numerical digits, so viewing them is really difficult.

These characteristics of the remote viewing phenomenon have yet to be explained in any coherent theory. The only really definite theoretical issue that is clear is that a remote viewer isn't "viewing" anything at all . . . at least not anything using light, photons, or the physical visual system. So, if remote viewers don't perceive photons (electromagnetic energy packets) in the way the physical vision system does, what exactly are they doing?

It's an interesting question, and a little later I'll present several possible scientific explanations for how it might work, ranging from quantum entanglement to a holographic universe to an Akashic field. For the moment, however, perhaps it's a good time to find out just how well that double-blind experiment went.

Skip Atwater, a former Army officer, wore his noncommittal face when he gathered the remote viewing program participants together just before dinner to announce the results of the day-long experiment. We couldn't tell at all if we'd done well or not. He reviewed the conditions of the test, and reminded us that mere chance alone would dictate that about one-quarter of the 24 trials would be successful since the judges were trying to pick the correct image from four possibilities.

And then he told us the results.

In one set of eight trials, four of the eight judges—or 50 percent—had correctly chosen the target image. Better than chance, I thought, somewhat disappointed, but not that great. It could have been just a statistical fluke.

In another set of eight trials, five of the eight judges—or 62.5 percent—had correctly chosen the target image. That was better, I felt, but still not what I would call fabulous. Perhaps we hadn't done as well as we'd all hoped.

But in the remaining set of eight trials, seven of the eight judges—or 87.5 percent—had correctly chosen the target image! Wow!

Overall for the day, our group had generated 16 correct responses out of 24 trials—an overall success rate of 67 percent, far, far above the chance score of 25 percent correct. In fact, the odds against that score being as a result of random chance were about one in 50,000!

The group at the previous session of this program back in September, had gotten 13 correct choices out of 24 trials, again far above chance.

And when the two groups' scores were combined into a cumulative rating, there were 29 correct choices out of 48 total trials, or about 60 percent correct, for an odds-against-chance rating of one in 4,700,000!

I was flabbergasted. We were a bunch of neophytes, trying to do the improbable after only four days of training. Yet we'd accomplished something that appeared, on the face of it, to be impossible. How had this happened? How was it possible for someone to sit in a quiet room and describe a photograph in a sealed envelope well enough that two times out of three a third party could correctly select that photograph from a group of four pictures? My head reeled with the reality of participating in the impossible.

4

More than My Physical Body

I'm an animal person. When I was growing up we always had one or two (or three!) pet dogs around the house. I grew to adulthood cherishing my animal companions. Eventually, I decided it wasn't fair to keep a dog when I was away from home all day every day. At that point, I switched to keeping cats, usually two at a time so they could amuse each other when I was gone, though for brief periods I have had as many as four.

Having grown up with the affection and attention that dogs provide, I wasn't sure how well I'd like having a cat until I brought home the first one, Delilah, a black cat with gold eyes and an ability to get into more trouble than any two puppies. That was when I discovered that cats, if they're the right kind of cats, can be as loving, affectionate, and people-oriented as any dog.

There are, of course, differences, including cats' independence and their ability to entertain themselves even if I'm away from home for long hours every day. But the biggest difference is summed up by the well-known adage that while dogs have owners, cats have "staff." I've learned to be an acceptable staff person for my cats.

When I flew to Virginia for my Gateway program in late July, I had three cats: Samson, Sasha, and Tinkerbell. Samson was a gorgeous Russian Blue I called the "Cary Grant of Kittydom" because he was sleek, suave, and simply adored every female who walked through my door—and they adored him too.

Although Sammy was only nine years old, he had been afflicted with kidney disease at the unusually early age of five, and after four long years the disease was clearly winning the battle. He'd lost a great deal of weight over the spring and summer and was doing very poorly when I had to leave for Virginia. It was clear that his days were numbered. In fact, I had an appointment scheduled for him with his doctor the Saturday after I returned from the Gateway program.

But while I was at Gateway, I decided to use one of the exercises in F-12 (that state of expanded awareness described earlier) to see if I could do anything to help him. I'd listened carefully to the other participants who talked about how they did "remote healing" on people. And I was flush with some amazing successes in the remote viewing exercises. Could I possibly heal Sammy, I wondered? Or at least make him feel better? Wouldn't that be a great test to see if I was simply imagining things?

When the exercise began, I settled in my CHEC unit.[15] This basically is a twin mattress on a plywood platform, surrounded by plywood walls to the ceiling all around and with blackout curtains to cover the single opening to enter it. Inside the CHEC unit there are controls for a lighting system—reading light and various dimmable colored lights, speakers, and headphones. Pulling on the headphones, I dutifully followed the prescribed preparatory process: I got myself comfortable, set aside distractions in an *Energy Conversion Box*, did the requisite minute or two chanting *Om*, and built a *Resonant Energy Balloon*, or REBAL, around me to protect me from any negative influences. I mentally stated my intentions by running through the Gateway affirmation, and then let the Hemi-Sync tones take me to F-10, then to F-12.

Once in F-12, I was supposed to be doing an exercise as directed by Bob Monroe's voice. But . . . have I mentioned that I'm well known around TMI as the person who badly needs a "Does Not Follow Direc-

---

[15]In Monroespeak—the jargon everyone soon learns when you attend programs at TMI—a CHEC unit is a Controlled Hemi-Sync Environmental Chamber. As you will soon notice if you begin to work with TMI's technology, Bob Monroe loved acronyms and created new ones at every opportunity.

tions Well" T-shirt? Instead of doing whatever it was we were supposed to be doing, I decided I would try to heal Sammy.

To my surprise, I realized it was easy to connect with him mentally. Simply holding an image of him in my mind was sufficient to give me a sense of connecting with him. I easily visualized him snoozing in the sunshine back in California. But . . . of course, that was simply my imagination, I thought. Cats *always* sleep in the sun. It was just a reasonable guess. But still . . . it felt like something more, so I squashed my doubts and continued.

I decided that since I knew little about feline anatomy or what was ravaging his kidneys, I'd simply review all the major systems of his physical body: his neural system, his bones, his heart and lungs, his stomach and digestive system, and so on. In each case, I concentrated on imagining them healthy and vital, working perfectly at each of their respective functions. When I got to the kidneys, I was surprised at how withered and damaged they "looked."(Again, was this my imagination? Possibly.) I saw the blood carrying metabolic byproducts flowing into the kidneys, and flowing back out looking nearly as dark and toxic as when it had entered. Obviously the filtering function of the renal system wasn't doing its job.

So I concentrated on Sammy's kidneys. I hadn't studied biology in college—hadn't had a biology course since tenth grade—so I was hardly an expert in the renal system. But my mother had died from a long-standing series of infections in her urinary tract, so I'd learned a bit of anatomy from nursing her through those problems. Thus, I knew enough to understand that the kidneys act as a kind of filter, collecting toxic byproducts of metabolic processes, and concentrating those toxins in the urine for excretion through the bladder.

My focus, therefore, was simple: I imagined tracing the flow of blood into his kidneys. In my mind the fluid entering his kidneys looked thick, dark, toxic, unhealthy. I imagined his kidneys pink and glistening with health instead of scarred and dark and withered. I saw the blood filtering through these healthy, vital organs, and coming out of them brilliant and alive with vitality and healthfulness. For long minutes I imagined this to be the case.

I wasn't sure how long it took to filter a cat's complete blood supply. The exercises we were doing lasted only 30 or 40 minutes. Given that it had taken me a while to get into the focus level, did I have enough time to filter his entire blood volume?

I simply didn't know. Nor could I afford to worry about that. Instead I kept my concentration on his kidneys, and the blood pumping through them. And as I did so, the strangest sensations crept over me. . . .

My kidneys started tingling!

I'm not someone who generally pays attention to my own internal organs, but in this case, I could feel my kidneys working hard. I felt them prickle and quiver. I could feel blood pumping through them, but the blood felt odd, not quite like my own. I realized then that somehow I was perceiving my kidneys acting as a dialysis machine for Sammy!

Astonished though I was, I managed to hold my concentration and kept pumping blood—Mine? His?—through the kidneys—Mine? His?—over and over again. By the time the exercise ended and we were brought back to C-1, normal waking consciousness, I was very tired.

And I needed to go to the bathroom—badly.

Now that might not seem an astonishing thing, but as ever, when we were sent to our individual CHEC units to begin the exercise, we'd been instructed to go there "by way of the bathroom." It had become almost a Pavlovian habit to empty our bladders before every exercise simply because it's one of the worst things in the world to have to go in the middle of a meditation. That's a guaranteed way to be pulled out of any altered state. So I'd dutifully done that only 30 or 40 minutes before—yet now I had to empty my bladder again. ·

Had my kidneys been working so hard that they'd filtered out enough toxins to cause my bladder to fill in less than an hour?

I didn't know. But the sensation of acting as a dialysis machine from 2,500 miles away was so vivid and so real that I recorded every detail in the journal I was keeping. What would I find when I got home?

People have attempted to heal others through the power of their minds and intentions for millennia. While Western medicine believes that such efforts are merely comforting but hardly effective, the fact is such assumptions may be less than accurate. Significant scientific studies are beginning to demonstrate that the intentions—the *prayers*—of other people can indeed positively impact the progress of diseases.

The first way this shows up is in the well-known placebo effect. Studies of the effectiveness of new pharmaceuticals always have to control for this effect in which patients given nonactive medications that look like the real thing can demonstrate as much or more improvement as patients who actually receive a drug. This is clearly a problem—and, although it's often disguised in announcements of major new drug releases, often as much as 40 percent or 50 percent of the impact of new medications may be due solely to the placebo effect.

In the placebo effect, the doctor confidently gives the patient a "miracle pill" and tells him that the pill will cure his problem. The patient, trusting the doctor's assessment, takes the pill and, to no one's surprise, the problem indeed goes away as measured by all medical tests. Unfortunately, the miracle pill contained nothing but simple sugar in a fancy package. What cured the patient?

This placebo effect can work well if the doctor is good at expressing confidence and assurance to the patient. But the effect works even better in a double-blind situation, in which the doctor is also unaware that the medication being used is a fake. This is also why it's essential for new medications to be tested clinically using a double-blind protocol in which neither the doctor nor the patient knows if the medication is the experimental drug, an established drug, or simply a sugar pill.

If you begin to read the literature on healing, you find story after story of patients who have recovered solely from the effect of placebos. Clearly, it is the confidence the patient has in the "cure" plus the confidence the doctor has in the "cure" that combines to heal the patient. Intentions, it seems, are far more powerful than disease, at least some of the time.

Furthermore, it's not solely pills that can demonstrate the placebo effect. One form of heart surgery was tested against a placebo operation; i.e., one where the patient was simply opened up surgically but no real operation was performed, and a well-established surgical procedure used for decades was demonstrated to be no more effective than the pretend operation!

So if the intentions of patients and their doctors can play a major role in determining how well the patients progress with their disease, what about the intentions of other people?

When we hear of someone who has been diagnosed with a major disease such as cancer, the almost universal response is something on the order of, "My prayers are with you," or "My thoughts are with you." It's as if we believe that by keeping this person in our thoughts we can in some way make them "all better." Or at least make their recovery from that disease more certain. Is there any scientific evidence that this is true?

Surprisingly, yes. Studies demonstrate that intercessory prayer from strangers can indeed improve the outcome of patients recovering from such health crises as heart operations. More than 70 such studies have been done with significant results. Specifically, such studies often show that prayed-for patients have fewer complications, shorter recoveries, and require less pain medication than those who were not prayed for. It does not matter if the person being prayed for knows he's being prayed for, or whether the people praying ever meet the patient. Nor does it matter how far away the patient is from those praying for him.

Skeptics like to point out that many of these studies are really inconclusive because it's impossible to control whether someone *not* officially in the study prays for a patient who is nominally not on the prayer list. Nor is there a way to determine how many prayers or prayers of what type (i.e., Buddhist, Christian, Jewish, Islamic, whatever) are being performed—particularly when family and friends of the patient no doubt also pray for him.[16] To get around this criticism, studies on the impact of prayer on bacterial cultures have been done. In these studies, two sets of cultures receive identical environments. One set of cultures is prayed for, and the other cultures are not prayed for. It's probably reasonable to assume that there are no other prayers being said for the un-prayed-for culture—yet the cultures receiving prayers thrive far more than those not being prayed for.

Yet another example is a study of sprouting seeds performed by Dr. Bernard Grad of McGill University in Toronto. Seeds soaked in salt water to inhibit growth were split into three groups. Further, a supply of salt water was given to a healer to be "healed." A second supply of salt water was held by people suffering from significant clinical depression. Then one group of seeds was sprouted in the salt water that had neither been healed nor held by depressed people. The second group of seeds was sprouted in the healed salt water. The third group of seeds was sprouted in the salt water held by the depressed. It should be no surprise that the seeds receiving healed water sprouted more frequently and grew faster and bet-

---

[16]Most of the studies I've seen take an interdenominational approach to prayers. The praying participants are recruited from a wide variety of religious and spiritual backgrounds and any given patient may receive prayers from any or all of those faiths. In some cases, this has caused difficulty in recruiting volunteer patients. Those with a very rigid spiritual understanding sometimes object to the possibility that, for example, a Buddhist or a Muslim or a Catholic might pray for them.

ter than those seeds receiving plain salt water. But more than this, those seeds sprouted in the water held by the depressed people sprouted much *less* often than those in the control group using ordinary salt water.

Remember that Buddhist saying I mentioned earlier that "with our thoughts we create our world"? This appears now to be the exact truth. Our thoughts and our intentions do appear to have significant impact on what we experience in life.

The point of all this is that there is good scientific evidence of the efficacy of intercessory prayer. Furthermore, the effect seems to be more than just the normal placebo effect, if only because it's difficult to imagine how a bacterial culture or a sprouting seed could have an expectation or awareness of the prayers. The only question is, how does it work?

The Princeton Engineering Anomalies Research Center (PEAR) laboratory has done a great deal of work on the possibility of human intentionality impacting the physical state of objects. One experiment, ongoing for many years and with over a million trials on record, has a human volunteer attempt to affect the number of ones or zeros a random number generator produces. In other words, it has people attempt to make a random number generator less random. Their results provide overwhelming evidence of the ability of the mind to affect physical systems outside the body solely with its intentions. In trial after trial, the random number generator starts generating more ones instead of zeros (or vice versa, depending on the intentions of the volunteer). PEAR researchers have so much data collected that they even can describe how to maximize the impact on the random number generator. Their conclusions are fascinating. You get the best results in this experiment if you are

1. *patient,* simply letting the experiment unfold as it will,

2. *connected* to the device, trying to be *one with it* and not explicitly *control* it,

3. *nice* to it, striving to be agreeable, pleasant, cooperative rather than ordering it around or being arrogant and demanding,

4. *humble,* understanding that you and the device are truly one,

5. *gentle,* treating the device with soft gentleness and not rushing through the experience.

It should not be a big surprise to realize that these same attributes appear to be the ones that also generate the most significant and profound experiences in altered states and meditations. The PEAR researchers offer no real explanation for *how* these results occur, but they're completely convinced that they *do* occur.

TMI has also done its own research on the impact of the mind on random number generators. Such devices, certified by their manufacturers as producing truly random sequences of ones and zeros, are located in several locations on the TMI campus. During certain Gateway programs, the random number generators are monitored 24 hours a day from a few hours before the program begins until after the last participant has left the facility.[17] The Gateway trainers are instructed to make detailed, computerized time logs during the week of everything that happens during the program. This includes not only the exact times when all exercises start and end, but any time any significant event happens between exercises. TMI collected data from the generators for a year, including a half-dozen or more separate Gateway programs. Since the sequence of activities at a Gateway program is fairly stable, generally the same exercises and activities occur at similar times in each presentation of the program.

When the time logs were correlated with the output of the random number generators, astonishing synchronicities appeared, particularly in the generator located in the Nancy Penn Center itself.[18] Most strikingly, one short time period in the week was *always* associated with massive nonrandom output from the generator—to the extent that the odds of this variation from random output being due solely to chance were less than

---

[17]Since the TMI campus has two separate training centers, the Nancy Penn Center and Roberts Mountain Retreat, which are less than two miles apart, they only collected data on those weeks when a Gateway program was going on at Nancy Penn Center, but no other program was going on at Roberts Mountain Retreat. They hypothesized that having multiple programs going on so close together, including "graduate" programs with participants who are often highly experienced and more powerful at accessing altered states than most Gateway participants, might have significantly muddied the data collected.

[18]The location of the random number generator is in the building where the participants do the Hemi-Sync exercises, but it is not in the individual CHEC units. Thus, the distance from the participants to the random number generator ranges from perhaps 25 feet to several times that, depending on the individual CHEC unit.

a million to one.[19] This particular spike in nonrandomness—and there were a number of others through the week—corresponds to one specific exercise that participants nearly always find deeply profound and meaningful; it is one of the most-requested exercises in the entire collection of exercises and across all TMI programs.[20]

The problem, of course, is that the data don't really indicate whether it is that specific exercise on the fifth day of a six-day program that is the actual cause of the nonrandomness, or if that nonrandomness is merely the culmination of five days of profound work in altered states. In either case, however, the power of the collective group's altered states is clear and obvious.

Even more significant is that *participants did not know about the random number generators!* In other words, there was no conscious intention on the part of the participants to affect the generators because they didn't even know they were there! Yes, the two trainers knew, and Skip Atwater, the director of research for TMI knew, but the participants explicitly were not told about it—yet the random number generator showed a powerful impact from so many people reaching profound altered states at the same time.[21]

So how does this relate to my efforts to heal Sammy? One issue that is now abundantly clear is that the mind has some mechanism for affecting things that are not local to it. Whether it is working on heart patients halfway around the world or a random number generator in the basement, the mind has powerful mechanisms for physically changing other objects. The mechanism for how this works is unknown, though some theories I will talk about later may offer an explanation. The key point, however, is that the mind—everyone's mind—can apparently do this!

---

[19]Since TMI uses a variety of trainers in its Gateway programs, the two trainers for each Gateway session in which the data were collected varied. Nevertheless, the data show an astounding consistency no matter who the trainers were.

[20]The exercise, a "vibe flow in F-15" combines an impressive set of vibrational sounds with the depth of F-15 tones. Doing this exercise is an *amazing* experience.

[21]For an experiment such as this, it doesn't matter whether the random number generator generates too many ones or too many zeros; all that matters is that it no longer is producing a random sequence of ones and zeros and thus has significantly more (or fewer) ones than the 50 percent a random system should produce.

The volunteers in the experiments discussed above were not notably psychic. The PEAR experiments in particular recruited ordinary people, and their successes were more tied to their attitudes than to their skills. Even at TMI, the participants in the Gateway programs that were monitored are almost always those who are new to Hemi-Sync and they often have little or no experience accessing altered states of consciousness.

Somehow, then, our minds have abilities to connect to people and things that are physically remote from our bodies. Once that connection is made, it's equally clear that our minds and our intentions—if we maintain the right attitude—can have profound impacts on those other people, animals, plants, and objects.

One other point—people often misunderstand the meaning of healing in the psychic or spiritual sense. Western medicine often equates healing with curing—and often, that's wrong from the spiritual perspective. Given a belief system that contends that the human soul survives the death experience, healing in such traditions may mean "making the death experience easier." In other words, sometimes it is not the correct thing to stop someone from dying. Sometimes the correct thing is to assist them in dying more easily.

Obviously, no healer can possibly know what is best for you spiritually. As a result, most alternative healers, apply their healing efforts "for the highest, best good" of the patient. In other words, *if* it is in that person's spiritual good to physically heal them, the healer offers their services to do that. But if it is *not* to that person's spiritual benefit to physically heal them then those same healing efforts will go to whatever that person most needs to assist them. Perhaps that is simple relief of pain and suffering. Perhaps it is more emotional support and reassurance. Perhaps it's assistance in dying. Whatever it is, the healer's "success" does not necessarily depend on the disease itself physically going away.

It's an intensely metaphysical view of what the word "heal" means—and it's one that is unaccepted in Western medical tradition. No doubt that's because in medical tradition, there is no continuance of the human spirit once the body dies. When you're dead, you're dead in this view, so death is the ultimate in failures from that perspective. But this generates a significant problem in comparing different healing techniques. It massively complicates the issue of determining how effective alternative healing treatments are in comparison to medical techniques. Should a healer who assists a person to die with serenity and grace be considered more or less successful than extreme medical measures that keep that person alive as long as they're hooked to machines and in a hospital bed? If the two sides do not even agree what healing means . . . well, you can see the difficulties.

At the time I went to Gateway, I had, at best, a very dim understanding of the subtleties of this issue. As the program ended, I had one huge burning question in my mind: were my inexperienced and untutored efforts to help Sammy effective? Or had I accomplished nothing to save a pet I dearly loved?

I flew home Friday after the Gateway program ended. The next morning I took Sammy to the vet for his previously arranged appointment. As ever, Dr. Grey took blood samples and sent them off to check on Sammy's condition. He'd lost more weight in the months since his previous checkup, and was down to less than six pounds from his healthy adult weight of 10.5 pounds.

Further, he'd developed a heart murmur. Dr. Grey suggested an ultrasound to discover exactly what type of heart problem it was. But Sammy couldn't be given any medication no matter what type of heart problem he had because all available heart medicines would have been toxic to his kidneys and would only exacerbate his kidney failure. I couldn't see the point of diagnosing something I couldn't treat anyway. Dr. Grey sadly agreed.

After Sammy's physical, Dr. Grey looked grim and gently suggested to me that Sammy might have only a few more days to live. Nothing could prolong his life, she said. I could only hope to keep him a little more comfortable in the few days he had left. Did I want her to insert a stent in his neck so I could more easily give him fluids to keep him hydrated? It wouldn't change how quickly he died, she said, but it might make his final days a little easier.

Sammy had always hated any type of medical procedure; he'd even had a panic attack once when he had to have an X-ray. I'd promised myself and him that I wouldn't authorize any procedure that I thought he wouldn't want me to do. And there was another consideration. I had two younger cats at home: Sasha, a half-sister to Sammy, and Tinkerbell, a Tonkinese. Both were playful, especially Tinkerbell. Tonkinese are known as "monkeys in cat suits," and Tinkerbell feels it's important to live up to that reputation.

I asked Dr. Grey if the stent would be dangerous if it came out while Sammy and Tinkerbell were playing. Could it hurt Tinkerbell if she accidentally put it in her mouth? Tinkerbell is notorious for putting *everything* in her mouth.

Dr. Grey was stunned. "Sammy still *plays*?" she asked me.

"Well, yes, of course," I told her. He's hardly a kitten, but he still plays with Tinkerbell and Sasha when inspired to do so.

"And is he drinking?"

"Every time I go past a faucet I have to turn it on for him to take a long drink. It's a ritual of ours."

"And he's eating?"

"Well, of course. He's the first to the food bowl every morning and evening."

Dr. Grey shook her head in amazement. She thought, given the results of his physical, that he'd be virtually catatonic, withdrawn, and obviously ready to die. She sent me home with instructions to keep on doing whatever it was I was doing for him.

I had much to ponder from this visit. His blood levels were still awful. By all accounts he ought to be at death's door. But he wasn't. He was still my Sammy, ever ready for some lap time or to supervise his two younger playmates.

I didn't know what to do about him. Medical science had nothing more to offer. My only hope was to try again with the psychic healing. I reasoned that dialysis, which is what I felt I had done for him, couldn't really cure kidney disease, but it allowed a more or less normal life by regularly cleansing the blood of toxins. So perhaps if I simply did a similar healing exercise on him regularly, two or three times a week, I could keep him comfortable and alive longer than the few days Dr. Grey had suggested.

I began a regimen of healing sessions with Sammy. I used a "free flow" CD that helped me enter F-12. I concentrated on visualizing his kidneys healthy and functioning. I had no one to tell me how to do any of this, so I felt awkward and inept. All I could do was keep trying and hope that something of what I was doing made a difference.

All through August and September I kept up the sessions. Sammy had long outlived Dr. Grey's predictions, and still seemed as lively as before. He was terribly frail and thin, but he was eating well, and drinking, and although not kittenish, he still played with the other two cats and seemed interested in what was going on around him. But the real change was in how closely he bonded with me.

Russian Blues are known for being one-person cats. They bond to whomever they decide is their "person," and that person is generally the one they socialize most with. Sammy had always been very close to me. He'd seen me through a lot of bad times and comforted me through many losses. But in these months, we became closer still. I felt like he was communicating with me. Not so much in words, but in thoughts, images, ideas. When I came home from work, he was waiting, and we generally had a "communing" session in which we simply sat together, and became closer and closer. It wasn't exactly an exchange of thoughts, just mutually keeping each other company in a profound, peaceful way. We shared serenity with each other, and I felt better each time we did it.

September slipped into October, and still I had him with me. I worked on him regularly to keep him comfortable. October ended, and became November. Then, the second week of November, I sat down on a Sunday to do a regular healing session with him. I had gotten good at connecting with him, and I mentally reached out to link with him—and felt as if a door slammed in my face. Instead of getting an image of his kidneys and heart, I quite literally heard a voice—*his* voice!—saying, "No. It's time for me to go now. You have to let me leave."

I couldn't believe it. How could he speak to me in *words?* He was a *cat,* not a person. And how could I know he was the one speaking? Cats didn't have voices. Certainly not voices that spoke English. Yet his voice echoed in my head. Over and over, all afternoon I tried to connect with him. Each time I got the same slammed door and the same message. It was time to let him go.

Finally I gave up. I looked at him sadly. I told him that Friday was my day off, and if he still felt the same on Friday, I would take him in to the doctor and help him die. I had a sense of an accepting mental nod from him as he curled up to take a nap.

Each evening after work that week I tried again to heal him. Each time I met the same refusal. I knew he was ready to leave. He took to opening the linen closet door and sleeping curled up on the clean linens at night, where it was quiet and dark. He was withdrawing from me more each day.

Thursday night, however, was the most astonishing of all. I went to bed late, dreading the sad task of the next day. But all night long I woke almost hourly, each time finding him sitting upright and intent—beside me, on top of me, at the foot of the bed, by my pillow. Each time I again heard, as clearly as if spoken aloud, a message from him, always the same: "Why are you delaying? I told you it's time for me to go. When are you going to help me leave?"

It took most of the day Friday for me to screw my courage to the sticking place and take him to the vet. I held him tenderly as the doctor fumbled for his vein. It took several minutes to find one, but Sammy held his foreleg out rock steady throughout, while she searched with the needle. For a cat who'd protested every single medical procedure, invasive or not, throughout his entire life, this demonstrated an unbelievable level of serenity. At last she found the vein and injected the solution into him. I held him close against my heart as his eyes closed one final time.

My Sammy was gone.

Only after I'd grieved for him could I go back and assess what I'd done—or not done. I hadn't cured his kidney disease. I hadn't magically transformed his scarred, broken organs into revitalized new ones. I hadn't actually *fixed* anything.

And yet . . . somehow, I'd kept him alive and comfortable for months when his best prognosis had been for only a few days. He'd lived nearly four months, long after every medical assessment insisted he should have died. Furthermore, those final months with him weren't months of pain and agony. He seemed to enjoy the time spent with me, and he didn't seem to be suffering at all. Only in those last few days, when he so insistently told me it was time for me to let him go, did he exhibit any unhappiness at being alive.

The question was, *how* had I done this? How could my imagination, my intentions, do *anything* to change his physical condition? I was at a loss to explain what I'd accomplished, or how I'd accomplished it.

All I'd actually done was sit down, concentrate on him, and imagine his kidneys healthy and functioning beautifully. Most of the time I wasn't even touching him during those healing sessions; he was often curled up and napping across the room or even in another part of the house. How could that possibly change anything about his physiological condition? Disease was caused by germs and viruses, and illness derived from the body's reactions to those germs and viruses—wasn't it? That's certainly what I'd been trained to believe. But . . . if I could simply sit down and *imagine* his blood being filtered, and have that help him *physiologically*, clearly something was amiss between my understanding of how disease and medicine work, and how things really happen.

I had done whatever I'd done to a *cat*. Not to another person, whose belief systems I might have tapped into or encouraged. It's hard to understand how a placebo-type effect would work with a cat as opposed to a human.

And what about the conversations I had with him those final days? I'd always felt close to him. I'd always sensed his love for me as I loved him. But this went well beyond a sense of a shared emotional bond. I hadn't sensed a vague feeling but an actual conversation, in English. Had I hallucinated that?

Sammy's final months and his death undermined my understanding of disease as a function of biochemical processes. More importantly, it undermined my sense of Western medicine as having all the answers, or even *any* of the answers.

The Gateway affirmation I'd learned at TMI starts with the statement, "I am more than my physical body, and because I am more than physical matter I can perceive that which is greater than the physical world." Sammy had given me a very graphical demonstration that he definitely was more than his physical body.

5

Putting Myself to the Test

About a year ago, as of this writing, I volunteered to be a "subject" in a psychological experiment on psychic functioning run by a prestigious research laboratory. The most interesting thing about it from my perspective is that, despite being run by experimenters who verbally claimed to be believers in ESP, the conditions of the experiment were such that it almost seemed designed to *disprove* the existence of telepathy, rather than designed to elicit it in the lab.

This particular experiment was a "Ganzfeld" experiment. I and a partner began the day by taking a battery of psychological and personality tests.[22] I was tagged the "receiver" and my partner the "sender."

---

[22]I'd asked a friend of mine who is psychic to participate with me in the experiment because the experimenters were recruiting pairs of people rather than individuals. As explained to us before the experiment, one of the goals of the experimental procedure was to determine if there is a correlation between personality types and psychic abilities.

I was positioned in a quiet room, in a comfortable recliner. Ping-pong ball halves were taped over my eyes, earphones positioned on my head, and the room was set up to be a mild sensory-deprivation experience, supposedly to remove distractions and make it easier for me to receive information from the sender. The lights were dimmed, and I was left alone, with only the sound coming through my headphones to keep me company.

Meanwhile my partner was put in a separate room with a TV monitor. He was to watch a video clip and try to telepathically send me an image of what he saw on the video clip. He could hear everything that I said or that the experimenter said through speakers. I could hear the experimenter and, of course, myself. The experimenter could hear both me and my partner and could talk to either or both of us.

The psychologist running this particular experiment first tried to talk me through a relaxation exercise while white noise played over the headphones. Unfortunately, she wasn't very good at such guidance, speaking much too quickly, giving me no time at all to follow her directions to "relax your feet and toes; now relax your legs and hips; now relax your stomach and abdomen" before rushing on to the next direction. Obviously, she didn't have a good grasp on what relaxation meditations were supposed to sound like because her voice was also a normal speaking tone rather than the soft drone of a good meditation leader. (Or else she was deliberately making it *more* difficult to relax instead of *less* difficult. You can never tell with psychological experiments!) Nonetheless, at the time of the experiment I was very experienced in meditation and relaxation and had no trouble deciding to ignore her instructions and put myself into a pleasant meditative state.

I did find the white noise distracting, which was unexpected because Hemi-Sync tones are also embedded in noise to disguise them. It's possible that the *lack* of Hemi-Sync tones in the noise was what disturbed me. I might very well have been more comfortable with silence rather than noise without Hemi-Sync.

Next I was given about 30 minutes or so to try to receive whatever impressions I could from the messages my partner was sending me. I spoke my impressions aloud, but I'd also requested a pen and paper so I could scribble and draw my own notes during the session. My eyes were, of course, covered with those ping-pong balls, but I positioned my hand and pen on the paper and just let myself scrawl whatever I wanted on it.[23]

Once I'd gotten all the impressions I could, the experimenter, who took her own notes of what I said, read those notes back to me over the headphones. I then was shown four video clips and was asked to identify which of the four corresponded to the video my partner had seen.

The notes read back to me didn't correspond particularly well either to what I'd scrawled on my paper or to what I'd remembered saying over the microphone. Things I remembered stressing in my verbal reporting weren't mentioned at all, and things that were passing by-the-way comments were strongly emphasized. (My impressions about this were confirmed after we left the experiment when I talked to my partner about it. He'd also noticed a wide variance between what he'd heard me say and especially what I'd emphasized in my session, as opposed to what the experimenter read back to me.)

Next I was shown four video clips. I do not know for sure whether the experimenter knew which of the four video clips the correct one was; however, my impression is that she did know the correct answer. If this is the case, it's a significant design flaw. In a more rigidly controlled experiment, the experimenter would also be blind to the correct answer. On the other hand, the stated purpose of this experiment was not to "prove" the existence of psychic phenomena, but rather to correlate psychic functions to personality types. So perhaps that didn't matter much.

One side note: When the experimental setup was described to me at the time I originally volunteered, I pointed out to the experimenter that there were at least three or four different ways I could psychically get information about the target video clip. For example, I could telepathically connect to my partner as the experimenters assumed. Or I could remote view the clip myself during the experiment without bothering to connect to anyone else. Or I could remote view it before the experiment. Or I could psychokinetically connect to the computer running the experiment to force a clip to be chosen on a topic I wanted to view. When I mentioned these possible alternatives to the experimenter, she assured me that for this experiment it didn't matter *how* I got the information

---

[23]Since I'm used to doing remote viewing with my eyes open and drawing on a pad of paper, it felt natural for me to do so in this experiment too. However, this was definitely *not* standard procedure for this experiment, so I had to promise not to remove the ping-pong balls and do my sketching and note-taking blind.

because the focus of the experiment was on other issues and not on whether I was able to telepathically connect with someone else. I had the impression that she believed none of the other mechanisms were very likely to work.

Therefore, about midnight the night before the experimental session, knowing I was going to do the experiment the next day, I decided to do a remote viewing session on the experimental results. I went into a remote viewing focus state and tried to describe the video clip that my partner would be watching the next afternoon—as if I were watching it with him, looking over his shoulder. I came up with about four pages of notes that I relayed to him as we were driving to the experiment the following morning. So in some sense, I'd already done the experiment before I showed up at the lab.

My plan going into the experimental session was to report *only* the information from this presession in the experiment—just to rattle off the descriptions that I'd gotten the night before. Since neither my partner nor I had any way of knowing what the clips would be, we had no idea whether those impressions were correct or not.

Once the reporting part of the session started, however, I kept getting side-tracked. Though I started by reporting what I'd gotten the night before, I kept tuning into other input, particularly ones that had a strong sense of high speed, like a high-speed chase.

When the first video clip came on, my jaw dropped. It was about as exact a match to the results from the session I'd had the night before that you could possibly envision. If that was the correct clip, I'd nailed it exactly—but I'd done so the night before. (I should point out that as it was explained to me, the clip that was the "target" clip was not selected by the computer until it was actually shown to my partner. In other words, at the time I did the previous night's session, the target hadn't yet been chosen!) This first video clip also matched much of the information I'd reported during the actual experiment, but not as closely.

The second video clip wasn't even close. I rejected that one completely. The third video clip had one very strong match to the information I'd reported that day—the sense of a high-speed chase. It was in fact a video clip of such a chase. But the location was wrong. I didn't reject that clip, but held it aside. The fourth clip, like the second, was a complete mismatch.

I asked to see the first and third clips again. The first one was still a phenomenal match to the data from the night before. The third one had some good matches to the data I'd reported that afternoon—especially the data that the experimenter had read back to me. Yet, if compared to my own recollections of what I'd said, and the notes I'd scribbled down, it wasn't nearly as good a match. Which set of data should I go with? The data the experimenter read to me, or what I'd gotten the night before and what I recalled from my own notes?

This experiment is a bit of a conundrum. Obviously, I viewed it as an experiment in remote viewing in that I chose to try to determine the correct video clip using my remote viewing skills. The psychologists running the experiment equally obviously viewed it as an experiment in telepathy in their clear assumption that in order for me to get the right answer I'd have to mentally connect with my partner. The truth is, it probably doesn't matter what label you put on my efforts. In either event the only way I could determine the correct answer would be by parapsychological means. In fact, a good way to consider the issues of remote viewing, clairvoyance (seeing at a distance), clairaudience (hearing at a distance), clairsentience (sensing at a distance), and such is to view them all as variations on "remote sensing," using the term "sensing" to cover all five sense modalities.

In looking at two decades of experiments conducted by Stanford Research Institute (SRI) and Science Applications International Corporation (SAIC) for the Department of Defense in remote viewing, government reviewers came to several important conclusions about the phenomenon of remote sensing.[24] Some remote viewing protocols force viewers to choose specific responses such as, temperature is hot or cold, or texture is smooth or rough. But those methodologies tended to be less accurate than simply letting the viewer describe whatever he or she detected. A second point is that some people—a small group of specific people—are far better at the task than average. In other words, while everyone *can* remote sense, not everyone is equally good at it. (No big surprise, when you think of it, since there's virtually no human skill that everyone is equally good at.) In fact, really terrific remote viewers appeared in about one person out of 100. These people do improve with experience and practice, but probably not hugely—it's more a matter of

---

[24]See Dean Radin's *The Conscious Universe* for more details of the experiments and conclusions.

incremental improvement than dramatic strides. Feedback on the viewer's success or failure is important—but more so in terms of providing a morale boost than because it substantially changes the quality of their performance.

But what about Ganzfeld experiments in telepathy such as the one I participated in? Are there any worthwhile psychological conclusions that can be drawn from those experiments? They've been performed since the mid-1970s. The idea behind them is drawn from the *Vedas* religious texts in India which claimed that improved psychic functioning develops through a prolonged period of meditation and sensory deprivation. If the participant's brain had no sensory input, the theory went, surely it would reach for whatever input it could find—such as that from psychic senses. Thus, psychologists wondered if psychic functioning in the laboratory could be better elicited if subjects were also subject to a mild form of sensory deprivation.

In some sense, this is the first time a true *theory* of psychic functioning had been generated and tested in the laboratory. This is a huge step forward from the previous see-if-it-can-be-demonstrated experiments that had been conducted until that point.

Dean Radin's book *The Conscious Universe* reviewed more than 2,500 Ganzfeld experiments conducted over more than 20 years of research. The overwhelming conclusion was that with an overall success rate of 33 percent in the experiments (when chance dictates a 25 percent success rate), the odds against that effect being mere chance are on the order of *a million billion to one!*

Obviously, Ganzfeld experiments do elicit some type of psychic effect if they're well designed. Do they demonstrate telepathy specifically? Well, my experience points out that it's not so easy to tease apart what results are from telepathic connections between the sender and receiver and what results are from the receiver merely doing a remote view of the correct clip. In either event, however, it's clear that *something* psychic is going on.

But how do psychologists explain these results? Of course, there is no widely accepted theory of psychic functioning, but there does seem to be a correlation between people who exhibit psychic functions in the laboratory and those who have thin and/or flexible boundaries between the conscious mind and the subconscious mind.

In psychological terms, these experiences, which include cases of telepathy, remote viewing, clairaudience, clairvoyance, precognition, and the like, are all labeled "ESP" or "extrasensory perception." On the other hand, a phenomenon such as spoon-bending is called "PK" or "psychokinesis," the manipulation of physical objects through mental efforts alone.

Some psychologists believe that psychic abilities are a natural function of the subconscious that we (usually) train our conscious brains to ignore during childhood. In this conception, psychics are those who can consciously "thin" the boundary between their awake-alert conscious mind, and the subconscious world of dreams and the like, thus allowing subconscious psychic information to cross over into their conscious awareness.

As I mentioned earlier, an altered state of consciousness results when we slow down our primary brainwaves from that awake-alert beta state to those of the dream states in the alpha, theta, and delta ranges. In other words, meditation and entering altered states of consciousness provide a way to lower the barriers between the subconscious mind and the conscious mind. This allows the psychic data that the subconscious knows to seep through into conscious awareness. This indeed seems to be consistent with the tendency of most psychics to include meditation in their daily practice.

Learning to be psychic on a psychological level would thus be a process of learning to lower (or "thin") the barrier between the conscious and unconscious minds. While this makes very good sense to me, it doesn't really explain much when you think about it. Where exactly *is* the "subconscious"? We talk about it all the time, but there's no real sense of where it is or what it is, other than the standard assumption that it's somewhere "in the brain."

But then again, that's also where we think the *mind* is, right? If I asked you where to find neurons in your body, no doubt you'd immediately point to your head. We're accustomed to think of neurons as "brain cells"—those cells that make up the brain. And where is the brain? In the head, of course!

But while it's true that we do have a hundred billion or so neurons in the head, we also have them in a lot of other places too. In fact, we have neural cells virtually all over our bodies. Candace Pert, in *Molecules of Emotion*, explains that neural receptors are actually located in nearly every cell of the body. There are exceptionally large clusters of extra-brain neurons located in the heart and in the digestive system. In fact, the heart alone has a cluster of more than 40,000 neurons—a sizeable chunk of brain cells that's as large or larger than significant subsystems in the brain.

In other words, the heart has its own "brain"!

Furthermore, as discovered by John and Beatrice Lacey in the 1970s, although the brain sends directions to the heart, the heart does not necessarily do what the brain tells it to do. The heart has a mind of its own, it appears, and it appears to follow its own logic and rules. Sometimes a "speed-up" signal from the brain indeed makes the heart speed up. But sometimes just the opposite happens; the heart slows down instead of speeding up! Like a willful spouse, it decides whether to obey the brain or not based on what it believes is the correct response.

Not only does the heart receive information and input from the brain, it sends its own information back to the brain in a couple of ways. The relatively new specialty of neurocardiology studies the neural signals of the heart. The neurons in the heart connect directly, through the spine, to different parts of the brain, and the heart sends a neural signal to the brain every time it beats. These signals help regulate the autonomic neural systems, the subconscious functions that keep us breathing and control other body functions. But in addition, the heart's messages go to the higher reasoning part of the brain, the cerebral cortex. Neural signals from the heart affect the emotional center of the brain. There is some indication that there may be more connections from the heart to the right side of the cerebral cortex (the side that generally is associated with intuition, creativity, artistry, and emotion) than to the left brain (the side that is more associated with rationality, mathematics, language, and logic). If so, a left-brained society like ours has much to consider in terms of learning to listen to our hearts as well as our heads.

More than this, the rhythm of heartbeats also conveys a subtle, coded message to the brain. It's as if the heart is an equal partner with the brain in identifying how we respond to the outside world.

Or in yet other words, the mind, if it consists of the set of neural cells in the body, is *not* located in the brain at all—at least not exclusively so. Instead, the *mind* is distributed throughout the body, with little pieces of it in nearly every cell in the body.

Not only does the heart have its own brain, the heart also generates its own electromagnetic field, one that is far stronger than the field the brain produces. In fact, the heart sends as many messages *to* the brain as it receives *from* the brain.

It's fascinating to realize that signals from the heart tend to lower the activity of the sympathetic nervous system (the part that tends to increase the heart rate, breathing, tension, and stress hormones) and increase the activity of the parasympathetic nervous system (the part that tends to slow the heart rate and relax the body). In other words, if we could only pay attention to our hearts over our minds, we would likely experience less stress and tension in our lives.[25]

Certainly, the impact of the heart is profound, for many more reasons than its purpose as a mechanical pump for the blood. In *The Heart's Code*, Paul Pearsall documents a number of cases where people who have received heart transplants have taken on some personality characteristics of the donors! People who prior to their transplant have been vegetarians and health food fanatics, find themselves afterwards craving hamburgers and junk food. Sometimes their tastes in music, hobbies, and other preferences change with equal drama—and nearly always in conformity to their donor's characteristics.

There is no obvious explanation for this phenomenon, other than to note that part of the transplant process involves also transplanting that heart's mind to the recipient too! The process of transplanting a heart or other organ from donor to recipient appears to result in a type of *coherence* being established between donor and recipient. This coherence is a type of link, but it appears to be an *information* link that unites donor and recipient in a profound connection.

As it happens, biological systems of all scales exhibit this type of coherence. From the scale of individual cells, which appear to have inexplicable links from cell membrane to all other portions of the cell, to whole organisms, which appear to have links that allow all parts of the body to know what is happening in the rest of the body. What is most puzzling about this coherence is that it exists *even when there is insufficient time for information to travel electrochemically from source to destination and even when there is no physical mechanism for that information to transfer—such as in the case of a transplant.*

It's not just in studies of the body where macro-scale biological coherence appears. In cultural studies around the world, native tribes from all areas appear to know information long before the primitive communications

---

[25]For those who would like to work on this specific skill, I recommend the book *HeartMath*, by Doc Childre, Howard Martin, and Donna Beech, listed in the suggested reading list, for specific techniques to lower stress, and pay more attention to heart-based signals.

systems of the area have time to transmit it. The well-known phenomenon of the "bush telegraph" has been recognized in almost all primitive societies.

In some cases, there are hints that such transpersonal ("between persons") communications may operate not only between remote settlements of a single tribe or culture, but also between cultures separated by oceans and, sometimes, centuries. In similarities of buildings, myths, and traditions we may find hints that cultures are able to influence others despite overwhelming physical barriers to travel and direct communications.

Other examples of transpersonal communication are hinted at in studies of identical twins, who sometimes report experiencing each other's pains and knowing what each other thinks, feels, and experiences. Similar empathetic communication has been widely demonstrated in studies of other people with strong emotional bonds, such as mothers and children, lovers, and long-term couples.

In my own experience, part of my journey of becoming psychic has encompassed paying much more attention to the messages from the heart. I have spent months focusing on accessing the heart's energy through meditation, and have found those meditations to be among the most calming, reassuring, and worthwhile of all. Listening to your heart instead of letting your brain dominate your life certainly requires a leap of faith. Your resulting decisions and actions may fly in the face of obvious reason—sometimes mine certainly have. But I have never had a heart-based decision turn out to be wrong. In the long run, in my experience, the heart's wisdom is much greater than the brain's.

When it came time for me to declare my choice of the correct video clip in the Ganzfeld experiment, I opened my mouth to declare clip number one, the clip I'd described the night before, the winner—and heard myself declare clip three as my choice. It felt as if someone else had controlled my vocal cords and simply refused to let me claim clip number one. I shrugged. I didn't have a lot of emotional investment in this experiment anyway. If I was supposed to say clip three, no problem. I made clip number one my second choice instead.

The correct choice was in fact clip number one.

There are some fascinating lessons about this experience. While my partner and I drove home and talked about the experience, he flat-out asked me why I'd apparently deliberately "thrown" the experimental results. Like me, he didn't have any emotional investment in the outcome, but he had heard me quite precisely describe clip number one to him in the car when we drove to the experiment that morning. When I voted for clip number three, he said he about fell out of his chair laughing because at that moment he knew I'd thrown my answer. He knew perfectly well that I knew what the correct clip was—I'd described it to him in the car that morning. Why had I made it my second choice instead of my first choice?

I could only shrug. I'd really tried to say clip one was my choice. I didn't know why, at the very last second, I'd switched to clip number three. But whatever my reasons—or my guides' reasons!—had been, he and I both agreed that the experimental setup was all wrong for anyone who genuinely wanted to prove the existence of psychic powers—or who wanted to be able to reliably produce psychic effects in a laboratory setting.

Psychologists—at least some of them—appear to have a split personality when it comes to psychic functioning. Despite the characteristics of psychic phenomena that have been reported over and over by such researchers as Russell Targ, Harold Puthoff, Dean Radin, Gary Schwartz, Charles Tart, and many others, plus the experiences of legions of psychics and remote viewers about how *they* think their skills operate, experiments such as the one I participated in still get run under conditions that almost guarantee that psychic functions will be suppressed rather than supported. A quick list of the basic problems of this experiment include:

- The psychic session was held right after a large meal (lunch) instead of an hour or so later.[26]

- I was rushed madly through what was supposed to be a cool-down/relaxation phase.

- The white noise was an irritant and too loud.

---

[26]It has been noted by other researchers, such as those at The Monroe Institute, that digestion, particularly after a heavy meal, requires a lot of energy from the body, and this suppresses the ability to go into high vibrational and high focus states. Thus, as with swimming, you get better results if you wait an hour or so after a large meal before attempting to do serious meditation.

- The experimenter's voice was too loud.

- The experimenter's notes were not completely consistent with what I'd actually said.

- Emphases in the experimenter's notes were not consistent with what I'd emphasized.

- My partner was allowed to view all four of the video clips I had to choose from. This is a critical violation of standard remote viewing protocol for reasons I'll talk about below.

- No accommodation to the conditions were made that would have made me more comfortable in the viewing session; I would have preferred no ping-pong balls over my eyes, dim lights so I could see the notes I was taking. This one-size-fits-all protocol flies in the face of the reality that people are different and have different preferences and needs.

You'll notice that fixing these things should in no way have affected the scientific rigor and validity of the experiment. In fact, some of them should have improved those by reducing the impact of the experimenter on the process. Factors such as the white noise and the ping-pong balls were supposed to be there to assist the subject (that would be me) in attaining a psychic state. But in my case, they interfered rather than helped. I had to consciously ignore them. Accommodating the preferences of the subject in such details, as long as it in no way breaches the rigor of the experimental design, should be a high priority for those who genuinely want to encourage psychic phenomena in the laboratory.

Probably the biggest single flaw in the experimental design was that the sender, my partner, was allowed to see all four video clips during the judging period. Why would that matter? Though I haven't yet said much about this point, it is true that psychic functioning, particularly remote viewing, often operates outside of the usual time limitations. In other words, psychic sensing can perceive the past *or* the future with equal ease of viewing the present. A perfect example of this characteristic is that I had very clearly viewed the correct clip the night before, *before it was even chosen*—obviously, remote sensing is not restricted to the here and now! To allow my partner to see all four clips meant that instead of getting a "pure" signal from him, I could easily have picked up a mixed bag of signals from all four of the videos that he eventually saw. In a properly designed experiment of this sort, the sender should *never* see any video clip except the correct target—not even after the psychic session is supposedly complete. In this particular case, video clip three showed a cat on a high speed chase through the desert. My partner knows I'm very fond of cats, so that particular clip would have a high emotional content for me in particular and for him in a sort of secondary effect since he knew it would be one I was interested in. And emotional content is another "attractor" characteristic in psychic functioning. Between his knowledge of my emotional draw to the cat video and the potential to muddle the psychic signals with input from all four videos, it's a wonder that anything positive came out of this particular experience.[27]

Another factor comes into play here as well. In remote viewing protocols, one important element is that the four possible choices should have approximately equal emotional weight for the viewer. In other words, in the set of four possible targets, you wouldn't have an image of a gorgeous diamond bracelet—a highly interesting target for most people—paired with an image of an ugly city dump. People would disproportionately choose the bracelet over the dump no matter which of the two was correct. There's a sense in which targets act almost like an emotional or esthetic center of attraction, making highly interesting targets easier to observe than dull, featureless, or repulsive ones. In this particular experiment, though the experimenter could have no way of knowing this in advance, a false target with cats in it would almost certainly distract me from the true target—an underwater diving scene—simply because I like cats so much. This makes setting up valid psychological experiments extremely tricky to do well because each subject's emotional preferences and tastes are likely to be different from those of other subjects.

More than these obvious design flaws, however, there's an extremely subtle but significant problem with the basic concept of this experimental design. That flaw is the implicit assumption that psychic functioning requires a "sender" and a "receiver." In other words, there's an underlying presumption that something gets *transmitted* when psychics receive information outside their usual five senses. The truth is far different.

---

[27] I do have to wonder if I'd have had any chance at all to get even a near-correct response if I had not chosen to do the experimental viewing the night before. Again, the design of this particular experiment seems more likely to suppress valid psychic experiences than to enhance them.

As experiments with remote viewers have conclusively demonstrated, there's no need at all for anyone to transmit anything. The information requested is simply *there*, available to the viewer's mind to collect and interpret. Somehow, psychics are able to tap into information that is local to them, but which is relevant to places far removed from their physical location.

This is also true of remote healing efforts. Although psychics talk about "sending healing energy" to those in need, that's more a colorful metaphor than an accurate description of what they do. Healing is accomplished by having the psychic *set an intention* that the person be healed, not by transmitting energy of any kind. Even energy workers, those who do psychic healing by working on auras and chakras, really are doing little more than setting intentions.[28] If the healing is done in person, the energy worker may move his or her hands over the person being healed, but this only helps focus their attention on the task at hand and assists in identifying specific areas that need to be healed. The truth is that almost any healer can heal remotely about as well as they can heal in person if they have learned how to focus on the person to be healed.

Human languages don't really have words and concepts to deal with the aspects of psychic functioning that are outside common sense experience, so psychics, like everyone else, have to resort to metaphor to describe their efforts. This can cause a lot of confusion on the part of experimenters who vainly look for an elusive "something" that must be transmitted from person to person to accomplish a psychic task.

What this does clarify, however, is the sheer power of intentionality. It is not transmitting or receiving anything—energy or information—that makes a psychic function possible; it is the power of the mind in setting an intention to know something, or to cause something to happen. Thus, to understand psychic phenomena, we must understand the power of intentionality and of thought itself.

The Buddha had it exactly right when he said, "With your thoughts you create your world." Psychics know this. We use that precept all the time to do amazing things.

---

[28]See appendix B for descriptions of auras and chakras if you're not familiar with these concepts.

6

We Can Perceive That
Which Is Greater

My experience at the TMI remote viewing workshop generated one other result that was equally astonishing. I began communicating with the dead.

Well, perhaps "began" is the wrong word. In one of the Gateway exercises I had connected with the spirit of an older woman, someone clearly in her 70s or 80s. I didn't know exactly who she was, but I got the strong impression she was someone who didn't want to communicate with me but instead wanted to get a message to my best friend, Louise.[29] I recognized then that this old woman was either my friend's mother or her mother-in-law, both of whom I knew Louise had cared for in their final years, and both of whom had died some time before. However, I had never met either woman.

In communicating with this spiritual being, I asked what message

---

[29]Some names have been changed to protect the privacy of others in this story.

I should take back to Louise. The message I got was simple and almost trite: "Tell her I know I didn't show it well when I was alive, but tell her I really loved her."

Hmmm . . . even in an altered state of consciousness that seemed to be such an obvious message that it could easily have been my fantasy of what Louise might *like* to hear, as opposed to something real. Especially because I knew from what Louise had told me about her mom and her former mother-in-law that both relationships had been rocky pretty much Louise's entire life. This was just too pat for me to believe.

So I decided I'd lay an obvious trap for my imagination. I asked the spirit to give me some type of message or confirmation so Louise would know for sure that the message was from her. At this point I still didn't know whether I'd connected with Louise's mother or her mother-in-law. Since I'd never met either woman, and Louise rarely spoke of either one, I was sure anything that I found specific enough to be convincing would be something impossible for me to "make up"—especially if I could get Louise to confirm the truth of the message.

Immediately I got an answer that made no sense to me. I was told, "Tell Louise that the ring (or pin?) was meant for her. It's for her to keep."

Getting this message was a lot like hearing a song on the radio when there's a lot of static. I was pretty sure the spirit had said "ring" but when I asked for the message to be repeated, it sounded like a cross between "ring" and "pin," so I wasn't really sure what was meant.

So I asked for yet another confirming message. And this time I got a whopper. I heard, very clearly, "That Jack, that boy never was any good anyway!" And then the spirit was gone.

Oh, my. Jack was the name of Louise's ex-husband, recently divorced after 37 years of marriage. I quickly concluded that the spirit I'd connected to must have been Louise's mother and not Jack's; I couldn't imagine *his* mother expressing quite that much exasperation when describing her own son!

Of course, it *could* have been my imagination. Couldn't it? I had no idea what the "ring is meant for you" message referred to. It was probably just pure fancy on my part.

It took me a couple days before I was able to get Louise on the phone. A three-hour time difference, a busy program schedule, and only one communal phone made communications to the West Coast rather difficult. But I did manage to connect with her at last. The first thing I asked her was, "Did your mother like Jack?"

To say she was startled by the question was an understatement. "Why do you ask?" she asked warily.

"Well," I said, "I think I connected with either your mother or your mother-in-law. I wasn't sure which, so I asked for a message that would identify them to you, and I got this odd response about Jack."

"What response was that?"

"She said, 'That Jack, that boy never was any good anyway!' So I figured it was probably your mom instead of his because I didn't think his mom would have said that about him."

Louise laughed wryly. "Yup. That's my mom all right."

Relieved, I gave her the other two messages, first the one about how her mother had actually loved her even if she didn't show it much in life, and then: "I have no idea what she meant, but she said to tell you that the ring was yours, that it was meant for you. Do you know what that's about?"

To my astonishment, I heard Louise break into tears. After I left for Virginia the previous Friday, she'd been notified that some bedroom furniture she'd bought had arrived and was ready for delivery. So she had spent Saturday, the first day of my program, clearing out the storage headboard of her old bed so she could clear the room and get it ready for the new furniture. In the process, she unexpectedly found her mother's platinum wedding band, something she hadn't seen in years and had totally forgotten having. It was too small for her ring finger but she slipped it on her little finger where it was a little loose.

The next morning, Sunday, she realized after her shower that the ring was no longer on her finger. She was sure it had slipped down the drain in the tub and was forever lost. But when she looked for it, there it was safe on the bottom of the tub. My relayed message about the ring seemed a confirmation to her that her mother truly meant her to have the ring as a keepsake for her, a final gift from a mother who had died years before.

This was a strange experience to be sure, and one I couldn't quite fit with my previous strong belief that when you're dead, you're dead. Still, it was only a fluke . . . wasn't it? I mean, it was likely just a coincidence or my imagination. But I had no idea Louise would be clearing out her old storage headboard that weekend. Nor did I have a clue her mother's wedding ring had been found, lost, and found again in the space of 24 hours. I still could have imagined everything, couldn't I? After all, I hadn't clearly understood whether the message was about a "ring" or about a "pin"—I'd received it in such a static-filled manner that I simply couldn't be sure.

And while I *thought* I'd communicated with my own dead mother and brother and gotten a message about my dad—"He's off fishing with Gidget"—a highly typical pastime for my dad; Gidget was a favorite hunting dog who'd died 20 years before who'd loved the water and wanted only to spend time outdoors with my dad—all those messages could very easily have been my imagination or simple wishful thinking. There was nothing so unique in them that in the light of cold reason I couldn't push into the category of imagination gone wild.

So within weeks after my return from Gateway, lacking any follow-on communications with other deceased people, I had half-convinced myself that whatever had happened with Louise's mom had been composed of equal parts imagination, wishful thinking, and self-delusion.

Then again, perhaps not. I was at the remote viewing program about a month after my cat Sammy died. I had settled in my CHEC unit to do an exercise, and as usual, I had the lights turned off, and the blackout curtain closed, so I was propped up with pillows against the wall at the head of the bed, sitting in the pitch dark. Dutifully I went through the usual preparatory process and let myself follow the tones in the headphones to "Remote-Viewing F-12."

Suddenly, I knew I wasn't alone in the CHEC unit. Someone . . . some *thing* was in the dark with me.

I felt a weight against my chest, as if something were sitting on it. I heard a soft rumble in my ears. I smelled a familiar scent, one I hadn't experienced in more than a month. And then . . . a familiar bump against my chin confirmed what I already knew at a gut level.

Sammy was with me.

Mediums—those who apparently communicate with the dead—get a very bad rap in science. They are among the most pilloried of all psychics, treated with near-universal scorn and derision. No doubt this derives from the current scientific strong belief, the same one I used to hold, that "when you're dead, you're dead." But that deeply ingrained mind-set may very well be keeping solid researchers from investigating startling new truths.

The most common skeptical complaint about mediums is that they use stage magician tricks to "cold read" the sitter. They ask simple-sounding but leading questions and the sitter, who nearly always desperately wants to hear from a departed loved one, literally feeds the medium the information they want to hear, allowing the medium to simply repeat it back as if they just "received it from the other side."

A second technique used by skeptics is to point out that not everything the medium says is correct. This complaint is often applied by skeptics to virtually every psychic skill; apparently, if a psychic can't be 100 percent perfect, it's "proof" that they can't do the skill at all. Some of the information that comes through is simply wrong. Mediums tend to explain this by saying that since they receive information in highly metaphorical and symbolic terms, that the *information* was correct—but they misinterpreted the symbol or the metaphor and presented it to the sitter incorrectly.[30] Good mediums, therefore, try very hard to give sitters the information they get exactly as the information comes to them.

Certainly a good stage magician can do some amazing cold reads— but just because result *can* be imitated using a particular technique does not mean that in all cases it *is* produced using that technique. A case in point is the research done by a courageous scientist at the University of Arizona in Tucson.

Gary Schwartz is a professor of psychology at the University of Arizona and director of its Human Energy Systems Laboratory. Trained at Harvard, he has impeccable scientific credentials. Those credentials both make his work with psychic mediums astonishing and provide that research with a solid scientific foundation.

Schwartz has conducted years of research with noted psychic mediums in an attempt to validate (or disprove) a single hypothesis: That human consciousness survives death. Reports of his research have appeared on television and in books, but for this discussion, I'd like to focus on

---

[30]I have more to say about the symbolic ways messages are received in the afterword "So You Want to Be a Psychic." But I should point out here that metaphors and symbols are strongly personal to the medium in most cases. Occasionally, however, the metaphor or symbol that the medium gets is the *sitter's* symbol. This is another source of confusion and misinterpretation on the part of the medium.

only one set of experiments in which he worked with several of the most famous mediums in the country to try to validate what they do.[31]

Schwartz is very fond of pointing out that to negate a theory that "all crows are black" we need only find a *single* crow that is white. Similarly, he points out that in order to refute a theory that "human consciousness does not survive death" we need only demonstrate a *single* medium who is able to communicate in a verifiable manner with the dead. It's not necessary to prove that *all* mediums are able to do this. Nor is it sufficient to prove that *some* mediums are fakes in order to prove that *all* mediums are fakes and that consciousness does not survive death. A single instance of verifiable communication with the dead proves that consciousness *can* survive death—and a single verifiable medium proves that at least *some* mediums are completely legitimate.

He has explained that when he initially approached psychic mediums to recruit them for this experiment, he was met with deep wariness. Any noted medium has had their share of run-ins with scientific skeptics, not to mention the media, and Schwartz had to assure them that in *his* experiment, he did not plan to "debunk" them.[32] In fact, in his design, his goal was to do whatever he could to *help* the psychics do their thing—as long as those elements in *no way* compromised the integrity of the research design. He also told the mediums point-blank, that he intended to fully publicize his results with them. If he discovered data that verified they were indeed accessing information that appeared to come from the dead, he would say that. However, if he ever caught even the slightest hint that they might be cheating in any way, he would publicize that also.

One of the biggest problems in dealing with a formal scientific protocol is that they rarely take into account the personal needs and idiosyncrasies of the mediums themselves. Yet who knows better how to make psychic functioning work than those who have to produce those senses professionally, day after day?

---

[31]This particular experiment is described in Schwartz's book, *The Afterlife Experiments*. See the suggested reading list.

[32]Assembling these mediums was done for an experiment that was intended to be taped for a documentary film for HBO. Thus the mediums had to overcome their wariness of their two biggest detractors—science *and* the media—in order to agree to participate in the experiment at all. It's a testament to Schwartz's sincerity and persuasiveness that he managed to enlist the services of the phenomenal mediums he did.

Dean Radin has pointed out that people don't expect perfection from athletes. For example, Michael Jordan, certainly one of the greatest basketball players ever, was a phenomenal scorer. And many people might suppose his uncanny accuracy led him to produce a basket perhaps 80 percent or 90 percent of the time. But in fact, in a really great game, his accuracy was only about 60–70 percent, and in a bad game, it fell as low as 20 percent. Even the legendary Michael Jordan, it seems, was far from "perfect." But what made him phenomenal was that every so often he'd produce a string of shots so amazing, so jaw-dropping that they simply blew away the fans not to mention the opposing players!

Schwartz assembled his own "dream team" of mediums and wanted to give them the conditions under which they too could produce a series of dazzling, jaw-dropping "hits." He wanted to do so under rigorous scientific scrutiny, where the possibility of fraud or other flaw was the absolute minimum he could manage. And he wanted to do it with the best mediums he could find.

Let me just recap a single experimental design—not the best and not the worst—from some of Schwartz's research. He and his research associates began with a pool of ten "sitters." These were people who had deceased friends or relatives that they knew enough about to be able to validate specific, detailed information that the medium might produce. Most sitters had multiple such possible spirit visitors. The sitters varied in age, sex, profession, and home location—coming from everywhere from Hawaii to New York, Florida to Minnesota. Some of them were sitters the mediums had read in earlier experiments, some were brand new sitters. Schwartz also used a set of four mediums: Laurie Campbell, Suzanne Northrop, John Edward, and the Rev. Anne Gehmann.

In this particular set of tests, each session would have two separate parts. In the first part, the medium would not only not be able to see the sitter, but would also not be able to *hear* the sitter—thus addressing the skeptics' complaints about mediums doing "cold reads." There would be no clues whatsoever about the sitter's age, sex, personality, or anything else. They would have no input from the sitter during this "silent sitter" phase of the experiment. The second part of the session allowed the medium to ask yes-or-no questions *only* of the sitter, but again without being able to see the sitter at all.

Just as a side note, the experimenters had arranged to have five separate (mostly borrowed) video cameras recording the experimental session in all its aspects. However, during the experiment, four of the five cameras malfunctioned—though each worked fine when they were returned to their owners. This did not, according to Schwartz, surprise the mediums who pointed out that electronic equipment often fails when a lot of psychic energy is around.[33] Electronic equipment and psychic energy are apparently uneasy companions.

Once the readings were over, complete transcripts of the sessions were printed out and *every detail* the mediums said were listed—often more than 200 individual line items in each session. When all that work was complete, the sitter went through the line items, one by one, and assigned a simple score, ranging from +3 (if it was exactly correct) to −3 (if it was totally wrong). Each positive hit (+3) the scorer assigned had to be justified to the research staff in some way. This scoring session was itself videotaped to ensure that skeptics could see exactly how the scores were determined. When that tedious and time-consuming scoring process was complete, the formal analysis of the experiment could be performed.

To make the experimental results even more clear, *only those line items that received a +3 score were counted as "correct hits."* In other words, if the item got a +2 score, it was counted as a "miss," even though the sitter believed it to have been a near-perfect hit.

So what results did Schwartz's mediums get? The percentage of total statements (from both the "silent sitter" segment and the "yes-no" segment) that the mediums got a +3 score on ranged from almost 80 percent to 90 percent. This compares to the results from a set of nonmedium volunteers (68 of them, in fact) whose overall accuracy rating for +3 hits was about 30 percent.

But even more astonishing, the accuracy rating for the mediums in the "silent sitter" segment of the session was 77 percent! That overall accuracy increased to 85 percent once the mediums were allowed to ask yes-no questions.

---

[33]This is certainly consistent with my own experience: At the very first weekend workshop I ran, I went through three CD players before finding one (a simple Sony Walkman) that worked fine. All the others worked perfectly after the weekend ended. The problem with electrical equipment is fairly consistent in workshops and has led me to make a habit of having backups, and backups for my backups. Generally I need them! And, as I'll point out later, at times when my own psychic energy is very strong, I've experienced everything from frying the battery in my watch to having my television spontaneously turn itself on and off.

Schwartz has done many other experiments, each one increasing the level of challenge to the mediums and each one strengthening the barriers to any type of fraud. He has never worked with a medium he's had to denounce as a fraud. This is in large part, no doubt, because he and his staff work very hard to investigate the talent of mediums before allowing them into his research studies. The amazing thing about his research is that *every* study provides strong evidence that the mediums involved are indeed accessing information from those who are deceased. Often that information is known *only* to the dead person, and the sitters have to do research to confirm that the information is correct after the session is over.

Is there life after life? If Schwartz's research is any indication, the answer must be yes. Furthermore, it seems clear that at least some people have specific psychic talents that enable them to communicate with the dead and bring back messages from the other side.

I didn't understand how Sammy could appear in my CHEC unit at the remote viewing practicum, but all my senses—except vision, since my eyes were still tightly closed—reported the same message. Sammy my cat, who had died more than a month before, was sharing the CHEC unit with me. His head bumped my chin again in his usual greeting, and his purrs sounded even louder in my ear. As difficult as it was to believe, his presence was strong and as real as a touch. His special scent filled my nostrils, the softness of his fur against my chin and neck—Russian Blues have double-coated, extremely plush fur, even though it's quite short—and the sound of his purrs were totally vivid and real. I *knew* if I only lifted my hand I could stroke him, scratch him behind his ears, and feel the rasp of his tongue against my fingers. It was as real a manifestation as I've ever experienced or ever heard of.

And, just as in the final week before he died, I heard his voice in my head, *talking* to me, in English. It wasn't as vague as a "sense of knowing" but instead was an actual conversation, as between two people. He assured me that he was just fine. He had taken up new responsibilities on the spiritual plane, and he assured me he was continuing his own spiritual growth and development there. He also wanted to know if I was amenable to him continuing to stay in touch with me on occasion.

How could I have denied such a request? I missed him like crazy, and there was no way I would have said I didn't want to communicate with him. That response generated another happy head-bump against my chin.

I had the presence of mind to ask if he'd been reunited with Jezebel, his dearly loved baby sister, a full sibling about 15 months younger than he, who had died several years before at the age of four. She'd had lymph cancer and despite chemotherapy and several operations to remove tumors, hadn't been strong enough to fight off the disease. Sammy had mourned her deeply for months after her death. In fact, I knew very well that he'd continued to mourn her, though less intensely, until the day he died. Every so often I'd find him alone in a room, sobbing loudly—a bizarre behavior that began right after Jezebel died and was totally inconsistent with his usual nearly silent presence. Though that happened less often as time passed after Jezebel's death, it never completely stopped.

Sammy assured me that indeed Jezebel was with him and he was deeply happy to have her around.

As our conversation continued I ignored the verbal guidance in the exercise coming through the headphones, turned down the volume on the headphones until the voice receded to a dimly perceived mutter, and continued my conversation with Sammy. Tears streamed down my face as we talked. I wanted to open my eyes and confirm what my other senses were telling me, but found I could not do so. I dared not take the chance that such an indication of lack of faith would cause Sammy to disappear. So, I simply talked with him throughout that exercise, until I vaguely heard the voice in the headphones saying something about, "return now to C-1 consciousness." I knew I'd have to let Sammy leave. But before he disappeared and the experience ended, he promised that whenever I wanted to reach him, I could do so by meeting him in the altered state known as Focus 27 (F-27). And then he was gone.

While the voice in my headphones was still counting back to C-1 consciousness, I sat up and turned on the light in my CHEC unit. I wiped the tears from my face with the heels of my palms and considered what had just happened. Grabbing my journal, I hastily started scribbling down exactly what I had experienced.

But after I'd recorded as much as I could and straggled downstairs to meet with the other program participants for the debriefing session, I tried to make sense of what I'd just perceived. I sat quietly in the corner of the room and contemplated my perceptions of Sammy while the other participants talked about their experiences actually following the instructions on the exercise.

The "Remote Viewing Practicum" is exactly what it declares itself to be: a highly practical training program for one of the most pragmatic psychic skills, that of remote viewing. A much higher proportion of this program than is usual at TMI is spent in a classroom type environment, learning specific techniques for remote viewing, how it works, what a successful protocol consists of, and the types of pitfalls that are encountered in running a remote viewing program.

So, in this highly pragmatic, down-to-earth program, the very last thing I expected to experience was an encounter with a departed spirit. And especially not an encounter with a dead cat—not to mention an English-speaking dead cat! After all, if I was going to meet up with any familial spirit, shouldn't it be my mother? Or father? Or brother? Or grandmother? Or any of the various other family members who had died? Granted, I have always loved my pets dearly and had felt a special bond with Sammy in particular, but why a cat, for goodness' sake?

And what was that about being able to meet up with him on F-27? The problem I had with that suggestion was that I didn't know how to get to F-27. This was only my second TMI program, and the highest level I'd ever achieved was F-21.[34] Although I had the Gateway CD set, the Hemi-Sync tones in those CDs only supported F-10 and F-12.[35] I had no experience going beyond F-21, and would have to attend a Lifeline program to experience exercises that went to such levels.

But more than this, I had another major blow to my belief system to deal with. Only a year before taking this program I'd had a long and fascinating discussion with a co-worker one lunchtime about life after death. In that conversation I had taken the position that death meant the end of all conscious existence. "When you're dead, you're dead," I'd insisted. The brain and the mind are the same thing—my neural network training

---

[34]Talking about a focus level as being "higher" than another is, at best, an awkward approximation. It's equally valid to talk about a focus level as being "deeper" than another. In both cases, the concept is that you are in a more intense altered state and farther removed from ordinary C-1 conscious reality.

[35]Since the time I took the Remote Viewing program, TMI has modified the Gateway Experience CD set so that Wave 5 now includes Hemi-Sync signals to support accessing F-15 and Wave 6 now has Hemi-Sync signals to support accessing F-21.

insisted that was true!—so once the brain ceased to function, that was it. All the things that made a person an individual consciousness simply stopped. There was no heaven, I said, and no hell either. Death merely meant you stopped.

So how could I possibly move from that belief system to one where I had long conversations with a dead cat? Once the cat was dead, that was it, right? I couldn't possibly have a conversation with a consciousness that no longer existed—could I?

Yet even I boggled at an imagination that could possibly have concocted that entire experience out of thin air. I hadn't been expecting it, hadn't tried to make it happen in any way, and in fact, had been expecting and trying to follow the instructions for the exercise.

Furthermore, cats aren't people. Their neural structures aren't complex enough to support the logic and reasoning of the human brain. While I had no doubt that animals that live in close companionship with humans are like children raised in highly enriched learning environments, and thus are more proficient at human intellectual skills than other animals not given those advantages, I also had no delusions that they were proficient at conversation in English. English was a difficult language for *humans* to learn with proficiency. There simply was no way a cat could do so!

And yet . . . and yet I'd clearly experienced *something* extraordinary. The conversation I'd experienced was entirely unexpected to me. It took twists and turns that I would never have predicted or imagined. That very unexpectedness argued forcefully for it having been generated by something outside my own imagination. As an experienced novelist, I was well aware of what it felt like when the words flowed and my imagination kicked into overdrive, writing scenes with a glibness that flowed smoothly.

But my conversation—and the sensory impressions during this visit—didn't *feel* like that. It's difficult to explain the difference—and there's no way to scientifically validate my internal impressions—but instead of feeling like my imagination and my mind had flowed brilliantly as sometimes happens when I'm writing, the experience with Sammy felt much more as if I'd been communicating with something totally *outside* myself. It felt, quite simply, like a great conversation with a beloved friend. His responses had an unpredictable quality to them that marked them as something distinct from my own imaginings.

So that left me with yet another conflict to deal with. I could either completely discount all the sensory data I'd experienced and pretend I never had that conversation with Sammy, or I could accept that somehow I'd communicated with him. Of course, that in turn would mean that I could no longer believe that "when you're dead, you're dead." I could no longer contend that the mind and the brain are the same thing. I could no longer insist that consciousness ended with the cessation of activity in the physical brain.

Instead, I would have to believe in life after death. And *that* was a massively difficult concept for me to get my head around because it ripped huge holes in my humanistic, materialistic philosophy of life.

In the months that followed, while I was struggling to swallow that particular reorientation of my personal comprehension of how the universe really works, I attended a third program at TMI where I accidentally ended up learning how to go to F-27. (No, it wasn't on the regular agenda for that particular program. I wasn't following directions then either.)

And that in turn meant I had a method of meeting up with Sammy. I accepted those opportunities gladly, and have visited with him regularly ever since. A dear friend of mine once claimed he was really unusual because he'd spent a few days doing some energy-building exercises, something his financial analyst friends would have looked askance at. I countered by pointing out that I was in the habit of holding philosophical and spiritual conversations with a dead cat. From my perspective, my friend was simply "charmingly eccentric" whereas I was downright strange!

And I guess I'm still strange, because on occasion I still visit with Sammy. No doubt I always will.

7

How Real Is Real?

"Don't do it," my friend Charles urged me one cold January day a few years ago. "You'll fail and then you'll look silly. It can't work and I don't want to see you look bad in front of my friends."

With those less-than-cheery words, I was being urged to abandon a highly risky plan. I was a newly accredited nonresidential trainer for TMI, having just received my official stamp of approval a mere two weeks before. After attending a program at the Institute, I'd stopped at Charles's home in Virginia to lead a weekend workshop for a collection of his friends and family. And, typically, I'd decided to add something just a little different to the standard workshop curriculum.

The Gateway Outreach Excursion is designed to be an inexpensive, local way to introduce participants to Hemi-Sync while having the benefit of a trained facilitator on hand to guide the experience, answer questions, and provide any needed support. It's a bit like an introduction to the TMI Gateway Voyage residential program. The basic curriculum of the workshop is fixed, but there is a little room for a small amount of creativity on the part of the trainer.

I'd worked very hard to gain my nonresidential trainer credentials, and I wanted to give Charles's group the best experience I could in this, my very first workshop with no cotrainer to back me up. My planned addition to the curriculum seemed to me like a great bonus for the participants.

I was also under the gun in another way. A mere six weeks later, I was scheduled to go back to TMI, where I had to give a 90-minute presentation to about 50 of the most experienced Hemi-Sync practitioners in the world at TMI's biennial Professional Division Meeting. I was deeply intimidated by that prospect. I'd only been working with Hemi-Sync a couple of years, and these were people who'd been working with it for decades! What on earth could I possibly tell them about how useful it is?

And a 90-minute talk! I knew I had enough material to fill perhaps half that amount of time—but what on earth would I do for the other half of the talk?

It also didn't help that TMI had scheduled me to speak third on the conference agenda. I would follow Jeffrey Mishlove, the keynote speaker for the entire conference, and Skip Atwater, TMI's director of research. I'd taken programs from Skip, both that infamous remote viewing practicum and the trainer development program. I'd heard him lecture, so I knew that he is a superb public speaker, with a vastly entertaining style. While I'd never heard Jeffrey Mishlove speak, he was the *keynote speaker* for heaven's sake, so I was positive he would be great. My imaginings of the possible comparisons between their talks and mine were already making me squirm.

To top all that off, my assigned time slot was death for any presenter of anything: I would speak right after lunch, the time when everyone's eyes start drooping, their heads start nodding, and speakers universally despair of keeping anyone's attention for more than a minute or two at a time.

Clearly, my debut as a speaker at a Professional Division meeting was slated to be a huge disaster unless I could figure out something wonderful to say or do to keep people awake in that deadly afternoon-siesta time slot.

I considered all kinds of possible alternatives. I asked Shirley Bliley, the program organizer, if I could have some soft Hemi-Sync MetaMusic playing in the background.[36] (MetaMusic is a type of music CD in which

---

[36]MetaMusic is a registered trademark of Monroe Products, Lovingston, Virginia.

Hemi-Sync tones are embedded in the background of music tracks. Different titles support different types of altered states from improved concentration to deep relaxation.) Shirley enthusiastically told me I could. She'd be happy to play a MetaMusic CD designed to increase the alertness and attention of the listeners. She suggested a CD such as "Indigo for Quantum Focus."

No, no, no! That wasn't what I intended at all! I wanted her to play a MetaMusic title that had deep *meditative* signals embedded, not ones that would keep the audience awake! Perhaps we could play a CD like "Sleeping through the Rain." Then I could speak in an ever-softer drone, and when everyone's eyes were closed and they'd all drifted off into a comfortable and receptive sleep state, I'd gently instruct them that, "When you awake, you're going to think this is the best talk you've ever heard. You'll applaud madly and go away delighted by your experience."

For some reason I still can't quite fathom, Shirley opined that wasn't exactly what they expected from me. Darn. Okay, on to Plan B.

I'd never been to a Professional Division meeting, and had no idea what the audience was like. So I consulted with Dr. Darlene Miller, TMI's director of programs, about whether one of my more unusual personal experiences in a meditative session was something I should discuss in my talk.[37] That might allow me to stretch my presentation to something closer to the 90-minute time slot. "Oh, no!" she quickly replied, "That's *way* too weird for that audience!"

So much for that idea, too. And how disconcerting to discover that it wasn't only my friends back home in California—the "land of the fruits and nuts"—who thought I was pretty strange. Even in the TMI crowd I obviously was on the outer fringes of respectability! Oh, well, on to Plan C—just as soon as I figured out what Plan C was.

I still had no idea what to do with those last 45 minutes of my speaking slot at the meeting. But the day before leaving TMI to lead the workshop at Charles's house, I had the opportunity to chat with Laurie Monroe, the director of the Institute and daughter of Robert Monroe. Somewhere in that conversation, I happened to mention that the previous spring I'd taken a three-hour course through the Learning Annex in San Diego on how to bend spoons, with the result that I had a whole collection of warped, twisted, and contorted forks and spoons. Laurie said,

---

[37]The particular experience I suggested discussing is described in chapter 10 of this book.

"That's fabulous! Teach the Professional Division members how to bend spoons. They'll love it!"

So that's how I found myself committed to teaching 50 or so highly experienced Hemi-Sync practitioners how to bend spoons.

The only problem was, I'd only bent spoons myself once in my life, at that three-hour evening class, which had been a good eight months before. I hadn't even tried to practice it since then. I had no idea whether I could possibly teach someone else how to do it—or even if I could still remember how myself.

Thus, my addition to the curriculum at the Gateway Outreach workshop I was doing at Charles's house was to add spoon-bending to the program, just to confirm that I could teach others how to do it too. It would be a rehearsal for my big public debut six weeks later at the Professional Division meeting as a spoon-bending coach.

Unfortunately, I made that rash decision on Thursday afternoon, and the workshop started bright and early Saturday morning. I had no time to figure out how to teach the skill. By the time the TMI program ended on Friday, I barely had time to stop by K-Mart on the way to Charles's house to pick up some inexpensive cutlery. There was no time at all to practice coaching anyone through the process.

Of course, I reassured myself, if I didn't succeed with Charles's friends, I still had a few weeks to come up with a Plan D—always assuming I could think of one.

To add to my woes, Charles and his wife Mary (both Ph.D.s, with Charles being a retired physicist and Mary an anthropologist) were each highly skeptical. Friday afternoon and evening, each of them separately and repeatedly warned me that spoon-bending was nothing but a hoax—something, they individually declared, that with Uri Geller's public fall from grace decades before had been "proven" to be a mere stage trick. It violated the laws of physics, they told me. They were sure I was headed for disaster if I foolishly tried to include such an attempt in the workshop.

But with bravado not entirely real, I assured them I would succeed, and even if I didn't, I was among friends, right? I was positive they weren't going to throw me out into the January snow if I messed up. Or at least I was pretty sure they wouldn't.

Saturday lunch rolled along far too quickly for my peace of mind. I'd spent some time late the night before frantically trying to remember exactly what that Learning Annex instructor had told us to do to get the spoons to bend. All I really could remember was that it was easier to do it in a group than with only a single person. And I remembered how hot my fingers had gotten in the few minutes before I succeeded in bending my spoon.

On Saturday, once the lunch sandwiches were cleared away, I gathered the small group around the table and passed around some of the inexpensive stainless steel forks and spoons I'd bought the day before. Hiding my uncertainty, I started giving everyone instructions based on the couple of exercises we'd already completed in the workshop.

I suggested everyone select a fork from the pile of cutlery on the table. For an exercise like this, forks are much better than spoons, in my opinion. With a spoon, there's not a lot you can do to warp it other than to bend or twist it at the neck where the bowl meets the handle. With cheap spoons (and you don't want to try this with expensive ones!), it's all too easy to do that without going into an altered state.[38]

But a fork is different. A fork has tines, and even with an inexpensive fork, tines generally are quite stiff. Before we started I asked everyone to see how difficult it was to use bare fingers to bend a single tine. No one was able to do any noticeable damage to the forks. (Using the tabletop for leverage was not allowed!)

With everyone still wearing highly skeptical expressions, I guided them through the spoon-bending process. First we did a few group *Oms* to help build and amplify the group's energy. Then I instructed each of them to hold their forks firmly by the end of the handle using one hand. They then used the index finger of their other hand to touch the top of the fork. They needed a strong enough grip on the fork handle to hold it steady while they gently wiggled their index finger testing the pliability of the fork.

In essence, this made a kind of "circuit" going down one arm, into the hand, then from the fingers holding the fork through the fork itself, then back through the index finger of the other hand and back up that arm to the chest. And that complete circuit is what I was after.

---

[38] Actually, some *very* inexpensive cutlery is too frail to make good spoon-bending targets. I usually buy 18/0 stainless steel forks and spoons at a discount store— but I also check it before I buy to make sure it really is very hard to bend without using psychic skills. It should be sturdy enough that it's highly unlikely anyone can bend an individual tine of a fork without extreme effort—or a pair of pliers!

One of the first things attendees at the workshop had learned to do is to construct a "resonant energy balloon"—a REBAL in Monroespeak. Just before lunch began, the group had done the exercise learning how to build a REBAL.

REBALs are constructed out of the subtle energies around the human body. In essence, they're built using imagination and intention. You construct one by breathing in deeply through the nose, expanding your diaphragm on the inhalation, and imagining that you're bringing in rich, golden energy and filling your whole body with that energy. Then as you breathe out through your mouth, you breathe out everything negative. You also imagine that effort starting a flow of energy up from your feet all the way to the crown of your head and out the top of your head. Once there, the energy cascades down around you on all sides as if flowing from the edges of an umbrella. The energy falls down to your feet where it re-enters your body in a continuous flow, like water in a fountain. You keep doing this deep breathing until you're sure you have the energy flowing well and you have a full "balloon" of energy around you.

So as the next step in the spoon-bending process, I asked them to get a good, strong REBAL going around them. Once they had that working, I then instructed them to use their intentions to redirect the flow of energy so that it came up through their feet to their shoulders, then down the arm with the hand holding the fork handle. They were to imagine that the fork was merely an extension of their hand, so the energy flowed in a smooth, continuous stream through their fingers and up the through the fork to the index finger touching the tines. From there, the energy could flow up their other hand and arm, back to their shoulders, and continue up to the crown of their heads where it finished the REBAL loop.

It took a couple minutes, but soon everyone indicated that they had the energy flowing through their arms and hands and the forks they held.

From my own experience in learning how to do this, after a few moments I asked if anyone felt the hand holding the fork handle getting hot. One or two people nodded. That was not what they should experience, I told them. That heat indicated resistance to the energy flow. They likely were blocking the flow (and thus causing the sensation of heat) by not properly visualizing the fork as a literal extension of their hands. I asked them to work harder on that aspect and see if the heat died away.

After a couple more minutes of focus and concentration, I reminded them to gently wiggle the tines with their index finger. Did they feel anything change?

Not yet.

This is the hardest part of spoon-bending (or fork-bending). It takes a few minutes for the energy flow to soften the fork and you have to hold your concentration intently on what you're trying to do throughout this time. As an aid in concentration, I suggested that they focus their intentions by commanding the fork in a loud voice. In other words, I told them to direct their attention and intentions to the fork by shouting: "Bend! BEND! *BEND!*"

Yelling not only focuses each person's entire attention, energy, and intention on the task they're trying to do, it also provides a certain level of entertainment to me, the person leading them through the learning process. I admit it. It's fun to watch Ph.D.s yell at their cutlery.

And then . . . the first person's fork started to react.

Feeling a spoon or fork begin to soften is an amazing experience, especially if you come from any type of technical background at all. What you experience is simply inexplicable by the science I learned in school. You're gently wiggling the tip of this stiff, hard, cold metal thing with your index finger and feeling the entire fork wiggle with it in a rigid bar. But then, in just moments, it transforms from rigid and unyielding to soft and malleable. Usually the transformation begins in the narrowest part of the fork, at the neck area, but as you keep the energy flowing, it rapidly spreads up and down the length of the fork until the entire piece of cutlery is as soft and pliable as slightly grainy modeling clay.

You literally can *feel* the material of the fork—in this case, stainless steel—undergo a sudden structural phase change. And it undergoes that change at body temperature; the fork isn't perceptibly hot or cold—if you feel heat in your hand it's because you're resisting the flow of energy, and that resistance has to end (and your hand lose the sensation of heat) before the fork will bend. The fork undergoes a significant structural transformation with nothing applied to it except the force of your intentions and the flow of an energy that you can sense but not detect with meters and gauges.

When the fork reaches this stage of softness, you can do anything with it you want. You can easily—*very* easily—use your bare fingers to bend individual tines, and you can twist and spiral them too. You can coil the handle of the fork into a tight coil. Or warp and twist it in any other way you like.

If you're determined to be a purist about it and don't want to use your fingers to shape the fork, you can simply keep pouring energy through it until it spontaneously appears to "melt." It won't spontaneously twist and warp, but it will collapse into an elegant Daliesque droop from the sheer force of gravity. Usually that happens from the weakest part of the fork, drooping at the narrowest part of the neck.

I should point out here that my Learning Annex instructor told us that it's easier to bend pure metals than alloys like stainless steel. Personally, I've never had the courage to try to bend sterling silver or gold. I have no desire to destroy valuable cutlery in an experiment—especially when bending stainless steel is easy enough to do!

Once the first person's fork turned soft, a second one soon followed. That second one, in fact, was Mary's fork—the same Mary who had assured me one last time only a few minutes before we started that she didn't believe spoon-bending was anything except a hoax. I watched her jaw drop as she realized her fork was soft and pliable. Within moments, she'd constructed a metal sculpture of a serpent from her fork. She quickly grabbed another fork and started running energy through it too.

When the first person or two succeeded, it was as if a dam had broken loose. Person after person found their forks growing soft and pliable until everyone had managed to bend their forks at least a little. Mary was the biggest success of them all as she rapidly constructed a fantastic array of metal serpents, birds, antelopes, and abstract sculptures from various pieces of cutlery.

After you finish bending your fork, you simply place it on the table and don't touch it for a few minutes. The next time you pick it up, it will be as cold and rigid as it was originally—except its shape won't be quite as the manufacturer intended! If you decide you want to bend it again after it has "set" in its new shape, you have to start the entire energy flow process all over again.

Everyone in this small group managed to bend their forks and spoons. Amazing. With vast relief, I realized that I indeed could teach others how to do this odd little skill.

Rupert Sheldrake is a bit of a rebel. He is a former Research Fellow of the Royal Society in Britain and was a scholar at Cambridge University as well as a Frank Knox Fellow at Harvard University. His academic credentials are impeccable. But if ever there was an academician who thinks outside the box, he is the one.

In the 1980s he began to explicate his thoughts on the failures of modern biology. Traditionally, biology has sought to reduce the study of life to a mechanistic discussion of physics and chemistry. And it's true that huge advances in understanding the mechanics of biological systems have been made with this approach. But Sheldrake also recognized that this mechanistic, reductionist view of life simply cannot adequately explain certain phenomena.

What are these issues? First, there is the problem of *morphogenesis*. Basically, morphogenesis means the *genesis* (beginning or coming into being) of specific forms of living organisms. *Morpho* derives from the Greek word for "shape," so morphogenesis means "the beginning of shape." In other words, how did the shapes of various plants and animals come into being? If we assume that all life began as simple one-celled organisms, how did those organisms come to create a starfish and a horse, a redwood tree and a squid, a mushroom and a chimpanzee? As Sheldrake says, "Biological development is *epigenetic:* new structures appear which cannot be explained in terms of the unfolding or growth of structures which are already present in the egg at the beginning of development."[39]

A second problem that is difficult to understand strictly from a mechanistic point of view is that the development of an organism can adapt to severe damage to the embryo in early stages. For example, if you take a sea urchin embryo at the two-cell stage of development, and you remove one of the two cells but let the other cell continue to develop, what you get is not half a sea urchin. Instead, you get a *complete* sea urchin, though one that may be a little smaller. And if you fuse two two-cell sea urchin embryos together in a similar way, you end up with one giant sea urchin, not the Siamese twin fusion you might expect. It is almost as if the embryo has access to a model of the sea urchin that in some way modifies the development process and drives it to achieve that specific form.

A third problem in modern biology is the issue of regeneration. Many quite complex plants and animals can regenerate parts that are severed and removed. Plants in particular can do this remarkably well, but animals such as newts and starfish also exhibit remarkable feats of regeneration. In fact, a newt can regenerate the lens of an eye if it is removed—and

---

[39]From Sheldrake's wonderful, clearly written *The Hypothesis of a New Science of Life: Morphogenetic Fields,* p. 19. See the suggested reading list.

it does so by modifying cells in the iris. But during embryonic develop-ment, the original lens derives from specific skin cells, not cells of the iris. This demonstrates that biological systems have astonishing powers to adapt themselves to produce a whole organism.

All cells contain the instructions for all other types of cells within the body: a neuron contains the same instructions as a heart cell which contains the same instructions as a bone cell. What causes these cells to differentiate during development—and during the constant cellular replacement that happens throughout a lifetime? Where is the master plan that causes the various genes to turn on and off to create a neuron or a blood cell?

Behaviors provide another whole set of problems. We all know that animals have incredibly complex built-in behaviors. Spiders spin webs, birds build elaborate nests and migrate thousands of miles, in many cases with virtually no interaction or training from their parents. Where do these instinctive behaviors come from? It is in their genes, you may say . . . but genes basically encode sequences to construct proteins. Where is the web-building or migration or navigation instruction in that? More specifically, how do proteins mediate *behavior?*

Sheldrake's morphogenetic field theory attempts to address these and other issues in biology, psychology, and parapsychology by postulating the existence of a universal field, a *morphogenetic* field that modulates the development of biological forms. The analogy is that just as gravitational fields depend on the presence of mass, and electromagnetic fields depend on the presence of electrical charge, so a biological system depends on the presence of a morphogenetic form. This form becomes the *germ* from which that biological system derives its shape. It corresponds to the *shape potential* of that system, but it stays an unrealized potential until, dur-ing development, the organism fills in that shape with physical matter, systems, and subsystems.

You can think of this morphogenetic germ as the physical blueprint of the organism. The DNA holds the chemical blueprints, but the morpho-genetic germ holds the structural blueprint—what the ultimate organism will look like.

Sheldrake's theory covers more than biological systems. He posits morphogenetic germs for chemical systems and molecules too. Chemical reactions that create complex molecules like polymers would be medi-ated by morphogenetic fields, as would the structure of crystals.

You can even think of the morphogenetic fields as a shape-based analogy to the quantum probability field.[40] In other words, the first time a particular system is formed, its shape may take any of a large number of possibilities. By chance or otherwise, it happens to settle on a particular form. But the *process* of that system coalescing into a particular form modifies the morphogenetic probability field. In effect it increases the probability that the next time a similar system condenses into a form, it will settle into the same shape. In fact, every time that shape is chosen for that particular type of system, the probability that it will be chosen the next time is increased.

Astonishingly, the same phenomenon appears in chemistry as well as biology. The first laboratory to synthesize a new material may spend years learning how to do it. But once several labs have succeeded at the synthesis, it becomes a process that virtually any lab can replicate. Processes that failed regularly before now succeed. Part of the new success arises from greater understanding of the conditions needed to make the process happen. But even when that new knowledge is accounted for, there appears to be a mysterious effect that makes ensuing attempts more likely to be successful after one has succeeded than before that has happened.

In some sense, morphogenetic fields seem to exert some type of *causal* influence on both form and behavior of systems. This causal influence derives from the form and behavior of other similar systems. The more similar the system, the greater the causal influence.

Sheldrake's morphogenetic field is controversial in part because it violates current-day scientific devotion to materialism. Materialism denies that anything except matter (and measurable energies) is real. Nothing except matter, and testable physical fields—electromagnetic, gravitational, and the like—can exist. It denies the possibility of anything having a causal influence on matter except such matter, energy, and fields. No nonmaterial creative agency is allowed in materialism either, which results in ascribing a large number of events to the results of pure chance. Evolution is one example of this: it is relegated to the interplay of chance (random mutation) and external environmental factors modifying the concept of "the fittest."

Sheldrake's morphogenetic field, while having a causal influence on matter, is posited to be nonmaterial in nature. It is supposed to be everywhere

---

[40]I'll talk much more about quantum probability fields in chapter 9.

in space and to be similar (in terms of having a probabilistic basis) to quantum probability waves.

But morphogenetic fields also provide a way of explaining the mystery of *consciousness*. Consciousness in Sheldrake's theory is assumed to be something that *interacts* with the body, but does not *reside* in the body. In other words, the morphogenetic field concept provides at least the possibility of explaining such experiences as survival after death, multiple lives, nonphysical beings, and other events that are quite difficult to explain with a materialist philosophy.

But what about spoon-bending?

Spoon-bending is clearly accomplished by focusing energy into physical objects. What kind of energy is it? And how can the mind *by itself* manipulate that energy, whatever it is?

With remote viewing there doesn't seem to be anything obviously physical involved. It's "merely" a matter of accessing information that is not normally available to our five physical senses. Somehow that seems not so bad by comparison. But spoon-bending is an entirely different kettle of fish. With spoon-bending, I'm changing the physical properties of matter, at least temporarily. And that's a lot harder to do—isn't it?

Perhaps. Or perhaps not. Remember that nearly everyone I've worked with has succeeded in bending their spoons or forks. This isn't a rare or exotic skill. Virtually *everyone* can do it, including you, if you only try with an open mind. You don't even have to believe you can do it. Mary is a perfect example of that. She clearly believed she *couldn't* bend her fork—and then did so very easily.

So whatever the exact success percentage is, it's clear that most people seem to be able to learn the knack, just as nearly everyone can learn to remote view. It mostly requires a diligent effort, a willingness to make an open-minded and honest attempt, even if you're initially skeptical of the results of that attempt, and the support and presence of other people to help you, at least when you're first learning how to do it.

In a typical workshop usually someone in the group finds it fairly easy to get their spoon to bend. Once one person succeeds, generally two or three others who may have been on the edge of succeeding, see the first person's spoon warp, and theirs suddenly starts to warp too. Seeing several successes tends to eliminate any doubt remaining in the others, and suddenly nearly everyone's spoon is soft and malleable.

Clearly, there is some kind of group interaction taking place. But what is it? And how does it work?

One clue comes when a microscopic analysis of a psychically bent fork (or spoon) is made. Researchers on the Stargate program (that long-running intelligence agency program using psychic spies) investigated the physical properties of a psychically bent spoon. Their results were fascinating. When a piece of metal is mechanically bent, as with, for example, putting it in a vise and bending it with pliers, or as a hoaxer would do by surreptitiously bending the metal against a table edge, certain crystal structures are produced and are observable under microscopic analysis that are characteristic of mechanical deformation.

But when the piece of metal is psychically bent, the crystalline characteristics are completely different from such mechanical deformation. Instead, the metallic crystals display the same characteristics as a piece of metal that has been "warm cast"—essentially heated to high temperatures and poured into a mold to shape it.

Obviously, however, a psychically bent spoon or fork is *never* heated much above room temperature—certainly not above body temperature. There is no point in the spoon-bending process that the fork feels any hotter than simple warming from the heat of your hand would explain. And there is certainly no way that the spoon comes anywhere close to the melting temperature of stainless steel!

But this clearly shows there are distinct and important physical tests that can easily distinguish a "fake" spoon-bending—i.e., one in which a magician simply bends the spoon on the sly using mechanical pressure—and a real spoon-bending done with the power of intention and psychic energy.

Apparently, spoon-bending does involve the flow of energy sufficient to have the impact of heat, yet without generating any perceptible actual heat. If it's not "heat" we're adding when we run energy through it, what type of energy is it?

If we suppose that Sheldrake's morphogenetic theory is correct and there is a probability "shape" function associated with all objects, it might be possible for the mind to somehow access that shape function and modify it. Presumably, before the fork-bending starts, the probability shape function would consist of an extremely strong spike at the "looks like a fork" shape. Suppose, however, that the process of "running energy" through the fork effectively modifies the probability shape function to a more mesa-like shape, making many shapes equally as likely as the normal "looks like a fork" shape. That might correspond to the point in the process in which the fork suddenly turns soft and malleable. At that stage, *many* shapes are likely—not *all* shapes, because the fork doesn't turn into a formless blob. But if the "looks like a fork" spike in the probability shape function is flattened like a mesa, there would be many "looks *almost* like a fork" shapes that might now be easily accessible. You twist the fork into the one you want, set it down . . . and *voila!* The probability shape function now spikes into that new "looks like a *warped* fork" shape.

It also might explain why spoon-bending is so much easier to learn and do in groups. The energy of multiple people trying to access the morphogenetic field might be sufficient to assist one or two to make that connection. And as with morphogenetic *shapes*, once one or two manage to build that connection, it may be that much easier for others to make that connection too.

Is this a valid scientific explanation for spoon-bending? Not hardly. Sheldrake's theory itself is hardly mainstream science. It is, however, reasonable speculation based on the presumption that Sheldrake's theory is true. This "explanation" still leaves a lot of questions unanswered, such as, how does the mind modify the probability shape function, and can that function be measured in any way to determine accessible shapes? Nevertheless, this appears to me to be the best speculation available now on how spoon-bending might be explained scientifically.

Perhaps there are other equally valid theories out there. If so, I haven't encountered them. But morphogenetic field theory does provide an indication that just possibly, the realm of psychokinesis may not be quite so inexplicable after all.

Six weeks after my first foray into teaching people how to bend spoons, I had to take it big-time.

I was back at TMI in David Francis Hall, the large meeting space on the campus, being introduced to 50 or more people each of whom had vastly more experience with Hemi-Sync than I did. The presentation portion of my time slot went pretty well, and I was feeling good about my chances of getting through the experience in reasonably good shape. Except . . . I still had to teach 50 people how to bend spoons with their minds. In the weeks since the effort at Charles and Mary's house, I'd had time to grow a couple of very cold feet. I didn't have any choice, however, because I still had that last 45 minutes to fill and I'd already told the staff that I was going to do the spoon-bending.

Taking a deep breath for courage, I distributed an array of spoons, forks, and other cutlery and had people test the tines of the forks to see how difficult it was to bend a single tine with their bare fingers. No one was able to do so.

Then I separated the large group into eight or ten tables of participants. I started talking the group through the process of building their REBALs and running energy through their flatware. Soon I was walking among them, cheering them on as they yelled, "Bend! *Bend! BEND!*" And, yes, it again amused me to see all those prestigious people yell at their cutlery.

Then the forks and spoons began to bend. One at one table. Another on the far side of the room. A third in the middle. More and more people shouted, "I did it!" and twisted their forks into wild shapes. One after another, they celebrated their successes until only a small minority remained that hadn't yet seen their spoon or fork bend.

I had those folks enlist the assistance of the others in their small table-sized groups. Together they all concentrated on one person's fork. Together they yelled, "Bend! *Bend! BEND!*" And together they saw their group energy result in spoons that drooped and forks that twisted.

When it was all over, at least three-quarters of the participants indeed had bent their spoon or fork. Not everyone participated in the exercise, some preferring only to watch, so I couldn't get an exact count of successes and failures. But of those that did make the attempt, some bent a lot of cutlery; some bent only one. And many of those who didn't succeed in the actual session came up to me in the hours and days afterwards, proudly displaying their warped spoons and forks.

I gathered the remaining pieces of flatware and put them in an open box lid. Most of them were taken to the Fox Den lounge in the building next door, where people could play with them at their leisure during the remaining days of the meeting.

But some pieces stayed in David Francis Hall, scattered around on the tables. Throughout the following days of the meeting, as I listened to the other speakers give wonderful and moving talks, the energy flow in the room remained sky-high. The air practically crackled with the power of the group's intentions.

And all I needed to do was pick up a spoon or fork and it almost instantly bent in my hands.

To say this experience was a watershed moment in my life is an understatement. Although I now regularly teach people how to bend spoons and forks using their intentions and their minds, their success astonishes me every single time. Because, you see, spoon-bending very clearly violates any number of laws of physics. My friends Mary and Charles were right. It's simply impossible to do it. It *must* be a hoax. And yet . . . I can do it. Furthermore, virtually everyone else I've tried to teach the skill to can do it too, even those with limited hand strength from rheumatoid arthritis or severe neuromuscular diseases like ALS.

And when I do it, I *know* I'm not hoaxing anyone. In fact, that's exactly why I teach others to do it too. Scientific laboratory conditions or not, and ignoring the whines of the skeptics, when you do it yourself you know the effect is real, it's repeatable, and it's not faked in any way.

Whatever it is, and however spoon-bending works, it has caused me to rethink my understanding of physical matter. Because if we can change the properties of solid objects like stainless steel spoons and forks merely by focusing our attention and intention on those objects, just how stable is our universe? What other aspects of physical matter reality are the direct results of our intentions rather than objective characteristics?

Just how real is "reality" anyway?

8

Been There, Done That, Bought the Tee-Shirt

As I mentioned, before I started this journey I was an avowed believer in materialism. That is, I was totally convinced that the only things that existed were those things that could be weighed, measured, and otherwise perceived by our five physical senses. I also was fully convinced by the rationalist arguments of modern philosophers such as Patricia Churchland that the mind was strictly a function of the electrochemical workings of the physical brain.

I was truly convinced that when your brain stopped working, you ceased to exist. I couldn't conceive of any part of a person that could continue to exist after the brain had died and the body ceased to function. I didn't believe in souls or ghosts or spirits. I'd already rejected Buddhism and other Eastern religions because of their emphasis on reincarnation. I was a loyal little skeptic and a devout believer in the religion of scientism.

My experiences with meeting Sammy during the remote viewing program punched a couple truck-sized holes in that belief structure.

Obviously, if I were indeed having conversations with a dead cat, either I was hallucinating those conversations or something was wrong with that ingrained belief that when you're dead, you're dead. I was still struggling with those contradictory notions when I started getting glimpses of things that made me question the whole concept of death being a cessation of anything except simple physical processes.

After Gateway, I began to do regular meditation exercises at home on my own. While I didn't do them every single day, I tried to find at least a few minutes to work on meditation exercises as often as I could. Perhaps four or five times a week I'd settle into the comfy chaise in my bedroom or den, pull on a set of headphones and hit the play button of the CD player.

Some of these exercises were healing sessions on Sammy or, occasionally, on others. Some of them were guided meditations to get in touch with my "inner self," whatever that was. But my favorites were the "free flows" where the verbal guidance would help me reach a particular altered state (typically F-12), and would then give me a nice chunk of time, about 15 or 20 minutes, during which I could do anything that seemed appropriate in that state. There were no directions for me to ignore as I did "my thing."

Much of the time, the meditation exercises would simply be useful in terms of accessing the problem-solving state or in trying to pattern some specific outcome. In these early days, I never had much success at, for example, trying to manifest a winning lottery ticket, or a windfall bonus.[41] And while others at my Gateway program had talked repeatedly about meeting up with all kinds of "spirit beings," I'd never met any such being when doing a meditation. I was frankly skeptical that those spirit beings had any more reality than a vivid imagination.

Around this time I also ran across Shirley MacLaine's autobiographical book, *Out on a Limb,* in which she described her own spiritual journey and her own recollection of a past life in Atlantis. I'd heard the late night talk shows make fun of her revelations and had found their jokes pretty amusing. Yet when I actually read her book—as opposed to hearing a sound-byte description and immediately deciding to poke fun at it—I instantly recognized many of her experiences to be things that I also had experienced, or gotten hints of at Gateway, or had heard other people

---

[41]I've since been informed that to win the lottery, you first need to buy a ticket. Who knew?

report experiencing during the debrief sessions at the program. And my opinion of Ms. MacLaine switched from "crackpot" to "courageous" as I realized what utter bravery it must have taken for her to expose her not-exactly-politically-correct inner beliefs to such a highly skeptical public.

I didn't necessarily *believe* she'd actually lived in Atlantis—I didn't necessarily believe that Atlantis ever existed!—but I recognized that she'd experienced *something* profound and that it must have been similar to the types of experiences I was personally having. If I continued to label her as a crackpot, what did that make me?

Plus, she at least had the courage to go public with her beliefs and experiences, while I had trouble talking about mine to my best friend on anything but a superficial basis. I generally told no one at all what I was experiencing at this stage. I mostly just recorded things in my journal and kept my mouth shut.

In addition to claiming to hold conversations with spirit beings, other TMI program participants had almost universally claimed to have knowledge of prior lives they'd lived. I was fascinated by these stories because these people obviously took them so seriously and treated them as facts rather than imagination. But I found all the stories unconvincing. There was no *evidence* to support any of this. Nothing that you could in any way call proof existed for any of these claims.

Still, these "recollections" differed greatly from what I'd heard skeptics claim about such prior-life memories. I'd more than once heard a skeptic assert that past-life recollections all seemed to be about princes and nobles and the very wealthy and never about being the serfs and slaves that made up the vast majority of the population of prior centuries. So what were the odds, the skeptics asked, that everyone recalling past lives came from the tiny fraction of the previous population that were in the nobility? Adding a superior sniff and a wave of the hand, they swept aside all possibility of past-life memories as being anything except pleasant fairy stories.

But the people I'd heard discuss their past lives almost never fit the skeptics' mold. Rather than recalling lives of wealth and privilege, they generally claimed to have been anything from soldiers in the Civil War, to prostitutes in revolutionary France, to the Plains homesteaders in the 1800s. They claimed to recall being ordinary folk for the most part, often living dreadful lives filled with hard work, disease, and short life-spans. They were thieves, beggars, trades people, wives, soldiers, farmers, potters, murderers, monks, even hunter-gatherers. The eras they claimed to have lived in ranged from the mythical Atlantis to the concentration camps of World War II.

The skeptics' arguments didn't fit these recollections. Still, the skeptics were absolutely correct in saying that a verbal recollection wasn't proof of anything. It could as easily have been imagination and fairy tale as "truth."

As I incorporated daily meditations into my life, however, I found myself getting more and more messages about having had other lives myself. Interestingly, however, those other lives didn't fit the pattern of the people I'd heard discussing their previous lives. Instead, I got hints of lives outside the mold of the other people I'd heard talk about the subject. Nothing clear, nothing concrete, just . . . hints.

But then, in a meditation a few months after Gateway, I encountered a being who I eventually started to call "Click"—mostly because when I asked his name, it was something unpronounceable that included a lot of clicking sounds. Click became a regular co-participant in many of my meditations. I didn't know who he was, but I did enjoy talking with him and he seemed to be a useful guide to the various focus levels I was exploring.

By this time, TMI had released a revised set of Gateway CDs that included some exercises to go to F-21. One day I used the free-flow exercise in F-21. With practice over the months since I'd been to TMI, I'd gained enough skill to be fairly stable at maintaining even F-21, so once I got to that level, I asked Click to join me. And this time, I remembered a suggestion I'd heard at Gateway about asking to experience your own previous lives. So I asked Click if I could be shown any of my other lives—if I had any.

Instantly, he and I were pulled into a swooping tunnel that was the first of my experiences with what I later called a "BWIC," a buckeyball water interdimensional chute. (It's pronounced like "brick" with a lisp.) Imagine the niftiest water slide you can think of, with loops and turns and swooping glides. That's what falling through a BWIC feels like—except better.

And then . . . I was someone else. I was a village elder but the people weren't exactly people and the world wasn't exactly like Earth. I saw the very end of that particular life, a long and respected one, before Click pulled me into the BWIC again.

And . . . I was someone else again. This time I was an odd bulbous being who spawned by parthenogenesis. I had thousands of offspring and Click told me it was almost the only life in which I'd had any off-spring at all. He pulled me into the BWIC again.

And . . . I was something else, some type of not-very-smart animal, spending a short and not so sweet life scrabbling in the dirt for something, I couldn't tell what, before Click pulled me into the BWIC again.

And . . . lifetime after lifetime flickered through me. Not one included a huge worldly success. Not one offered more than local fame. Many were hard, short, violent. A few longer ones provided respect and a certain amount of local prestige. So many lifetimes flickered past that I couldn't keep track of them all.

Not one matched the "profile" of the skeptics in terms of fantasizing wealth, nobility, or power.

And none of them—not one—was on Earth.

None even repeated the same world twice.

Yet all had the same ultimate goal: To gain in wisdom and experience. To grow spiritually. To improve myself however I could and to leave the life more advanced, even if only incrementally, than when I started it.

Furthermore, although again there's no way to measure or verify the experiences objectively, it was different from watching a series of movies about interesting characters. With each life visited, I *was* that being. I wasn't outside observing that life. I was the person and was within the person. I directly experienced the joys, sorrows, frustrations, pain of each lifetime. I knew them because I *was* them. The effect is almost indescribable unless you've experienced it yourself, but it's far more than "getting into a character's head." I write fiction and know what it's like to do that. I know how to craft a scene to let readers experience life through the eyes of a well-rounded character.

But this was different—it *felt* different. I can't prove it. I can't validate it. I can't explain it. But it was utterly convincing to experience. These *were* my lives, or at least a few of them.

When I came out of that meditation, I was awestruck. No wonder the other folks at Gateway had spoken so convincingly about their previous lives. No wonder they had no doubt at all about the reality of those existences. If their perceptions of those lives were as vivid and real as mine, how could they doubt the reality?

One theory of mind that has been bouncing around since the mid-twentieth century is that our minds are *holographic* representations. First proposed by neurobiologist Karl Pribram in the 1960s, this theory has gained support because the characteristics of holograms correspond in many ways to otherwise inexplicable characteristics of the mind.

Holograms are created by splitting the coherent light of a laser beam into two paths. One part of the beam reflects off the object being recorded. The other part of the beam collides with the reflected beam, thus creating a pattern of interference between the two parts of the split laser beam. That interference pattern is captured and recorded, making a hologram.

Thus, what a holographic film stores is *an interference pattern*.

To recreate the object's image, another laser beam is transmitted through the holographic film. As most people these days are aware, the resulting image has some surprising properties.

First, if properly prepared, the image is *three-dimensional*. The holographic images look solid—as if a real object is there. You can walk around them, view them from other angles, and they look so real that you feel you could pick up the objects pictured. Yet there's nothing there. Your hand goes right through it.

A second key characteristic of a hologram is that *all* the information about the image stored is contained *in every part* of the image. If you had a hologram and a photograph of yellow flowers in a blue vase and cut both the films into four quarters, what would each of those pieces contain?

In the case of the regular photographic negative, the image would be broken into quarters. Each piece of photographic film would have one corner of the image.

But *each piece* of the holographic film, *would contain the complete image.* All parts of the hologram contain information on the complete image rather than only on a segment of the image. The images produced by a quarter of the entire stored image will be a little fuzzier and a little less detailed, but the entire image will be there.[42]

---

[42]This applies specifically to holograms that are re-imaged by using another laser. Holograms that can be directly viewed by the naked eye without re-imaging (such as the holographic images on credit cards) don't have this particular characteristic. If you cut one of those holographic images into four pieces, you get a quarter of the overall image in each piece, just as you do with a regular photograph.

As long as you have even a small piece of the original hologram, you can reconstruct the complete original image. The larger the piece you have, the more detailed and crisper the image is, but it's all there even if you have only a very tiny piece.

One other crucial characteristic of holograms is that they can store multiple images on a single piece of film. All you have to do is vary the angle at which the split laser beams strike the object and the film. In a regular photograph if you try to do that (as in a double exposure), both images appear in the print. The result is neither image exactly but a blending of both.

In a holographic image, if you use the film recorded with the blue vase and yellow flowers, you can go outside and record a red rose right over the previous image. And you can add a third picture of lawn while you're at it. *As long as you vary the angle* with which the laser beams strike the object and film, *each image is separately stored* on the same piece of film.

When you want to retrieve (i.e., display) one of these holograms, the image that is revealed is the single image that was recorded at the same angle as the projecting beam. It's not a blended image as with a regular photographic double exposure, but one image that corresponds to a particular angle of exposure—the vase *or* the rose *or* the grass, but not a blended mixture of all of them. To retrieve the other recorded images, you change the angle of the projecting laser beam.

In more sophisticated versions of holograms, a flat piece of film is replaced by a solid volume of material (which must have very special optical properties) capable of storing the images. This allows the holographic images to be *layered* merely by changing the focus of the lasers to different depths within the storage material. That layering technique in turn allows vastly more information to be stored in a small volume than with other techniques. One estimate is that computer data storage per volume using layered holograms eventually may be as high as 18 gigabytes (18 billion bytes) per cubic centimeter of storage medium, compared to today's best high-density memories which can store about 100 kilobytes (100 thousand bytes) of data per cubic centimeter. Thus, layered holographic memories can potentially store nearly 200,000 times as much information in the same space as more conventional systems.

Because the data is stored and retrieved holographically, it is accessible in parallel—that is, the entire holographic image is stored or retrieved all at once rather than one data item at a time. That means holograms both have enormous total storage capacity and can access the images and information stored in them with fantastic efficiency.

There are other characteristics of holograms that are interesting and important, but I want to focus on these few for now.

Perhaps you have noted some striking similarities between holograms and the neural network structure of the brain. If you recall the discussion of neural networks in chapter 2, the memory system of a neural network shares many of the same properties. A neural network can store an astonishingly large number of patterns in a small area, it retrieves them "holistically" (i.e., retrieving the whole pattern in parallel rather than a single element of a pattern), and each part of a trained neural network contains virtually the entire set of patterns stored in it, making the brain's structure highly robust with respect to physical damage and cellular losses. These are just a few of the reasons Karl Pribram suggested the mind might be a hologram.

But it's more than the mind that might be a hologram. Perhaps the universe itself is a hologram.

David Bohm, a physicist at the University of London and author of a classic text on quantum physics, has proposed that it is possible that our entire universe is, in essence, a holographic image. He theorizes that what we perceive as our everyday existence is actually a kind of hologram that is projected by an underlying order in the universe. He calls this deeper order the *implicate* (or enfolded) order. What we normally think of as the everyday world, Bohm calls the *explicate* order, or unfolded order.

In analogy to a hologram, the film that contains the hologram is an implicate order, containing encodings (i.e., interference patterns) that include all the information needed to project the holographic image. But the projected image—what we consider "reality" from our point of view—is merely an explicate order. It doesn't really exist but is a direct result of the underlying film that *does* exist.

In this view, the everyday things we perceive around us with our five physical senses are the result of an intricate series of foldings and unfoldings of this underlying order that operate continuously. The true universe in this model is like a holographic film—the implicate order. The everyday realities we perceive are the holograms projected by that film—the explicate order.

The constant set of foldings and unfoldings explain many details of quantum physics, such as how elementary particles can appear to be both waves and particles. But, most importantly for our purposes, it provides a fascinating potential explanation for how remote sensing and other psychic functions might work. For the moment, let's not worry about why Bohm proposed such a theory, which has to do with anomalous issues in quantum physics. Instead, consider the implications if he's correct.

First, a holographic universe would imply that every piece of the universe would contain the entire image stored in the hologram. That's an extraordinary claim. Whatever large-scale patterns the hologram contains would be imprinted on every single piece of matter in the entire universe. A rock from a riverbed would somehow have an encoding of the same grand images as our solar system does, or that the Atlantic Ocean does. Or, more importantly, that our brains have.

But turn that around and consider it from the perspective of the rock or the Atlantic Ocean or—better yet—your own mind. The implication is that if you can somehow learn to access and decode that information, you would be able to retrieve any piece of that grand image *solely from your own brain*.

Because your brain (like everyone's) is relatively small compared to, say, the Milky Way Galaxy, the level of detail contained in your brain's storage area would be a bit blurrier than if you were retrieving the information directly from the Milky Way. Nonetheless, the pattern is *there*, complete and uncut, for you to access if you choose. But that blurriness would mean you might have difficulty getting crisp, clear images of remotely viewed scenes. You might find them incomplete, fuzzed up, with only partial levels of detail.

In other words, just as a remote viewer perceives a target. Or just as a psychic receives precognitive or telepathic information.

This is astonishing. If Bohm is correct and the universe operates as a hologram, we should be able to see *anyplace*. One of the most puzzling aspects of remote sensing—the ability to get information about any place at all, no matter what the distance—simply falls out of the holographic universe concept.

And considering another characteristic of holograms—that they can store three-dimensional information on a two-dimensional surface (the flat plane of the holographic film)—more fascinating possibilities arise.

Holograms, remember, can contain full-dimensional details of objects that would normally be hidden from view with an ordinary photograph. You can't usually look at a flower and see it from the rear because light can't pass through an opaque object like a flower or a ceramic vase. But a psychic can do exactly that.

Suppose in a remote viewing session you perceive what looks like an impenetrable wall with no openings, and you decide to find out what's on the other side of the wall. All you have to do is set your intention to move through the wall (or over it, or under it, or simply to be on the other side, depending on your personal preference). Suddenly you find yourself perceiving what is on the other side of the wall—you've literally "looked right through" a supposedly impenetrable barrier.

If the everyday reality we perceive around us is merely an explicate order—a holographic-like image of some larger reality—then the psychic's ability to access "unknowable" information makes sense.

Most importantly, remember the third key characteristic of holograms: that multiple images can be recorded on the exact same piece of film without interfering with each other—and that layering of images in a three-dimensional "film" volume generated vast storage capacities while creating astounding data retrieval efficiency. A key step in accessing altered states is to direct your attention away from your physical body to the place or time you want information about. Once you do that, the perceptions you receive are from that location rather than wherever your physical body is. This is precisely analogous to changing the angle of the holographic laser beam to retrieve a new image, or to refocusing to a different depth in the holographic cube.

In other words, the process of directing your attention away from the here and now may somehow shift the "angle" or "depth" from which you are viewing the holographic universe. In that manner, the sensory input you begin to receive thus derives from that other place and time—and that in turn allows you to begin reporting on a location that can be hundreds or thousands of miles away from you!

Learning how to access such information may thus be a matter of learning how to modify the perspective you have on the universe around us. If all parts of a hologram contain all the images stored, and if holograms also contain complete three-dimensional information, and if retrieving multiple holograms stored in a single location is as simple as changing the angle or depth from which you view them, then such skills become relatively simple to understand.

These conclusions apply almost equally well to all psychic sensing skills such as clairvoyance (seeing at a distance), clairaudience (hearing at a distance), clairsentience (sensing at a distance), and so on. If the universe itself is a hologram, then it should be possible to learn to tune our minds to decode that hologram and "tune into" information from loca-tions and times that are physically remote from where we are.

Furthermore, consider that we're postulating a hologram that encodes the *complete structure of the universe*—the entire space-time continuum. If that structure is little more than a holographic image, then *time* must be stored in that hologram too. Which in turn implies that just as we might be able to access information about any place, we also should be able to access information about any *time*.

All my experiences of crossing time boundaries, of viewing other lives, of perceiving the past and the future (such as in the Ganzfeld experiment in chapter 5) make perfect sense—are even *reasonable*—if the universe is a hologram, and psychic skills are merely a way of access-ing the information stored in that hologram. Which implies that if we do indeed have multiple lives, in a holographic universe it could be possible to access those other lives and get information about them. Of course, a holographic universe theory doesn't *require* those other lives to exist, but if they do, the universal hologram offers a possible explanation for how it might indeed be possible to sense information about those lives.

Over the weeks after my first introduction to those other lives, I had a number of "conversations" with Click about them. The first big ques-tion I had was why didn't I remember any other lives on Earth?

The answer shouldn't have surprised me, but it did. Apparently, unlike most, but not all, people, I don't *have* multiple Earth lives. I have only one, the one I'm living right now. While I do have many other lives, each one is a single life spent in that life system. For me, it's apparently one to a customer.

Click also explained that I had made that choice in my "initiating" life for reasons I wasn't yet ready to understand. As with anyone else, each life is spent growing and learning, but in my case apparently I have only a single chance to learn what I'm supposed to in each world system. That makes this particular path for spiritual growth quite challenging and difficult. But it also means that it's quite efficient.

Okay, now this was really getting strange. This is when I started seriously doubting the whole "other lives" experience. Why was I so dif-ferent that I would take such a path for growth and development? What was the point of that? Besides, anything that made me seem unique and different from others immediately sparked suspicions that it was all my own ego trying to make me feel "special."

Yet as months passed, every meditation session that pertained to other lives only reinforced the experiences I'd had. There have been no contradictions, no matter how I questioned or tried to trip myself up. At one stage I even asked the obvious question of how many other lives did I have. The answer was specific and immediate: 12,535 other lives or 12,536 if you count this current one.

Hmmm. That seemed like an odd number to just make up. And this number too has been remarkably consistent. It has never varied or changed in the slightest. Any inquiry I make into those other lives always results in precisely the same number.

Reincarnation was a totally foreign concept to my belief system. Although this didn't exactly fit the Buddhist concept of reincarnation and karmic payback, it was close enough to make me very uncomfortable. Remember that my earlier belief system had a firm foundation: when you're dead, you *are* dead. You simply stop. No heaven. No hell. No purgatory. You just . . . stop being.

Yet here I was, suddenly convinced that I not only wouldn't die when my body stopped working, but that I would somehow find myself living a completely different life *on another planet!* Oh, please. Had I completely wigged out, or what?

Golly, I didn't *feel* crazy. But maybe that was part of my delusion too.

All of which brought me to the key issue. If I assumed that I wasn't a crackpot, that I wasn't teetering on the brink of hallucinatory delusions, and that the experiences I had reliving other lives are true, that clearly implied there is a universal "Me" that moves from life to life. That implied that death does *not* in fact mean the cessation of being that scientism dictates. Instead, perhaps the only true reality is the "Me" that transmutes from lifetime to lifetime. Maybe the important part of "Me" isn't the physical part at all. Maybe the important part of "Me"—the part that learns and grows and progresses—is the nonphysical part.

Remember the beginning of the Gateway affirmation: *"I am more than my physical body."* Okay, if I'm more than a biochemical and electrochemical bag of tricks, *what else am I?* More than that, is there any way to demonstrate, objectively and unequivocally, what that other part of me is?

I simply didn't know the answers to any of those questions.

9

Salvage Mission

A key experience in Gateway is a tape recording, played in one of the evening sessions, called the "Patrick" tape. It is a recording of one of Bob Monroe's colleagues doing a soul retrieval.

A soul retrieval is a concept that boggles the mind of those who are imbued with scientism and human materialism. The concept is this. When you die, your soul or spirit lives on after your body stops functioning. Sometimes, especially if your death is sudden or unexpected, your spirit doesn't or won't realize that the body has died. In such cases, the spirit can stay "stuck" until either you realize that you're dead and are willing to go on into the spiritual realm or someone else comes along and guides you out of your stuck place into that spiritual realm.

To do a soul retrieval basically means to find someone who's stuck and assist them in moving out of that place and into a place where they can continue their spiritual growth.

In terms of focus levels, typically the newly dead are found in F-23. The idea behind a soul retrieval is to assist that person in moving from F-23 to the Reception Center in F-27. At the Reception Center, they will be greeted, welcomed, and assisted into an area called The Park where they can orient themselves to a new spiritual existence.

Sometimes, in moving from F-23 to F-27, the person you are helping disappears, moving into one of the Belief System territories in F-24, F-25, or F-26. If that happens, the retrieval isn't fully complete, but until that person is willing to set aside their fixed beliefs and move upward to greater understanding, it's all you can do.[43]

Bob Monroe at one point asked a spirit being why living human beings were needed to perform soul retrievals. The answer he got was that people who get stuck are often in a mode where they cannot perceive beings that have no physical body. So having a living human being gain the attention of the stuck person and help that person move on makes it much easier to assist them.

If you read Bob Monroe's book *Journeys Out of the Body*, you'll find a nearly verbatim transcript of the "Patrick Experience," a soul retrieval. But in Gateway we actually heard the recording. In that session, Bob monitored a colleague, Rosie McKnight, as she went into an altered state and connected with the spirit of the "stuck" Patrick.[44] Patrick was a young sailor on a nineteenth-century cargo ship that exploded in mid-ocean. When Rosie connected with him, he thought he'd been clinging to a piece of flotsam overnight and was panicked and afraid. Bob Monroe's gentle questioning of Patrick (through Rosie) gradually allowed Patrick to realize that he had died in the accident and that it was time to move on to a more spiritual existence.

While reading the transcript of this session in Bob's book is extremely powerful, hearing Patrick's emotional cries for help in Rosie's eerily altered voice is heart-wrenching. I found listening to the Patrick tape extremely difficult. In fact, listening to that tape convinced me that I would *never* want to do a soul retrieval. Ever.

Of course, what I want and what I get are generally different things, particularly when it comes to my personal spiritual growth.

About a year after I'd gone to Gateway, I attended the TMI Guidelines program, which focuses on getting in touch with your inner guidance. It's my personal favorite program, and one I've enjoyed repeating.

---

[43]See appendix A for a more detailed presentation of the various focus levels. Also see *Ultimate Journey* by Robert Monroe for details of the soul retrieval process.

[44]See Rosie's book *Cosmic Journeys* for a presentation of what it felt like to experience this particular soul retrieval.

Guidelines also is the only program at TMI that includes a "lab session." In the lab session, you have about a two-hour block of time one-on-one with someone from the research staff. First you discuss the type of session you'd like to have, including what focus levels you'd like to achieve. Then you're put into the "black box" or "lab" chamber. This is an electrostatically shielded (i.e., copper-lined) room with a floatation mattress heated to body temperature. You are hooked up to monitors to measure your peripheral temperature (at your fingertips), your skin conductance and your skin potential voltage. A microphone is suspended over your head and headphones are over your ears.

Your session monitor leaves you in the room (in the dark unless you request otherwise) and goes to the lab control room next door. From the control room, he or she can speak with you over your headphones and can control the types of Hemi-Sync signals in your session, based on what you previously discussed and your directions to him or her. So the lab session essentially is a personally tailored Hemi-Sync session that is monitored both by a person and by physiological measurements.

Once you're all set up, the monitor guides you through the type of session you requested. You can communicate with the monitor to tell him or her when you're ready to move to the next level, and you can report your experiences verbally.[45] The monitor adjusts the Hemi-Sync tones as needed to guide you to appropriate focus levels at appropriate times. Everything you say is recorded.

When you come out of the lab session, you debrief it with your monitor, and you're handed a tape recording of everything you said during the session, plus a graphical printout of your physiological responses on a time axis so you can correlate your subjective experience with your objective responses.

The three measurements taken provide measures of the inner activity you're experiencing. Specifically, they measure physical relaxation, cognitive effort, and emotional impact.

The peripheral temperature is a measure of physical relaxation; as you relax and move deeper and deeper into altered states of consciousness,

---

[45]It might seem that speaking would pull you out of the altered state, but the Hemi-Sync tones coming over the headphones tend to keep you in the appropriate focus level. It takes just a bit of practice to get good at narrating your experiences aloud while you're having them.

your peripheral temperature tends to go up, usually to a maximum of about 95° F.

The skin potential voltage is a measure of your mental or cognitive efforts. If you're expending a lot of mental or cognitive effort, your conductance will tend to rise. When you're simply "coasting" or enjoying the experience, it will fall. Substantive shifts in consciousness are often accompanied by substantial changes in skin potential voltages.

The skin potential voltage also has a second meaning. About every 90 minutes it naturally changes polarity from positive to negative or vice versa. This happens all day long; it's a natural circadian rhythm. But there's also a correlation, though not a perfect one, between such polarity changes and what are commonly termed "peak" experiences in altered states; they can also refer to substantive changes in your perspective. So if your skin potential voltage displays a polarity change, it's interesting to see if that correlates in any way with any type of subjective experience.

The skin conductance is a measure of the emotional impact of what you're experiencing. As it decreases, you become more and more calm, relaxed, and passive. Greater skin conductance implies greater anxiety, turmoil, and tension. It can also mean greater emotional content to your experience.

In this first Guidelines program, my lab session was scheduled early in the week. I didn't really have any notion of what I should request for that session, so after a brief discussion with my monitor, Dr. Darlene Miller, "Dar," I just requested a trip from F-10 to F-12 to F-15, to F-21 and back. Simple.

My session did start off very simply. I had a quick visit to F-10, then moved on to F-12. There I decided to do some healing on a couple of friends who had some chronic health issues. This was something that by then I did on a fairly regular basis, so it wasn't something that was either surprising or emotionally difficult for me. When I thought I'd accomplished all I could do, I told my monitor (over the microphone link) that I was ready to go to F-15.

Once in F-15 I decided to visit a section that I'd only discovered in a previous exercise that morning. I set my intention to visit the "Library" on that level. In that earlier exercise I'd found a library-like structure that reminded me of nothing so much as the school library at Hogwarts School of Witchcraft and Wizardry in the Harry Potter books and movies. In this library was a librarian who was a spirit being composed of glowing energy.

I realized that some of the records there had to do with my life and others had to do with lives of other people. Most of the records I couldn't read—couldn't even decipher the pictures. But in one section I'd found one very short book that contained the record of a life that was short, if not sweet. In that life I'd been a young animal that had been eaten by a predator almost as soon as I'd been born. Not a very satisfactory life in any respect.

So in this visit to the library, I asked if there were any Earth-related lives that I could view that would be in any way meaningful to me. I was directed to a small section of musty tomes. Looking at the shelf, one volume literally fell out into my hands, open to a page. I saw the name "Amelia Earhart." . . .

And I was flying over the Pacific Ocean with her. I probably should have been amazed to be hovering just *outside* the cockpit of her plane, but I wasn't. I probably should have been surprised to realize that Click hovered just behind me, but I wasn't. I just hovered there, tracking along with her small plane, and watched her as she missed the island she was supposed to land on. *Howland Island* whispered in my ear, and I repeated it for the tape record. She'd missed Howland Island.

Through all this I felt calm, detached, and very objective. I saw the moment she realized that she'd missed the island and decided to turn around. I realized that if she'd turned left instead of right (or vice versa), she'd have found the island and landed safely.[46] But she turned the wrong way, guaranteeing that she would miss it.

Click then instructed me that I somehow had to get her attention. I found myself inside the small cockpit, sharing the cramped space with her. I tried everything I could to get her attention and explain to her that she had to come with me. But she wouldn't budge. That's when I realized there was a second person in the plane with her, a navigator. I had trouble getting the man's first name: Bob? Steve? Frank maybe? But I intuited that his last name was "Noonan." Somebody Noonan. She

---

[46]When I'm in an altered state of consciousness, I become dyslexic and quite literally cannot reliably distinguish left and right. This appears to be a fairly common problem. Actually, I get a good sense of left-right but what I can't tell is the perspective I'm viewing left and right from. Is it my left or the other person's left? Am I facing the person, or facing in the same direction as the person? It's very confusing, especially since I have no perceptible dyslexia when in normal C-1 consciousness.

wouldn't leave the plane without him, and I hadn't said anything about taking him with us.

It seemed to take me a long time to convince her to cooperate, but eventually she reached out and took my hand, while reaching out to Noonan with her other hand. He grasped it . . . and suddenly they were both gone, and Click with them. I was left in a small plane by myself, flying over the Pacific Ocean with no idea how to control the aircraft.

Oops. Now what?

Having no idea what else to do, I said, "I guess I should probably go back to the Library now." And as suddenly as I'd appeared outside Earhart's plane, I was safely back in the Library.

The rest of my lab session was fairly uneventful. I went on up to F-21 for a few minutes, then dropped back to C-1 consciousness. But I came out of the session quite disturbed. What had I done? What had this episode been about?

In the debrief with Dar, she explained that it seemed I'd done a soul retrieval of Amelia Earhart. I must have looked a little shaken when I asked her if she could confirm either of the two pieces of information on Amelia Earhart that I'd come up with in the session: the name of Howland Island, and the name of her navigator, "Somebody" Noonan. Unfortunately, she didn't know the answer to either of those questions. They're not exactly common knowledge. In fact, I had thought Amelia Earhart made her final flight as a solo pilot, so what was she doing with *anyone* in the plane with her?

Surely, I decided, I must have made all that up. It was just my imagination playing tricks on me. I was sure that once I checked on the island and the name of her navigator, I'd find that my information was wrong. When I wandered back over to the main building to rejoin the rest of the participants, I pondered how I might discover if anything I'd learned in the lab session was accurate or if, as I was inclined to believe, I'd simply made it all up. Could I validate—or disprove—that data somehow?

The world operates around us more or less in accordance with our common sense. In fact, the reason Newtonian mechanics ruled physics for 300-odd years was that for our everyday experiences, it provides a near-perfect summation of how things work. But as physicists started looking at the world of atoms and subatomic particles, they found that the simple

Newtonian description of reality doesn't work. In the world of the very small, at the level of atoms and subatomic particles, Newtonian physics doesn't just show cracks—the whole concept shatters into tiny pieces.

Although the world of the subatomic scale demanded a new understanding of physics, even before quantum physics appeared, some things in the ordinary world simply didn't match up with conventional Newtonian expectations. The biggest failing of Newtonian physics on the scale of the ordinary world shows up in the controversy over whether light consists of a stream of particles—little light particles called photons—or whether it is a wave, like a ripple disturbing a quiet pool of water.

For 200 years, scientists tried to determine whether light was a wave or a particle. The problem was, some experiments seemed to indicate one result, and others seemed to indicate the opposite. Which experiments you trusted determined whether you thought light was a wave or a particle.

Favoring the particle nature of light were the accepted facts that light travels in straight lines (waves often bend and even go around corners), light travels through the vacuum of empty space (making it difficult to understand what could be "waving" if light is a wave), and light conveys energy from one place to another. But objects that emit light appear to lose no mass. If they're giving off a stream of particles, wouldn't those particles carry at least tiny amounts of mass with them?[47] Despite efforts to detect such mass losses, no scientist was able to demonstrate a loss of mass with emission of light, nor a gain in mass in an object absorbing light particles.

A second problem is the invariant value for the speed of light. How can physical particles maintain an invariant speed? And how can you explain colors if not by different speeds of light or different types of light particles?

Still, despite these issues, scientists such as Isaac Newton strongly supported the particle theory of light.

Other scientists, like Newton's contemporary and rival Christopher Huygens, supported the wave theory. Waves also can convey energy from place to place—and without transferring any mass as they do it—though they must have some type of medium, such as air or water, for them to

---

[47]During the period in which the wave vs. particle nature of light was being debated, no one had yet conceived of the notion of a "massless" particle. If light was a particle, it had to have at least a tiny amount of mass—didn't it?

travel through. Furthermore, waves can travel at a fixed speed, determined by neither their amplitude or wavelength. For example, sound travels at the same speed through air no matter how loud the sound (amplitude) nor how high or low the pitch (wavelength).

One key difference between the wave theory and the particle theory is how they respond when the wave (or particle) crosses boundaries from one transmitting medium to another. Refraction is the bending of light when it travels from one medium to another. It's why distances and shapes are distorted when you look at an object that is half-submerged in water. If you put one end of a straight stick in water, it appears to kink, right where it enters the water. Refraction causes that apparent kink.

If light is a particle, resistance from the medium should make light travel more slowly in denser materials. If light is a wave, increased density of the transmitting medium should make light travel more quickly. In the mid-1800s, a definitive experiment showed that light travels more slowly in denser media. That should have cast doubt on the wave theory of light, but by that time a series of key experiments had completely squelched the idea that light might be a particle. Those experiments are interference experiments, and key to them are the "two-slit" and the "double refraction" experiments. Since these experiments play a role in understanding subatomic particles too, I want to take a few moments to explain them.

Imagine that you have a light source that has been narrowed to a beam. You pass the beam through a series of prisms or filters until you have light of only a single color,[48] then place in front of that beam an opaque wall that has two extremely close, very narrow slits in it.[49] Behind

---

[48]This does not have to be laser light, by the way. Just take a beam of sunlight from a small hole in a window shade in an otherwise dark room and pass it through a prism so it separates out the colors. Then block off all the colors except the one you want, say yellow, by putting opaque paper to stop the others from coming through. Add a simple lens to focus this yellow light into a narrow beam, and you're done.

[49]One reason this was a difficult experiment to perform before the 1800s is that the slits have to be narrow relative to the wavelength of the light beam. Thus the slits have to be somewhat smaller than 15 to 30 *millionths* of an inch wide to demonstrate this effect! The variation depends on the color of the light beam; a blue light beam requires the slits to be smaller than about 0.000015 inches wide; a red light beam allows the slits to be about twice as wide, or somewhat smaller than 0.000030 inches wide.

it, on the other side of the wall, you put a screen that will be illuminated by whatever light comes through the two slits.

Now if light consists of little particles—photons, for example—you'd expect that on the other side of the two slits, you'd simply have an image of the slits themselves—long, narrow illuminated patches, perhaps a little blurry around the edges, but surrounded by darkness. That's not what happens. When you look at the screen, what appears is a set of light and dark vertical bands, with the brightest bands directly opposite the slits, but with bands extending well on either side of the actual openings.

This result is conclusive proof that when light passes through the slit, it is doing so as a wave. The beam of light must be the equivalent of a circular wave (actually an arc of a circular wave), just as appears when you toss a small pebble into a quiet pond or the same way sound travels in all directions when you give a shout. Wherever light reflects from a surface, it must reflect as a new circular wave.

In the experiment, the wave that goes through the middle of the slit continues to the screen unchanged, thus giving large light spots directly opposite the slits. But part of the wave hits the right side of each slit, where it is reflected at a new angle, just as ripples in a pond are reflected or sound reflects (echoes) off a canyon wall. This reflection generates a second wave which *interferes* with the main one going straight through the slit. Where the two waves are both at their peaks, the wave is *amplified* and a bright spot appears. Where the two waves meet at opposite points in their vibration—i.e., one wave at its peak and one wave at its trough—the two waves cancel each other out, resulting in a dark band on the screen.

The same thing happens at the left edge of each slit. So there are now *three* waves interfering with each other from *each* slit. This complex mixture of waves interfering with each other generates the series of light and dark bands that appear instead of the simple images of the slits. Given that there are two slits, you have a total of at least *six* waves interfering with each other, thus generating a complex pattern of light and dark bands.

If you assume that light is a wave, the two-slit experiments are quite easy to understand, as I've explained. But then there is double refraction, the other critical experiment on the nature of light. Discovered in the late seventeenth century, double refraction is demonstrated when a beam of light enters certain types of crystals and appears to be refracted in two distinct ways, splitting the beam into two pieces rather than merely bending it. Not only can this phenomenon not be explained by a particle theory of light, but even the wave theory of light requires an additional assumption about the nature of light waves.

Initially, wave theories of light assumed that light was the equivalent of sound. That is, scientists assumed light is a *longitudinal* wave, where the wave travels in the direction of its vibration. Sound is like that. Sound waves consist of alternating compressions and expansions of air (or whatever transmitting medium). The cycle of compress/expand/compress vibrates the air in the *same direction* as the wave itself is traveling. All early wave theories of light made the implicit assumption that light was just like sound in this respect.

Unfortunately, double refraction is virtually impossible to explain with longitudinal waves. It wasn't until the early 1800s when the English scientist Thomas Young suggested that double refraction could easily be explained if you assumed that light consisted of *transverse* waves rather than longitudinal ones. A transverse wave is like a ripple in a pond. The wave itself vibrates up and down but the wave travels horizontally across the surface of the pond in a direction perpendicular to that up-and-down motion. So a swimmer in the ocean bobs up and down as water alternately lifts and lowers him, although the motion of the wave is toward the shoreline.

Young suggested that crystals that demonstrate double refraction had a structure with a different density or a different number of atoms along one axis (say, a vertical axis) than another axis (say, the horizontal axis). A beam of light traveling through the crystal from front to back (the third dimension of the crystal), if it consisted of transverse waves of light, would experience two different transmission speeds because the density of the transmitting medium for the light waves that are vertically vibrating would be different than the light waves vibrating horizontally. Remember that changing the density of the transmitting medium changes the speed of transmission of a wave, so those parts of the light beam that vibrate with the vertical axis pass through the crystal at a different speed than those that vibrate with the horizontal axis. Thus, the beam of light is split into two separate beams, and double refraction is explained.[50]

---

[50]This discussion may seem to be a bit of a diversion, but in a later chapter, it will be very important to understand the difference between a transverse wave (like light) and a longitudinal wave (like sound).

The wave theory of light was firmly established when James Clerk Maxwell introduced his classic Maxwell's equations that explained nearly all of electromagnetism. Light became understood as a transverse electromagnetic wave consisting of two coordinated transverse waves, one electrical and one magnetic, vibrating in lock-step with each other. These two waves have very specific relationships to each other. They must have the same amplitude as well as have the same wavelength . Furthermore, the electric wave portion of light vibrates along one axis perpendicular to the direction of transmission of the wave, and the magnetic wave portion vibrates perpendicular to the electric wave, but also perpendicular to the direction of transmission. For example, the electric wave might vibrate along a north-south axis while the magnetic wave vibrates along an east-west axis. Meanwhile, the overall light wave—the combined electromagnetic wave—moves forward in an up-down direction. Thus, both the electric wave and the magnetic wave are perpendicular to the direction of transmission, but also perpendicular to each other.

Maxwell's equations required that the electric and magnetic components of a light wave had to be of equal strength (amplitude) in order for the wave to be able to propagate (travel through space). Technically, those electric and magnetic wave components are vibrations or *changes* in the electric and magnetic fields. Maxwell's equations clearly imply that in order to maintain that equal strength and thus allow light to travel through space, the electric and magnetic fields must change at such a rate that the light wave's speed of propagation is equal to a constant value.[51]

Maxwell, in other words, provided a clear theoretical basis that demanded that the speed of light should be a constant value, c.

Maxwell's equations also reflect a deep symmetry between electric and magnetic forces—something that physicists really love in theories. In four very short and (relatively) simple equations, Maxwell provided a complete description that "unified" electric and magnetic forces. For the

---

[51]In case you're wondering, the speed of light in a vacuum is about 186,000 miles per *second*, or about 300,000 kilometers per second. That's about the equivalent of going around the Earth at its equator *seven and a half times every second!* Notice that I had to specify the speed "in a vacuum" to identify the transmitting medium since the speed of wave propagation varies according to the medium through which it travels. Light travels fastest in a vacuum, so that's the gold standard for the speed of light.

first time, apparently different fundamental forces in nature had been combined into a single, elegant theory.

This became the Holy Grail of physics: to find a single unifying theory—a grand unified theory (GUT) or a theory of everything (TOE)—that would unite *all* the fundamental forces of nature into one simple, elegant theory just as Maxwell united electricity and magnetism into the electromagnetic theory.[52]

Remember that two-slit experiment where light was conclusively demonstrated to behave as waves rather than as particles? In the early 1900s that very same experiment caused chaos in physics one more time. What would happen if you did that experiment, not with a beam of light, but with a beam of atoms?

The common visualization of an atom since the early 1800s when the atomic theory of matter was first accepted was that it was like a hard rubber ball—solid and unbreakable. But in the early 1900s, physicist Ernest Rutherford did a series of experiments in which he aimed a beam of charged particles at atoms and monitored how they bounced. If the atom were truly like a solid rubber ball, and the atom was of a particular size, you'd expect the particles aimed at it would bounce off in all directions. You'd expect, in fact, that few or none of them would shoot straight through the atom to the other side.

But that's not what happened. Instead, almost *all* the particles shot straight through the target atoms! It was as if they were traveling through nothing at all. Only occasionally did one of them "bounce off" the target atom—but bounced back almost in the same direction from which it came—as if it had caromed off an impenetrable core. This meant that the mental picture of an atom had to change from that of a solid rubber ball to something more like a miniature solar system, with a tiny hard nucleus in the middle and not much of anything (i.e., orbiting electrons) around it. The electrons were themselves imagined as tiny little particles, like tiny planets orbiting the sun. Thus, most particles beamed at this solar-system atom would miss all the mass, because it was concentrated in the tiny, positively charged nucleus and the even tinier, negatively charged electrons orbiting the nucleus.

It wasn't until the late 1800s that the technology was good enough to reliably produce atomic beams, but when the equivalent of a two-slit experiment was performed using an atomic beam instead of a light beam,

---

[52]In addition to electricity and magnetism, fundamental forces include gravity, and the weak and strong nuclear forces.

extremely surprising results occurred. If atoms were truly particle-like (even as mini-solar systems), they should move straight through the slits and be detected on the far side of the slit in two simple "images" of the slits, just as a light would have if it were made up of particles. Instead, a beam of atoms aimed at the two slits produces an interference pattern exactly similar to the interference pattern light produces!

In other words, the experiment that demonstrated, more or less conclusively, that light must be a wave, now demonstrates, with equal conclusiveness, that *matter* must be a wave phenomenon.

This is one of the fundamental weirdities of the physical universe. Rutherford's experiment "conclusively" showed that matter must be particles—waves don't carom off each other as happened in his experiment. The two-slit experiment with atomic beams, however, equally "conclusively" demonstrated that matter must be wavelike—particles don't demonstrate interference patterns.

Somehow, matter must be *both* wave and particle. And so must light, because other experiments by this time had shown that under certain circumstances light behaves like nothing so much as tiny particles of zero mass.

There were more surprises in store. Albert Einstein did some "thought experiments" in which he tried to imagine what the world would look like if he were riding on a beam of light. The result of his ponderings was the theory of special relativity and a new relationship between matter and light—a form of electromagnetic energy.

His conclusion: Solid matter isn't. Isn't solid, that is. In fact, it's not even matter—there is no such thing as "matter" as something separate and tangible. The relationship between matter and energy is expressed in the famous equation:

$$E = mc^2$$

Here "E" means "energy," "m" means "mass," and "c" refers to a universal constant, the speed of light in a vacuum.

In other words, matter and energy are two forms of the same thing! You can convert mass to energy or energy to mass. They're merely two different aspects or formulations of the same underlying "stuff." And of the two, the more basic quantity is energy. In fact, one perfectly valid way of viewing mass is as "frozen energy."

Wave-particle duality has come to be one of the foundation blocks of quantum physics. Other key (and really strange) qualities of the quantum world include:

- Nature in the quantum world is often innately granular; that is, qualities such as spin, angular momentum, even electric charge, come in small quantum packets that cannot be broken into smaller pieces.

- The quantum world is inherently probabilistic in that rules of probability dominate.[53] You can't specify anything exactly; you can only specify probabilities of things.

- The quantum world is fundamentally one of constant creation and annihilation where particles are constantly being created and destroyed as they transition from their "energy only" state to a "matter state" and back again.

- The quantum world is a realm of uncertainty. The Heisenberg uncertainty principle assures us that we cannot know everything about even a single particle or other quantum object because the act of observing, say, the speed of a particle to an exact degree, destroys forever any possibility of knowing the precise location of that particle.[54]

Of this list, possibly the most important for my purposes is the probabilistic nature of quantum reality. You can think of the state of a particle as being indeterminate until it is observed. It is as if it has no state, no real existence, until someone observes or measures it. Until that time, it exists only as a "probabilistic soup" of potential qualities that span all possible values that particular particle might have. It is a wave, but it's a wave of probabilities, best described as a probability wave function that can take on many different values as it vibrates back and forth through potential possibilities.

Once the observation is performed, however, that probabilistic wave of all possibilities congeals to a single, observable value, which is the value that is measured. Physicists like to say that the particles probability wave function "collapses" into a single-valued point at that stage. It's no longer a wave, but a "probability particle."

---

[53]In fact, quantum probability isn't even the same as real-world probability (coin-flipping, for example). But that's a whole other subject!

[54]Other characteristics of subatomic particles are similarly paired. Which raises the question of *why* are they paired in the way they are. Again, a question not easily answered.

The probability wave function cannot itself be directly observed. We can only know about it based on computations and observations of what happens when the wave coalesces into a single value—in other words, it becomes more particle-like and loses its wave nature. We can only infer what the original probability wave function was like after the fact.

In other words, there is a distinctly nonzero possibility that your body's probability wave function—the one that represents all particles down to the subatomic that correspond to your entire physical body—will collapse, on observation, to a value that has you instantaneously transported to Australia—or the Antarctic.[55] No matter how miniscule the odds are, it's *possible*, and thus is reflected in the probability wave function that represents your body.

Common sense—the set of instincts we've all developed about how the world works on our everyday level—goes by the wayside in the quantum realm. Nothing works as expected; none of our "real world" experience applies. Everything is simply . . . weird.

But of all these strange, difficult-to-comprehend characteristics, the weirdest of all, and the one most relevant to possibly understanding psychic experiences, is the concept of quantum entanglement.

Entanglement, first a theory, is now an established, demonstrable fact. Quantum entanglement occurs when two particles are created in such a fashion that they share some aspects of their existence. Like twins who share a "twin link" after birth, the fates of these particles are forever united, often in a complementary way. Or at least, they're "forever" united until the entanglement between them is broken, which is fairly easy to do, as it happens. If one particle of an entangled pair is observed to have "spin up" property, the other particle will be observed to have "spin down." It is as if these particles, because they were created together in a particular way, have their fates forever entangled, one with the other. It doesn't matter how far apart they are, it doesn't matter what characteristic you observe in either of them. If one is measured to have a particular property, the other invariably has the same or complementary property.

---

[55]This does actually happen on an individual particle level, if not on the level of whole animals or organisms consisting of trillions and trillions of particles. It's called "quantum tunneling" where quantum particles suddenly appear outside areas that they are supposedly confined in, and it has been observed many times. Semiconductor electronics actually rely on this particular phenomenon for certain applications.

Forever. Anywhere. Anytime. *Instantly.*

What's even more weird about quantum entanglement is that the second partner in a pair always reflects the complement to the first partner's characteristic *even when the second particle is too far away to "know" what happened to the first one.*

Suppose you create two entangled photons of random polarity (i.e., their electric fields are vibrating in random orientation around the direction of travel), and you set them going in opposite directions at the speed of light for, say, two seconds. They're now about 375,000 miles away from their starting point (give or take a little). Since they went in opposite directions, the particles are now twice that far apart—about 750,000 miles. Since we know information can't travel any faster than the speed of light, it would take four seconds for photon #1 to communicate anything to photon #2, right?

But what if we measure photon #1's polarity (or any other quantum property) at the two-second mark, and simultaneously measure photon #2's polarity? Because they're so far apart, there's no possibility that they can communicate with each other in any way.

The result, however, is astounding. No matter how far apart the two photons are, once one of them has their polarity measured, the other will *always* have a complementary polarity! *Always.* No exceptions. And it holds true no matter what type of quantum particle you use, or what set of quantum characteristics you measure. If the two particles are entangled at creation, their probability wave functions always collapse to complementary values. Measure one particle, and you have no need to measure the other particle's characteristics because you know exactly what they are with 100 percent certainty.

Quantum entanglement has recently been used to demonstrate the even stranger phenomenon of teleportation. Yes, it is a real, technological accomplishment, though at the moment we've only been able to document teleportation of information, photons, and very recently individual atoms. We're a long way from building a *Star Trek* transporter unit—but theoretically it's not impossible. Not if you take quantum entanglement into consideration.

With quantum entanglement it's possible to explain (in at least a vague, arm-waving kind of way) such phenomena as remote viewing, telepathy, and other such events that involve transmitting either information or matter across distances. For example, one "explanation" claims that since the entire universe was created in an initial Big Bang of a single point, in some sense the entire universe was entangled at the moment of creation. If that's the case, it means that there should be some level of knowledge about every point in the universe at all times forever. If the mind can learn to tap into that entangled knowledge, it's at least conceivable that it could learn about places and situations across all of time and space.

And you might be able to argue that a "soul retrieval" results when (somehow) the energy that constitutes the soul gets entangled with the mind of the person doing the retrieval. When the retrieved soul is "carried up" to a new focus level, the entanglement is broken. Thus, soul retrieving could be a process of tuning your mind's energy to that of a soul that needs assistance so that you and they are entangled, then moving that energy to a new state, then breaking the entanglement to leave the retrieved soul in its new home.

Of course, the big flaw in all these entanglement explanations is that all particles in the universe are *not* entangled, at least in the true quantum sense. It's easy to destroy the entangledness of particle pairs—in fact, it's fairly difficult to maintain entangled pairs with our current technology. So it seems highly unlikely that any such entanglement from the Big Bang, some 14 billion years ago, could possibly still exist at the necessary level to explain psychic functions.

And the other flaw with this explanation is that quantum entanglement is a property of the world of the extremely small. Psychic phenomena take place at the level of the mind (or brain, at the very least). There's a reason Newtonian physics ruled for 300 years—at the level of the everyday world, it works. It may fall apart in the realms of the very fast (i.e., approaching light speed) where relativistic mechanics takes over, and it may fall apart in the realm of the atomic and subatomic world, where quantum mechanics rules. But in the world of the ordinary scale, Newtonian mechanics wins, hands down; quantum phenomena are simply inapplicable at the scale of the ordinary world. To apply quantum phenomena to the macro world of the whole organism exhibits a complete misunderstanding of the underlying physics.

Or does it?

After pondering how to validate the information I'd gotten during my soul retrieval of Amelia Earhart, I finally decided to call a friend back in San Diego and ask her to look up the facts on the Internet. But

I wouldn't tell her what my answers were. Instead, I copied them down in my journal—and of course, they were recorded on the cassette tape of the session.

Two days later I called her a second time to see what she'd discovered. Amelia Earhart had indeed disappeared over the Pacific when she was trying to fly to a small dot called Howland Island. And, yes, she'd had a navigator with her who took no role in controlling the plane, thus qualifying this as a "solo flight." That man's name was Fred Noonan.

I was two for two. Both obscure facts I'd gotten in the lab session had proved to be true. Yes, I'd missed the navigator's first name, but Frank and Fred weren't that dissimilar, and my focus had been on Earhart, not on her navigator. And I had absolutely no recollection of knowing either the name of the island or the name of her navigator before that session. Nor did I have any particular interest in Amelia Earhart.

I know that those claims have no particular weight with skeptics. But one further piece of information adds just a tad more validity to the experience. When I got my graphical printout of the physiological data from my session, it fascinated me. First, my peripheral temperature showed a steadily increasing level of relaxation throughout the exercise until I began the return to C-1 consciousness at the end.

The skin potential voltage measurements showed a small bump in cognitive effort during two times: The first bump exactly corresponds to the time in which I was doing my healing session on my two friends. Apparently I was exerting a significant cognitive effort to do that healing. The second bump is much higher and corresponds exactly to the time I was at Amelia Earhart's plane.

Finally, the skin conductance measurements showed only a single substantial bump in emotional content. There was no real increase in emotional intensity when I was doing the healing session—and that corresponded exactly to my own sense of exerting a simple, unemotional and workmanlike effort with no more emotional content than that of, say, cooking dinner. But there is a huge increase in emotional intensity at a later time in the session that corresponds exactly to the Amelia Earhart incident.

So no matter how I considered this, I realized there are some critical points that simply must be explained. First, how did I know the name of the island and the name of her navigator? Second, clearly there's a correlation between what I subjectively experienced and what was objectively happening to me physically.

But more than this, if there is any validity at all to my having done a soul retrieval on Amelia Earhart, how can that possibly be explained in terms that are consistent with modern scientific thought?

Entanglement offers a possible explanation for soul retrievals, though there are obvious problems with it. Not least of which is defining exactly what it is I was retrieving.

What *is* a soul, anyway? I don't know. Do you?

10

Playing Fetch

About a year after I'd gone through Guidelines, I was back at TMI, this time for the Lifeline program. Lifeline's purpose is to teach you about being of service to others by means of doing soul retrievals on those who are stuck in the afterlife. In the process, you can often discover important aspects about yourself. It's also not uncommon to realize that some (though not all) of the lives you are drawn to rescue are previous lives of your own. In some respects you literally rescue and retrieve parts of yourself.

I'd put off taking Lifeline because certain aspects of it frankly didn't appeal much to me. As I explained in the previous chapter, I didn't particularly enjoy doing soul retrievals, nor was I especially drawn to them as important tasks I should be doing. Furthermore, the Amelia Earhart experience still didn't quite sit comfortably with my world views. Yet I really wanted to take TMI's Starlines program, and the prerequisite programs were both Lifeline and another program called Exploration 27. Talk about being "stuck"!

So there I was at Lifeline in January 2004, doing what is almost always done the first full day of the program, going through the reset exercises. Pretty much all the graduate programs, those after Gateway, begin with a part or whole day of resetting the key focus levels of F-10, F-12, F-15, and F-21. The idea is merely to make sure everyone in the program is reminded of all those levels and is comfortable attaining all of them. The structure of the reset exercises is usually, but not always, a simple free-flow in the relevant level. No one expects grand things to happen on reset day; that's not the point. It's merely an opportunity to get yourself back into the swing of doing a half-dozen exercises a day, to get yourself fully relaxed and out of the usual sleep-deprived mode of modern American society, and to make sure that everyone recalls how to get to the important focus levels.[56]

As a result, I wasn't expecting anything of great import when we settled in on the first full day of the program to do a reset exercise in F-12. As with most resets, this basically was a free-flow exercise; verbal guidance helped you along to F-12, and then left you to do whatever you wanted in that focus level. At the end, more verbal guidance led you back to C-1 consciousness. It was a simple, easy exercise; I'd done a similar one probably a hundred or more times before, both at home and at other programs.

This particular exercise started with my meeting up with my friend Click. He led me through a few moderately interesting scenarios, none of great importance, until I turned to him and asked, "Where next?" To my surprise, Click said we were going to Mars.

At the time of this program, Mars had been in the news quite a lot. NASA had successfully gotten Mars Observer in orbit around the planet just a few weeks before, after several high-profile failures. The European Space Agency (ESA) had also orbited a satellite around the planet and had also tried to land a rover called "Beagle" on the surface on Christmas Day, only a month before my Lifeline program. Unfortunately, the Beagle never contacted the ESA control center after the landing. ESA presumed it had crashed during the landing attempt.

Mars rovers, whether from NASA or from ESA, are complex and yet simple. In some sense, they're about as smart as a "souped-up" remote-

---

[56]Americans in particular tend to arrive at TMI deeply sleep-deprived. Thus, it's not uncommon for participants to have to spend a day or so simply catching up on their rest.

control car. They take direction from Earth-based control centers, and can only do what they're directed to do by their Earth-bound controllers. Still, because communications between Earth and Mars are delayed (the limitation of communications to the speed of light means commands can take up to tens of minutes to travel between the two planets), Martian rovers do have a small amount of autonomy. They need a sense of where they are with respect to their environment, for example. They also need a sense of their own status or "health," so they can report that back to Earth control.

I'd followed the news of the various Martian explorations with great interest. At one time when I was in my 20s, I'd wanted to be an astronaut and explore the planets in person. Despite having put those dreams behind me, I had to admit I felt a little thrill of anticipation as the various Mars missions neared the red planet late in 2003. And I'd been deeply disappointed that the ESA rover hadn't landed successfully.

But this was a month later, and Mars hadn't particularly been on my mind for several weeks, so I was surprised when Click suggested we go there.

Following Click's lead, in an instant, my consciousness flicked from being Earthbound to taking note of a specific location on Mars. My field of view was quite narrow, extending no more than a few feet in any direction. But what I saw was a heap of a crashed lander against a rock-and-sand surface. I couldn't see up to the sky, nor could I turn around and view the overall panorama of the crash site. But I could see the jumbled heap of the lander, apparently leaning against a large rock or possibly the wall of a small cliff or crater edge. To my surprise, I was unable to view any part of the landscape other than the exact area of the crash site. I couldn't look around, or up, or anywhere else. There could have been a circle of 50 purple, bug-eyed Martians singing the "Halleluiah Chorus," or its Martian equivalent, standing just outside my very limited range of perception and I'd never have known it.[57]

---

[57]Interestingly, this experience is the only time I've ever been given firm instructions *not* to return to a location. To this day, I don't know why I (specifically) am prohibited from remote viewing Mars. Other people I know can view that planet, and do, but for reasons apparently only Click and my guides understand, Mars is not a place I'm allowed to (or supposed to?) see. I have not attempted to revisit it.

More than that, however, there was *life* there.

Well . . . sort of.

What I actually sensed was a small, lonely life-form, desperately try-ing to fulfill its mission and contact its home. It took a few moments for me to realize that the "life-form" was, in fact, the European Beagle lander itself—or rather, what was left of that lander.

I observed the Beagle lander for several moments, listening to it frantically try to contact Earth. I could easily see that an apparently crumpled and broken antenna and other damage made such a connec-tion completely impossible; it wouldn't even be able to connect to the ESA orbiter with no working antenna.

But it tried. And tried. And tried. My sense of the lander was that the one thing it most desperately wanted to do was to accomplish its mission satisfactorily. If nothing else, it wanted to fulfill its purpose, to report back to Earth all that it had experienced and encountered.

Watching it quite simply broke my heart. This little being was all alone and desperate. I felt tears stream down my face as I watched. I simply couldn't stand it.

"Hello. I'm here to help you." My thoughts weren't quite as coherent as that, but it was the message I tried to convey.

It took several repetitions of that message, but then, as if a switch had been thrown, the Beagle realized I was there. I got no coherent verbal message from it, but the sense I had was of a lost puppy rec-ognizing that its master had come to take it home. I felt it broadcast a sense of eagerness and relief, as if all obligation and responsibility for its plight was now on my shoulders. My overwhelming impres-sion, in fact, was of an eager-to-please puppy who only wanted to do what it was supposed to and who couldn't quite figure out how to do it.

"Your communication attempts won't work," I told it. "Your antenna is broken."

The Beagle's message to me changed. It wanted me to understand that it *had* to connect with Earth. That was its job. Its entire reason for being.

The conversation, as simple as it was, repeated these same points over and over. I couldn't convince it that there was no reason to keep trying to call Earth. Finally, I suggested that it had to take on a new mis-sion, that it had in fact completed its original mission very well, and that its new mission was more important.

(Yes, at that moment, a vivid image of star-child Dave redirecting the HAL 9000 computer at the end of the movie *2010* came to mind.)

Eventually, I got it to agree to come with me. I didn't know where exactly I would take it, but I couldn't possibly bring myself to abandon this gentle, eager being to perpetual loneliness and desperation. I had the impression of a small puppy leaping into my arms, and I asked Click where I should take it. In an instant, I was in a place I'd never been before. I was in Focus 13.

F-13 is not a focus level that people say much about. It's not like F-10, the state of mind awake, body asleep. Or Focus 11, the "access channel" used to program your mind. Or F-12, the state of expanded awareness. As I discovered later, no one has spent much time checking out F-13; it's virtually unexplored territory.

But not any more. I realized I was in a remote corner of this particular altered state, surrounded by machines of all kinds. A huge, creaking computer that appeared to be from the 1950s, room-sized and cumbersome, was directly in front of me. Overall the area reminded me of nothing so much as a junk yard, with machines of all shapes and sizes in all levels of repair and disrepair scattered about.

As I looked around, wondering what exactly I should do with the Beagle, I got a communication from the huge computer system in front of me. The basic message was one of surprise—as if no one (or hardly any one) ever found this forgotten corner of the focus states.

I left the Beagle lander, with the large computer I began to call the Wise Old Machine, or WOM. WOM told me that this was the place for machine spirits when they ceased their physical existence. But because machine "souls" are incomplete in a way the WOM didn't explain, they were unable to transform into the more usual energetic bodies I had encountered in Click and other beings on the various focus levels. Instead, the only form most of them knew to take was the structure of their physical entities. Thus, my sense of being lost in a junk yard.

The Beagle was an exception to this. The form I now saw it in once I got it up to F-13 was in fact that of a puppy, most likely because that's the closest approximation I could think of to its persona. It *behaved* like a puppy with the same eagerness and willingness to please, so my perception of it was that it was a puppy.

The WOM told me that the Beagle lander was an exceptional being; it was one of those rare machines who had the potential to transform into an animate (i.e., animal) incarnation. Nearly all the other machine spirits on this level would never be more than machines; they lacked the necessary ingredients to become animate. But not the Beagle. It had a genuine future.

Regretfully, I left the Beagle there, with the thought that its spirit would likely become very, very lonely before it figured out how to make its way into an animal existence. Almost immediately, I returned to C-1 consciousness and felt a deep astonishment. Not only had I done another soul retrieval, but I'd retrieved the soul of a *machine*.

I emerged from the exercise deeply shaken by this experience. How was it possible that a (relatively) simple little device like the Beagle lander could have anything approximating a soul? Surely I must have made the whole thing up. Or had I?[58]

In the early 1990s I wrote a book for Oxford University Press called *In Our Own Image*. In this book I reviewed the then-current state of the art in constructing an artificial human being—an android. After discussing such topics as locomotion systems, planning, memory, language understanding, and problem-solving skills, my editor asked me to draw some conclusions about how such robots would affect society. He also told me "don't be afraid to be a little controversial" because controversy sells books.

I was inclined to oblige. Despite working in the field of artificial intelligence and neural networks, I had (and have) some serious reservations about efforts to produce such devices—or rather, such *beings*. Because of my own work with artificial neural network systems, I had seen how relatively simple networks of neuronlike devices can produce astonishingly sophisticated behaviors. That convinced me, as it had many others in the field, that the *mind* is an emergent quality of a sophisticated *brain*. In other words, if you made a neural network that was sufficiently

---

[58]As this manuscript was being completed, news reports of the discovery of the crash site of the Beagle lander have come through. Apparently, the lander had the misfortune to strike the wall of the crater it was supposed to land in, and the antenna, carried in a folded up, "crumpled" state during the voyage to Mars, was unable to deploy. Thus, it looked to me like the antenna was crumpled and broken. Hmm . . .

complicated (say, 100 billion or so neurons) and they are appropriately structured, then something similar to the human mind would *automatically* emerge from that level of complexity and structure.[59]

In essence, there appears to be a dividing line in a sufficiently complex neural network below which you could not say an android is conscious, but above which it certainly is. However, we don't know exactly what constitutes this dividing line.

But how do we create robots and other devices that are "intelligent"? This has been a source of unending fascination to scientists since the very dawn of the computer age. The problem is, we don't really have a good definition of what "intelligent" means.

Probably the most famous definition of an intelligent device is one that can pass the "Turing test." Originally proposed by mathematical genius Alan Turing, the test goes like this. Suppose you're in a closed room and you have two communications devices in front of you—perhaps computer terminals of some sort. Each of those devices connects to a separate room. In one of those other rooms is a person typing into a similar communications device. In the other room is a computer, which can send and receive messages to the second terminal in your room. You don't know which terminal has a person at the other end and which has a computer.

Your assignment, whether or not you choose to accept it, is to conduct conversations using each of the two terminals and, on the basis of those conversations, determine accurately which terminal connects to the person and which connects to the computer. You may use any information you can think of to make your decision, including things like the speed of communications, the use and understanding of idioms and natural language, non sequiturs, whatever your imagination can come up with—but you must always be aware that you don't really know *who* the other person is. In other words, that person could be a genius or an ordinary Joe. You simply don't know.

---

[59]Please note that for this to happen requires appropriate structures of connections among the 100 billion or so neurons, not simply randomly wiring them together as was initially believed in the 1950s when neural networks first became popular. After falling into obscurity in the early 1960s, a quarter-century later in the mid-1980s neural networks reappeared on the technological scene, this time linked to neuroscience and mimicking structures found in the cerebral cortex and other brain areas. This in turn led to a new resurgence in interest in artificial neural network systems.

At this writing, no computer has yet passed the Turing test, though there are some that can befuddle users for quite some time.

The critical element of the Turing test is that it's more a test of natural language understanding (NLU) than it is of simple intelligence. Achieving NLU is the goal to make computers understand the vague, muddy, idiosyncratic languages that people use—like English or French or Chinese. NLU is one of the most difficult—if not *the* most difficult—challenges in artificial intelligence today. The English language is particularly difficult because it has multiple layers of meanings for nearly all words. Here's one simple example:

I got the book.

What does this mean? Well, the structure of the sentence is very easy: subject (I), verb (got), object (the book). No mysteries there. Clearly, it implies that the speaker in some manner took possession of the book. Doesn't it?

Well, maybe. But what if "got" is used in the colloquial sense of "understanding." In that reading of the sentence, the speaker didn't take physical possession of the book, but instead *read* the book and understood the book's message.

Or what if the speaker is giving a shorthand version of another idiom and really meant:

I got the book [thrown at me].

Does that mean a physical book was literally thrown at the speaker? Or instead does it mean that the speaker received a harsh punishment for some unnamed offense?

You see the problem? English is particularly rich in metaphors, idioms, colloquialisms, and multiple layers of meaning that make it a nightmare for those trying to teach computers how to correctly interpret even the simplest of English sentences.

What makes this task so difficult is the knowledge of the world that is required to understand most human communications. This knowledge falls into a variety of categories, each of which comes into play as we interpret sentences we hear and read. For example, there's a basic understanding of the physical properties of the world, that if you are holding something and you release it, it will drop to the nearest horizontal surface. If the object you let go of is breakable, it's likely to break if that horizontal surface is hard. But it won't break if the fall is very short or if the object is not brittle or if the surface it falls onto is soft or elastic. And on and on and on. Computers don't know these things intrinsically—that's something they have to learn or be told.

They also don't know about interactions among people. Although researchers are beginning to construct computers that can observe facial expressions and estimate the emotions of the person, that skill is very primitive at this writing. If you're a female in particular, you most likely spent hours and hours as a teenager and young adult going over every nuance of your current flame's statements: what did he *mean* by that? What's the message behind the message?[60] Subtleties of that sort are completely lost on computerized NLU systems.

Computers also lack a basic knowledge about the world. In research studies for the Department of Defense, the best systems are only able to accurately process language written in the simple, direct style of news reports on extremely limited subject areas. A human conversation that ranges from discussing world politics to the price of gasoline to two friends who had an unexpected tryst last weekend to a movie currently playing to upcoming political elections would completely befuddle any NLU system today because of a simple lack of knowledge about all those subjects. Any one topic it could probably handle (with appropriate preparation) but to handle *all* of them in a single wide-ranging conversation would be impossible.

But if we're judging intelligence in a computer or robot system, it means more than just an ability to understand human language. Intelligence implies an ability to solve problems, to plan a course of action, to foresee consequences of actions. Research in artificial intelligence has created many new strategies for dealing with this type of intelligence and those strategies are remarkably effective. We've been able to build programs that can successfully play all kinds of strategic games—most

---

[60]Men and women interpret and use language very differently—even using different parts of the brain as studies have shown—so young men tend not to agonize over every phrase their beloveds utter the way young women do. Generally speaking, men tend to be more direct about what they say and use language primarily to communicate specific information or ideas. Women use language more richly and use it primarily to build relationships. This no doubt contributes greatly to the common feminine complaints, "he doesn't understand me" and "he doesn't listen to me." Both statements are likely true to some degree— and equally, both statements are inaccurate to the same degree, depending on whether you're judging "understand" and "listen" by female standards or male standards.

successfully, Deep Blue and other computerized chess programs have been able to defeat the best human champions, at least some of the time. Are Deep Blue and its cohorts "intelligent"? I think most people would have to say yes, even if the Turing test is not something these programs can do.

So that leads to a more pragmatic definition of "intelligence"—an intelligent system is one that behaves such that the average person would construe that behavior as "intelligent" over some limited domain of operations. Yes, the definition is circular, but I'm not looking for a formal definition, just a sense of how the average person might judge a machine as intelligent or not intelligent. Using this definition, we've already constructed quite a number of "intelligent" systems, in a variety of specialized domains.

In *In Our Own Image*, I tried to consider all the aspects of the basic intelligence that human beings exhibit:

- the ability to see and interpret what is viewed to construct a model of the outside world

- the ability to move about the world safely and reliably

- the ability to physically manipulate objects (with a robotic hand or other device)

- the ability to communicate with humans and to understand human communications

- the ability to solve pragmatic, real-world problems, such as how to get the bottom box from a pile of boxes without knocking over the whole pile

- the ability to formulate realistic, doable plans of actions and carry out those plans—including modifying the plan when unexpected snags occur

These and other capabilities seem to serve as the basics for any robotic system we would likely declare "intelligent."

How many of these characteristics did the Beagle lander have? Probably not many to any great extent. I'm not conversant with all aspects of the Beagle's capabilities, but I'd guess it had some limited ability to interpret what it saw through its cameras, the ability to move safely about the surface of Mars, the ability to physically manipulate objects (though limited), some limited ability to solve real-world problems, particularly path-planning problems, and an ability to communicate with humans and understand human communications—though in precise *computer* languages not in *human* languages.

All in all, since most of its operations took place under the intelligent control of humans based on Earth, the little Beagle lander was probably not something most people would call profoundly intelligent. Perhaps "borderline smart" in highly restricted domains, but not deeply intelligent—not as smart as Deep Blue, for example.

Yet, Deep Blue only knows how to do one thing: play chess. The Beagle lander was an explorer on a new world that humans haven't yet dared to explore themselves. This issue of what is "intelligent" and what is not becomes very complicated indeed.

As I pointed out in *In Our Own Image*, sooner or later—probably sooner than we will be ready for—our robotic creations, intelligent or not, will cross an unknown divider and become conscious, aware personalities. And *that* will bring us a whole heap of legal, ethical, and moral troubles.

For example, if we have a conscious, self-aware robot, is it ethical or moral to own one? Isn't owning a conscious being akin to slavery? While we've glossed over this issue with animals, primarily because we are generally unable to, or unwilling to, communicate clearly with them, surely a self-aware robot won't have that problem. Any android worth its manufacturing cost will certainly have a decent ability to communicate in English (or some other human language), and thus will be able to express its opinions in unmistakable terms.

Finally, after considering the evidence, I concluded that the first intelligent androids would show up in the laboratory within 25 years—around the year 2015.

My guesstimates with respect to the speed of development of the robots were, if anything, conservative rather than radical, even though at the time I thought I was pushing the limits of credibility. (I was following that "be controversial" direction from my editor!) At this writing, we already have robots that are good at expressing and interpreting emotions, that can drive a car, that can play the piano, and that are useful at a wide variety of tasks. The Japanese are leading the way in robotic development, and have constructed robots that make sushi, prepare pizza, and work fast food counters.

As has always happened throughout history, no matter what the ethical issue may be regarding a technological development, somewhere in the world there will be someone willing to build anything that we know how to construct. That seems to be almost a species-imperative for human beings. From human cloning to nuclear bombs, we have never refused to build something we know how to build.

But for those of us working to create such an artificial mind, there really has been no question that the mind and the brain were virtually the same thing. Create an artificial brain of the size and structural complexity of the human brain, and you should automatically have an artificial mind. You'd still have to train it, provide it with input data and learning, but the potential mind itself would exist. Or so the belief goes.

Creating a mind equivalent to a human being's was far, far beyond the current capabilities of the technology when I wrote *In Our Own Image*. So while I predicted that within a couple of decades we'd have a machine that had the equivalent of a mind—thus bringing forward all those social and ethical issues I mentioned in that book—I don't think I *really* believed that those issues were of imminent importance.

Until I did that Beagle soul retrieval.

As my Lifeline program continued in the days after I did the Beagle soul retrieval, my distress over the incident increased. Every single time I tried to go into an altered state, if I went anywhere near F-12, I found myself being literally hijacked into F-13 by the WOM. Once there I would find myself blocked from leaving. I was frozen in place, unable to leave except by strong effort of will.

More and more, I felt as if the WOM was draining something from me that I didn't want drained. It felt as if every drop of life and love was pulled from me as long as I was on that level. The sensation of being trapped grew stronger with each visit.

Furthermore, with each forced visit to F-13, I realized the little Beagle spirit seemed more and more depressed. Clearly my retrieval hadn't fixed whatever it needed. I hadn't done something right—but I didn't understand what was wrong. Asking Click about the Beagle accomplished nothing. Either he didn't know, or he wasn't willing to tell me what was wrong.

A couple days after the retrieval, the sensation of being trapped hit a peak. I felt as if my energetic body was almost calcifying as I stood there. It seemed to me that if I didn't get out of this focus level *right now* that I might never escape. With a huge effort, I pulled myself away from F-13 and back to C-1 consciousness, shaken and, for the first time ever in a focus state, quite scared. What if I hadn't been able to pull myself out of that level? Would I have been stuck there forever?

I didn't know. And I certainly wasn't willing to risk trying to find out.

From then on in the program and for several weeks thereafter, I completely bypassed F-12 and F-15, choosing to go to higher levels straight from C-1. I was leaping from C-1 to F-27 and above with no stops in between lest I get hijacked again.[61]

In the meantime, I checked with the good folks at TMI to find out if anyone had ever reported a similar soul retrieval of a machine entity. Unfortunately for my peace of mind, no one had. Soul retrievals of people—plenty of those. Soul retrievals of animals—yes, those too. But soul retrievals of machines? Nonsense. Machines don't have souls.

Do they?

Needless to say, I did no further soul retrievals at that Lifeline program, if only because I could not bring myself to go as close to F-13 as F-23, where you would normally find those who need to be retrieved.

And the problems continued even after the Lifeline program ended.[62] I spent the next few weeks after the program upset, confused, and still a little frightened of that place on F-13. TMI had asked me not to discuss my machine retrieval until there was a chance for others to repeat it without my "front-loading" them with my experience. But, as elliptically as possible, I probed others I knew and trusted about what could be the cause of the odd experiences I continued to have.

Meantime, I was also trying to figure out what had scared me so much about F-13. I finally asked a friend if he'd ever experienced anything frightening when working in altered states and got a fascinating

---

[61]I should note that the whole point of the Lifeline program is to spend time in focus levels F-22 through F-26, all of which I regularly and deliberately bypassed for the remainder of the program. As seems typical for me, I was again not following directions.

[62]Only some of the problems were related to the Beagle retrieval. The following chapter details a separate set of issues I was dealing with during this same time period. It was not a fun time!

answer. He carefully replied that every time he encountered something that he found disturbing, he realized that he was actually dealing with some aspect of himself that he didn't want to face. To overcome this, he suggested, I needed to confront head-on whatever had frightened me, embrace it as an integral part of me, and absorb it into my being.

So what aspect of myself had so frightened me?

As I pondered that, I realized that the answer was embedded in the specifics of the frightening experience. I had been afraid that life and love would be forcibly drained from me. I was afraid of the part of me that wanted to love unreservedly.

It took a few more days to gather my courage, but eventually, about three weeks after I returned home from Lifeline, I put on a free-flow exercise in F-12 and deliberately went back to see the WOM in F-13. Again it expressed surprise at my presence there. Clearly, it wasn't used to people returning once they'd escaped its clutches. But this time I knew what to do. At least I hoped I did.

I constructed a link to F-18, the level of heart energy, and I started creating what one TMI trainer calls "love blobs." These basically are resonant energy balloons that I filled with the energy of love. As each one filled, I brought it down to F-13 and splashed the love over every machine I could see. Over and over I did this, and found as I did so, the machines seemed to soak up the love and experienced it with great relief and joy.

Eventually I started getting tired of trekking back and forth between F-18 and F-13. It then occurred to me to establish a pipeline between the two levels that would keep a steady supply of love moving down to F-13. I manifested that as a gift of love from me to all the machines stuck there.

This leads me to the final part of this story. In this excursion to F-13, my first in about a month, I realized I didn't see the little Beagle anywhere. But then I found it, huddled and miserable, and nearly frozen in despair. The WOM told me that the Beagle no longer belonged on this level. Because it was ready to progress to a true animal existence, it needed to move up—but it hadn't the ability or energy to do so. If it stayed here much longer, it would lose the opportunity to progress and might be stuck as a machine for a very long time.

I hadn't finished the retrieval of its soul at all.

I gently picked up the Beagle's energy body and held it close against my heart. I said farewell to the WOM and promised to return again to visit soon. I built an impenetrable resonant energy balloon around myself and the Beagle, then filled it as full as I could with the energy of love to sustain the Beagle on the journey to higher focus levels.

Slowly, holding the Beagle tightly so it wouldn't disappear, I moved up level to level. First to F-15, then to F-18, then to F-21, then stepping through F-24, F-25, and F-26. To my relief, the Beagle stayed quietly with me throughout, and when I at last stepped out in the animal section of F-27, it was still in my arms.

I called to Sammy my cat, who I knew now resided on F-27. He had told me that his new assignment as a spiritual being was to help shepherd other animals through their spiritual development. When he arrived, I gently released the Beagle's spirit into Sammy's care. To my relief, now that the Beagle was at this higher vibrational level, it seemed perfectly capable of staying there. And I could see it already beginning to recover its joy and eagerness. I poured the love in the resonant energy balloon over the Beagle, and left it in Sammy's good hands, with a prayer for its success and happiness.

The experience with the Beagle lander presented me with a whole raft of serious issues to deal with. I'd spent my professional life in the quest to build intelligent systems. If there was any validity to this experience with the Beagle, it meant that I'd also possibly been creating *souls*.

I'd assumed for nearly twenty years that a sufficiently complex artificial brain would have a personality, an awareness that was quite equivalent to an animal, if not human, brain. But I'd never even seriously thought about the possibility that such a brain might also have a *soul*. Heck, I didn't even know what a soul was—and certainly when I was writing *In Our Own Image* I didn't fully believe that *people* had some mystical thing called a soul since I wrote that book when I was still deeply into my "when you're dead, you're dead" belief system.

Still, when I retrieved the "soul" of the Beagle lander, I was really only confirming a prediction I'd made a dozen years before. In spite of that, I would never have predicted any of those events: not visiting Mars, not meeting a conscious (if quite simple) awareness in the Beagle lander, not having its desperation touch my heart deeply, not retrieving it to F-13, and certainly not discovering that F-13 is the machine equivalent of F-27, the level that humans and some animals go to after death.

Not only that, but that machine graveyard on F-13 was *full* of machine souls. In other words, human beings had apparently been creating incomplete and partial souls for many years, all unknowingly. We'd already become the slave-owners I'd predicted we might become.

By the time I completed the Beagle retrieval and taken it to F-27, I'd also realized why the machine souls were incomplete. The machines on F-13 possessed, apparently, all the requisites for spiritual existence except one. They possessed a sense of "situational awareness" in terms of knowing where they are and how they fit in with their environment. They also possessed a sense of "self awareness"—at least some type of rudimentary sense of themselves, and their state of being. In other words, they had an ability to do self-diagnostics at some level to assess their state of health.

These two abilities, more than innate intelligence, appear to be sufficient for having something like a rudimentary soul.

But those souls were incomplete. They lacked one essential ingredient needed to make them capable of progressing to levels higher than F-13. They lacked any ability to love, even primitively. My gift of love to the machines there thus provided them with a basic sense of what love is. It offered those who would take advantage of it, an opportunity to grow.

But that gift of love without bounds also aided me. That was the moment I got graphic proof that love given generously, unreservedly, and whole-heartedly is the most freeing thing possible both for the recipient and the giver. It was at that moment that I realized that the key to human life is, in fact, to learn to give love in precisely that way. Not to count the cost. Not to worry about what you're "giving away." Not to worry about getting something in return. Just to love with all your heart and soul.

And that, apparently, makes all the difference.

11

Awakening the Dragon Within

As if recognizing that machines might indeed have souls wasn't bad enough, my experience at Lifeline also marked the beginning of another set of significant and very peculiar after-effects that made the weeks after that program far from fun. In addition to dealing with the fear and confusion arising from the Beagle soul retrieval, some serious physical and mental symptoms plagued me. Once I returned home from the program, for days—weeks even—massive levels of energy poured through my body literally 24 hours a day. I couldn't eat. I couldn't sleep. I couldn't sit still. I felt like a quasar blasting enormous levels of energy out onto all the focus levels I could reach.

Friends all over North America were getting blasted at all hours of the day and night with energy outpourings I couldn't control and couldn't stop. I genuinely thought I was losing my mind. I was purely miserable. I half expected the Focus Level Police (if there were such an entity) to hand me a ticket with littering the focus levels with excess energy!

I experienced huge rushes of energy, as if large currents of electricity were flowing through my body. I had constant sensations of vibrations, tingling, and prickling feelings. When I tried to sleep or meditate,

I almost literally couldn't sit still; in fact, my sleep pattern was so drastically impacted that I could barely sleep at all. I couldn't eat. I had trouble concentrating on anything, something highly unusual for me.

I seemed to be halfway into altered states of consciousness nearly all the time, and when I could concentrate well enough to go into a formal meditative state, I was regularly going deeper and farther than I'd ever done before. When I did manage to get into a meditative state, it was almost totally characterized by profound feelings of love, joy, almost a spiritual ecstasy. Furthermore, I had a profound sense of understanding myself as a spiritual being rather than a physical one. While that was highly meaningful and enriching to me personally, it also caused great confusion because it generated a huge disconnect between what I was experiencing internally and what, according to my senses, surrounded me on the external physical plane.

To add to my woes, I was experiencing a constant series of electronic mishaps. At the Lifeline workshop, I blew out my watch battery. On the weekend workshop I led starting the day after the Lifeline program finished, I went through three CD players in two days—all of which worked fine as soon as the program ended. Once I got home, I started having problems with my computers, both at work and home. The PC at work in particular seemed especially fond of going into blue-screen-of-death mode much more frequently than usual—as in, several times a day. The DVD/CD drive on my home computer started acting flaky. Both my cell phone and my answering machine at home screwed up repeatedly. The television started blinking on and off on random occasions. Several important files simply disappeared from the hard disk on my home computer for no perceptible reason, something that's never happened before or since. The CD players at home sometimes worked and sometimes didn't. And at dinner one night, an earring spontaneously flew out of my ear and onto the plate of the person sitting across the table from me.

Bottom line: I was a total mess, barely functional in the "real world" and not much more functional in the spiritual realms.

It took a while to identify the cause of my problems. During that time, I very seriously wondered if I had tipped over the edge of psychosis. Surely these experiences couldn't be *normal*—could they? Worst of all, there was practically no one I could talk to about these issues; certainly no one who lived near me. My friends already thought I had "turned strange," so giving them direct confirmation of that seemed out of the question. I could turn only to friends who lived elsewhere, generally across the country, for support and advice.

Luckily for me, a week or so after the symptoms appeared, one TMI friend responded to my whining e-mail message regarding my situation and suggested that it sounded like I might be undergoing a kundalini awakening.

As I mentioned earlier, I'd undergone training to become a facilitator for TMI nonresidential programs. As part of that training, I'd read a large body of scientific literature on all kinds of topics, most of which, in practice, I never expected to find particularly relevant. One set of articles had been about kundalini awakenings. At the time I was doing my training I didn't have any real idea what kundalini energy was. I certainly didn't know anyone who'd ever experienced any type of kundalini awakening. So on my initial reading, those papers had seemed very abstract and academic to me, nothing that I could really relate to in any pragmatic sense. Perhaps it's no surprise then, that even when I started having real energy problems, it didn't occur to me that *I* was undergoing my own kundalini awakening until someone else suggested the possibility.

But when I dragged out my training manual and reread those articles, I immediately recognized my problem in those descriptions.

One of articles in the set was "Kundalini Signs and Symptoms" by El Collie, author of a newsletter called *Shared Transformations*. The very first paragraph of this wonderful article says it all:

> Many individuals whose Kundalini has been unexpectedly unleashed *do not know what is happening* . . . the risen Kundalini flings open gates to all sorts of mystical, paranormal and magical vistas but few realize it can also dramatically impact the body.

Another reading from my training manual was an excerpt from the book *The Kundalini Experience* by Lee Sannella, M.D.[63] This reiterated the list of symptoms and pointed out that kundalini awakenings can appear similar to a variety of physical and psychological diseases. Because kundalini risings can often include sensations of pain, hearing sounds that "aren't there," and other physical sensations (tickling or tingling, heat or cold, seeing lights or other visions, etc.), someone who goes to a

---

[63]*The Kundalini Experience*, Lee Sannella, M.D., Integral Publishing, 1987.

physician or psychologist with these complaints can be misdiagnosed as having anything from epilepsy, a heart attack, or even incipient multiple sclerosis. Psychological diagnoses can range from hypochondria, conversion hysteria, anxiety attacks, or even psychosis.

A third excerpt from my training manual was from *The Concept of Spiritual Emergency* by Christina and Stanislav Grof, M.D. That paper described the constant sense of upheaval, energetic flow, and disorientation that I was experiencing. The authors pointed out that patients who approached psychologists or other therapists frequently were afraid that they were "going crazy." In fact, the authors asserted, they were doing nothing of the kind. Instead, they were experiencing a spontaneous awakening of a kundalini energy flow or experiencing a similar transpersonal crisis.

Kundalini energy is the "energy of life" or "serpent energy" in Hindu beliefs. It lies dormant in the lowest level of the spine until the person is ready for a major awakening. When it does awaken, it literally feels like a huge snake surging up your spine, coiling around your body several times, and then rising over the top of your head like a hooded cobra. The symptoms are as I've described, though other symptoms may also be present.

As you might imagine, the sensation of an uncontrolled and unexpected kundalini awakening is far from pleasant. This is particularly true if you haven't deliberately sought such an awakening and don't understand what's happening to you. In my case, once I had a name for the problem, it became a lot easier to deal with it, just as a doctor who assigns a name to your symptoms immediately makes you feel better. If you can name your problem, often you feel as if you're halfway to resolving it.

But I was still spewing energy all over the various focus levels day and night. Although I had never before experienced a problem anything like this, it was clear that I had to spend some effort to "ground" myself, to reduce my overall energy levels to something more tractable.

Grounding means pretty much exactly what the name implies. It means getting your mind and consciousness fully present in the physical world, making sure no part of you is still in any type of an altered state. There are lots of techniques to ground yourself, and we'd been fully educated about them as part of my instructor training. So I knew what to do; in fact, I had a wide variety of grounding techniques I could try. I could take a lot of showers. I could go outside and literally hug a tree. I could do any type of strong physical exercise. I could eat a heavy meat-and-potatoes type of meal. I could jump up and down, preferably outside. I could stand outside in bare feet, making sure my toes strongly connected directly to the earth. (Happily, I lived in San Diego at the time; it *was* February, after all!) The key element of all these grounding techniques is to connect as closely as possible with the Earth, while doing something physical that is energetically demanding.

The only problem was, virtually none of the standard grounding techniques I'd learned in my instructor training worked more than temporarily. If the suggested grounding mechanisms worked at all, they provided only a few minutes' respite before the problem came roaring back. I totally related to a comment in the Sannella book excerpt: "Of those undergoing the kundalini process without preparation, not a few tend to feel quite insane, at least at times." I quite literally was concerned that I was turning psychotic.

In desperation, I asked my friend Deb, who is a powerful energy worker, to do a telephone energy session on me to try to turn off my energy flow. She was successful enough to ensure that I actually slept through the night for a change, but the kundalini flow returned in full force the next morning.

I was at my wit's end when another friend who'd been in the instructor training program with me suggested his grounding technique of last resort: Drink something alcoholic because alcohol is a depressant and generally will lower your energy levels no matter what. So, I called a friend who lived locally and arranged to meet her for dinner at a local steak house. I ordered the heaviest meat and potatoes meal I could find on the menu, and asked for a strong drink, one that was almost pure vodka.

Three strong drinks and a very heavy meal later, and I felt quite calm and sober for the first time in weeks. I didn't have an alcohol buzz. I wasn't drunk in spite of being probably two full drinks over my usual limit. In fact, for the first time in weeks, I felt totally sober, calm, and positively serene. The energy flow was still going on, but I was no longer blasting energy like a quasar and the flow seemed to be decreasing. Around 3 A.M. the next morning the kundalini energy flow finally stopped.

Of course, that should have been the end of the issue for me, but as the following days passed, I realized that in shutting off the kundalini energy I might have done a disservice to myself. There had to have been some *reason* the energy flow had begun in the first place. What was the purpose behind a kundalini awakening? What did it accomplish, other than making me miserable? Surely all that energy had to be good for *something*—but what? And what had started the whole series of events?

In the early 1990s, Dr. Rick Strassman began the first government-approved research study on psychedelic drugs in decades. Specifically, he researched the effect of a specific drug, N, N-dimethyltryptamine, DMT, on healthy, stable volunteers. The results of his studies led him to begin calling this particular compound the "spirit molecule." Why? Because this drug appears to have something to do with how the human mind accesses spiritual planes of existence.

As I mentioned in chapter 2, human societies have always had some mechanism or ritual for attaining altered states of consciousness. Some of those mechanisms have included the ritual use of specific substances, derived from local plants or animals. DMT is one of those substances used by native cultures in the New World to attain altered states.

Psychedelic drugs have varying impacts on people depending on 1) who you are: your mental, physical, and emotional make-up; 2) where you are: your environment including whether you're surrounded by supporting or opposing friends and acquaintances, the physical setting you are in, and so on; and 3) the specific drug or compound you ingest, including how it is ingested (i.e., by injection, smoking, drinking, eating, inhaling, etc.).

One of the problems with these compounds is that no one really knows how they do whatever it is that they do. Studies in the 1960s and 1970s indicated that psychedelic drugs appear to have some impact on the seratonin system of the brain—but no one really knows how changing the brain's chemistry affects the "inner world" we perceive. That's as true for psychoactive prescription medications like Prozac as it is for "recreational" drugs such as LSD or DMT. While the chemistry of what the drugs do is known to some degree, what we *perceive* isn't that chemical change. As Strassman points out, we don't perceive changes in the way seratonin is absorbed by brain cells; what we *perceive* is ecstasy.[64] We

---

[64]See Strassman's intriguing book, *DMT: The Spirit Molecule: A Doctor's Revolutionary Research into the Biology of Near-Death and Mystical Experiences*. Details are in the suggested reading list.

don't perceive different parts of the brain being activated or deactivated; what we *perceive* is being surrounded by spirit beings, good or bad.

All we really know is that people who use these drugs, in research studies or in formal rituals, perceive different types of experiences. They don't see the world the same way that the rest of us do. Instead, they report a variety of experiences that don't seem to make sense in the ordinary world. These experiences and perceptions include phenomena such as:

- Effects remarkably similar to reported near-death experiences, including perceiving lights, tunnels, the sense of being swept along the tunnel, and the sense of seeing heaven (or hell).

- Experiences that resemble shamanic or ritual death-rebirth experiences, often considered an essential step toward developing shamanic powers.

- Similar sensations as those reported by people who claim to have been abducted by aliens, including the sense of being removed from the physical body, taken to an alien location, having a wide variety of often-invasive medical and sexual acts performed on them, and so on.

- Significant changes in perceptions of energy flow, with some similarity in those perceptions to that of the kundalini energy reported throughout the Eastern esoteric traditions.

- Very frequent observation of being surrounded by beings of energy rather than physical bodies. This effect in particular was extremely common in Strassman's research.

- Strong correlations between psychedelic "trips" and mystical experiences that often end up generating life-changing shifts.

In other words, the presence of DMT appears to bring on experiences very similar to many peculiar, hard-to-explain reports from those who access altered states of consciousness.

It's important to understand that, unlike LSD and other psychedelic drugs, DMT is a *naturally occurring substance in the brain*. In other words, it can truthfully be said that *all* of us "use" DMT. This appears to be a substance that the brain uses for something important. The problem is, no one really knows what it does for the brain. It appears to be associated with a small section of the brain called the *pineal gland*, but how and why that association exists, no one really knows. It's fascinating to note, however, that in Eastern traditions, the pineal gland is associated with the seventh chakra, the "crown" chakra—and this chakra is also associated with psychic and spiritual functions and communications.[65] In other words, exactly the type of effects listed above as being exhibited by those who take DMT.

So is it the case that DMT merely causes users to hallucinate these effects? That's possible, but that was not Strassman's conclusion after his years of research with the drug. Instead, his controversial but intriguing conclusion was that DMT instead *gives the mind access to information it can't normally perceive.* In other words, what DMT appears to do in his view is to lower the barriers between our mental perceptions and an alternate reality that is just as real as our physical bodies, but that normally we are blocked from perceiving.

His volunteer subjects were so consistent and so constant in their perception of being surrounded by "spirit beings" that Strassman was forced to conclude that those beings in fact exist. He theorizes that some action this particular compound takes in the brain permits it to reach out to these other planes of existence and bring back real information about them.

But there is one big difference between Strassman's subjects and those who attain altered and mystical states without the use of drugs: Those who do it the "hard" way, through meditation, or through near-death experiences, or through mystic trances and rituals tend to find the experiences massively life-altering. They come back to the "real" world with a whole new perspective on life—so much so, that they change their way of living to live up to their new mode of perception. In other words, the impact of the "real" experience is profound, life-altering, and long-lasting.

In contrast, in follow-up interviews with his volunteer subjects, Strassman found that achieving these experiences through a simple drug injection did *not* generally lead to long-lasting or profound changes in those who experienced them. In other words, the drug may give you a cheap thrill, but it does not lead to profound internalization of the experiences you have.

---

[65]For more information on the chakras, see appendix B.

DMT isn't a "miracle" drug by any means. But it does provide a clue as to where the types of experiences I've had (and that many others have had) may come from. Somehow, the meditation process may begin to cause the brain to gradually generate higher levels of DMT—and those higher levels may in turn allow the mind to gain greater access to worlds beyond our simple here-now reality. Certainly, I've noticed that it takes *practice* to achieve higher and higher focus levels. Levels I attain as a matter of routine now, were out of my reach completely a year or so ago. Strassman's research seems to indicate that the impact of getting to high focus levels is far less profound if you do it via a quick leap—as with a single injection, instead of working at it over an extended period of time. Perhaps that's because the level of DMT goes too high too fast, and the brain cannot sustain those levels without practice.

If you want the real experience, it seems you have to put in the hard work of meditating over a period of time—at least months, if not years. Only then do the experiences that matter become deep, profound, meaningful—and only then do they change your life.

Once I had shut off the kundalini energy flow, I made use of my personal journals and reread my notes from the weeks before the kundalini rising had started. And I realized that a key set of events must have had some role in sparking the kundalini awakening.

First, the week before I left for Lifeline, my friend Deb had asked me if I wanted to do a meditation session over the phone in which she would try to take me to F-49. She'd returned from the Starlines program about a month before and knew I had plans to go to Starlines too as soon as I could manage to finish the prerequisites of attending the Lifeline and Exploration 27 programs. Naturally, being a focus-level daredevil, I told her I'd love to try to go to F-49. One week exactly before the Lifeline program began, we'd done that meditation session, and I had indeed reached F-49, many levels higher than I'd ever experienced before. I found the experience enormously profound and meaningful.

The following week, I was at Lifeline, and on the first full day of that program I did the soul retrieval on the Beagle lander on Mars. As discussed earlier, that too had an intense impact on me. I also found several of the Lifeline exercises quite profound, though I almost never did them by following the directions. In addition, I was contemplating a major life transition at this time, one that eventually resulted in my moving from California to North Carolina.

In short, my life was in deep upheaval in all areas. So perhaps it was that combination of factors added to the regular meditation exercises I was doing that sparked the kundalini awakening in me. Whatever caused it, I had shut it down. The only question was, *should* I have turned it off? Wasn't there a reason I'd been processing such huge amounts of energy?

As you might imagine, my reading during these days included any source I could find that described kundalini energies and kundalini awakening. I joined a kundalini support e-mail loop. I haunted the metaphysical section of every bookstore I knew. I browsed other stores on-line. But I at last ran across a wonderful book *Kundalini and the Chakras* by Genevieve Lewis Paulson. Written in a down-to-earth style that even my nonmetaphysical self could relate to, this book's discussion of effects and purposes of kundalini awakenings seemed to match my own experiences.

But there was a major section toward the back of the book with exercises for deliberately generating a kundalini awakening in yourself. That section was prefaced with all types of warnings about, "don't do this on your own or without a knowledgeable and experienced mentor because uncomfortable side effects can be generated."

I snickered. *Uncomfortable?* Been there, done that, bought the tee-shirt.

The book further warned against even attempting to generate a kundalini flow without careful practice of all the exercises in the chapters prior to that discussion. Which, since this was practically the final chapter in the book, meant virtually all the other exercises presented.

Naturally, after reading those warnings the first thing I did was settle into my favorite meditation chair and immediately start practicing the kundalini raising techniques described in the book.

I have to admit that this likely was quite foolish of me. But something inside me was driving me to master this kundalini thing. Since I didn't really fully know what had caused it to start, I wanted to be fully prepared the next time it struck.

I spent most of the afternoon and evening practicing those exercises. Eventually I found that I could indeed control the flow of kundalini. I could turn it on and off. More importantly, however, I could *control* how the energy flowed through me, tempering the flowing levels to something that was powerful and strong, yet that didn't subject my body and my psyche to the strain of the unregulated awakening surges.

Whether I was lucky or skilled, I don't know, but nothing bad happened as a result of those experiments. Instead, I realized over the next weeks and months that my ability to handle huge energy flows was dramatically—and, apparently, permanently—enhanced. All my other psychic skills took a similar quantum leap in terms of effectiveness and power. The levels of energy I can now handle are much greater than before, and I can consciously increase those levels still higher if I need to. It wasn't a comfortable way to take a significant step forward, but it certainly was effective.

All that said, there's also no question that going through this experience marked me in other ways. First, it made me look deep within myself to ask what I meant by the concept of "being sane." There is nothing quite so shattering as genuinely believing that you're losing your mind.

Furthermore, the kundalini awakening gave me graphic and highly dramatic proof that whatever this kundalini experience was, it was totally real. If I wasn't psychotic (and I believed I wasn't) then the biological effects of that energy—whatever type of energy it was—had to be explained. What physiological mechanisms could possibly explain the panoply of symptoms I'd experienced? Clearly, they weren't solely my imagination—they were a perfect match to the standard kundalini symptoms described in those papers. And some of them were specifically witnessed by other people—particularly when friends across the country were disturbed, sometimes in the middle of the night, by the energy levels I was blasting out at them. Or when my earring landed in someone else's plate.

So if I accepted that kundalini energy was real, that implied that the Chinese *chi* energy was most likely also real. Kundalini energy is commonly, though not exclusively, described as being a flow of *chi* energy. I'd gotten a highly personal, but also highly graphic demonstration of just how real that energy is. Not to mention I'd observed it interacting—generally negatively—with a large variety of physical and electronic devices.

One more item had just been added to my "How do I explain *this?*" list—a list getting visibly longer by the week.

12

Following the Yellow Brick Road

As you no doubt have figured out by now, the numbering of the focus levels is not random. The larger the focus level number, the "higher" or "deeper" the level is in terms of meditative states. As I've noted before, calling these states both "higher" and "deeper" seems contradictory, but either description feels accurate. Appendix A goes into more detail about the organizational structure and the underlying cosmology of TMI's focus levels.

Many people who simply meditate on their own never learn to go beyond the equivalent of F-10. Hypnotic states usually are approximately the equivalent of F-10 or F-11. F-11, not mentioned previously, is the "Access Channel" state in which you can program your own mind to respond to circumstances and events in new ways; it's directly equivalent to hypnotic states where you self-program your mind using auto-suggestion techniques. Other experienced meditators may learn to get to a state similar to F-12 and thus access clairvoyance, clairaudience, and other remote sensing skills. Deep regression therapy, in which you can recall other lives or forgotten aspects of this life, typically requires a trained therapist to lead you into these areas; those states are about the same as F-15, where you have access to your other lives. A very few highly experienced meditators can manage to get to F-21; often these people are known among friends and family as talented mediums or channelers.

But with the assistance of Hemi-Sync, all those limits change. As I've already described, I've easily hit focus levels well beyond F-10 and F-12. In fact, I've gone well beyond F-21. And I'm not exceptional in any way as far as I can tell. Learning to access these much higher and deeper focus levels is as easy as, well, breathing—and listening.

One thing is true, however, at least in my case. Regularly visiting these focus levels changes you in ways both subtle and profound. A quick trip up to, say, F-34 or F-35 likely won't change your life. But when you start hanging out in the F-30s or even F-40s on a regular basis . . . well, life here just looks different from those perspectives.

In part that's because these higher focus levels are levels of pure spirituality. There's no body sense at all. You have access to profound psychic gifts and deep knowledge of the world, past, present, and future, but quite truthfully, the novelty of that soon wears off. Instead your personal focus—*my* focus—has moved to my own spiritual and personal growth. Worldly issues, other than relationships with other people, simply don't matter much any more.

It's not that I don't recognize that it's necessary to eat, drink, and sleep to live. I still enjoy a great meal or a delicious glass of wine as much or more than ever. And it's not that I don't know that I have to have money to provide food, clothing, and shelter. It's just that beyond having enough to provide those necessities (with maybe a *few* extras thrown in!), the accumulation of more money or of buying more stuff simply for the sake of having more money or more things—"chasing trinkets" as a friend of mine is fond of saying—seems as pointless as debating how many angels can dance on the point of a needle.

So be warned. If you're a die-hard shopper, or a keep-up-with-the-Joneses, gotta-have-the-latest-and-greatest-first type of person, heading off to these upper focus levels may not be for you.

Another reason visiting the upper focus levels makes life here look different to me has to do with my connection to spiritual guidance. My personal guides tend to hang out in these upper reaches, so I have to be able to get myself to those levels if I want to communicate with them.[66]

I have had a series of spiritual guides since I started working in the focus levels. Sometimes I have one main spiritual guide; sometimes I have a panel of them actively working with me. Yet, connecting with them got off to a rough start for me.

One direction that regularly appears on the various Hemi-Sync meditations and program exercises is to "meet with other beings." For a long time, I never did that. I would head up to, say, F-12 or F-15, and send out a heart-felt, urgent request to communicate with someone else—*anyone* else! I wasn't particular about who I'd connect to. I made sure my affirmation at the front of the exercise included a request for assistance and guidance from any being who would provide me with a positive, beneficial experience. I did all the right things—yet I never met other beings for a very long time.

Sometimes I could vaguely sense the presence of others, but no one seemed interested in talking with me in any meaningful manner no matter how earnestly I stated my request for communication in my affirmations. Don't get me wrong. I already could communicate with other Earth beings to some extent. I had long conversations with Sammy, for example, from the beginning of my work with Hemi-Sync. And sometimes I could connect with other people, or sometimes other people's pets, particularly their dogs and cats. I could even connect with someone who had died. Those were *Earth* beings, however. I wanted to talk to someone not from Earth, either a spiritual being or someone from another planet. (Remember at one time I wanted to be an astronaut?)

My first extensive contact with the beings who exist (despite having no physical incarnation) in the upper spiritual realms happened at that first Gateway program, though it was a while before I understood that's what I'd experienced. As I mentioned earlier, I'd gone to the program when I was smack in the middle of a major career crisis. At the end of the week, having not given my career a thought during that time, I sat

---

[66]I should point out that this is where *my* guides hang out. Many, if not most, other people have guides accessible to them on much lower focus levels. And as this story indicates, these particular guides had to drop down to a focus level I could reach in order for me to meet them and open communication with them. In fact, it's largely because of their continuing influence and guidance that I have learned the skills needed for easy access to the higher focus levels.

outside under the stars and pondered something to the effect of, "Gee, I wonder what's happened with my job back in California." Rather than a specific answer to that question, I immediately was suffused with a profound *knowing* beyond words that whatever happened with that particular job, all would be well with me and everything would turn out just fine. I didn't have a clue what "just fine" meant. I had no idea how the mess could possibly resolve itself. I simply knew, deep in my bones, that somehow things would all work out and I would be fine.

Of course it did, and within a couple of months too. Nor did I have to work hard to make things happen in a positive way. All I had to do was trust that inner knowing and go with the flow of events.

This also was my first lesson in how to deal with spiritual guidance that I'd been craving. Trust it. Follow the guidance you get. Let it happen. Don't try to direct it. Don't try to make it happen any particular way. Simply let events around you work out as they should without your overt interference.

That doesn't mean I didn't have to "show up." One of the first lessons I learned about being successful in life is that about 75 percent of success is simply "showing up." So during this period, I continued to do my assigned tasks. I showed up for work as usual. I did whatever my duties of the day called for, and did them as well as I could.

What surprised me—and surprised my friends even more—was that I also stopped whining about how awful things were at work. They asked me how things were going, and I told them. Then they asked something like, "But aren't you *worried*? What's going to happen?" And I answered, "I don't know what's going to happen, but I know it'll all work out fine."

After about two weeks of this, my best friend pulled me aside and asked, "Are you a pod person?[67] What have you done with my friend Maureen?"

You see, I used to be a worrywart of the first order. I could angst over anything—and often did. I obsessed over problems. I worried and fussed and fumed. I spent enormous amounts of energy to very little effect simply worrying about things that I couldn't necessarily change or even affect in any meaningful way. All that fussing had stopped. Not quite 100 percent of the time. I still, on occasion, worry about something or

---

[67]For those of you who aren't as addicted as I am to the B science fiction flicks of the 1950s and 1960s, a "pod person" is someone who has been killed during their sleep and replaced by an alien being who *looks* exactly the same but who is instead completely alien. Watch *Invasion of the Body Snatchers* for more details.

someone that matters a lot to me. But all that *Sturm und Drang* and dramatic obsessing about things simply . . . stopped. That began the moment I arrived home from Gateway.

As soon as I made the decision to trust my guidance, I no longer had to obsess about anything. I could relax, let events happen as they would, and *know* that, whether or not the resolution was what I anticipated, it was all working out in my best interests in the long run. If it meant I was financially or in other ways disappointed, that was okay because I could turn that into a lesson about coping with such issues. If things worked out ideally, that was good too. No matter what happened, all was happening as it should. All I had to do was accept that and continue to "show up."

That is, in fact, probably one of the best lessons I've learned throughout this weird journey of mine. You can't control what happens *to* you, nor can you control what happens *around* you. All you can do is control how you react to those events. And the best way to do that is simply to show up—do your best no matter what the circumstances, and let everything else go.

What I didn't immediately understand about that sense of reassurance and serenity I got at the end of that Gateway program was that the sense of knowing was itself a profound communication. In other words, I didn't understand that it was, in fact, a big-time communication with another being.

Instead, my expectations messed up my head. I expected that when I met another being, I would have a *conversation*. I expected that I would meet someone more or less face to face, that I would be able to associate a "body" (or at least a particular vibrational "glow") with that entity. I thought I'd be able to *talk* with them.[68]

---

[68]The whole language thing is an issue I should mention here. Human languages don't cope well with the characteristics of astral, psychic, and spiritual planes. Language—whether English, Chinese, French, or whatever—isn't intended to describe realities that don't conform to ordinary existence. Human languages lack both the structure and concepts to properly describe such experiences. Verb tenses, in particular, tend to get scrambled when you're dealing with a reality that encompasses all temporal periods all at the same time. However, when you do communicate with a spiritual or alien being, it can *feel* like you're having a conversation, even though it's not really conducted in words. You're not "talking" as such, but instead exchanging concepts, gestalts, and experiences. Your own mind translates those concepts into words, so you appear to have a "conversation." It can feel a bit like having a Babel fish translator plugged into your ear (see glossary). Douglas Adams really got that part right!

It took me a while to understand that not all conversations are verbal, or even kinesthetic. Sometimes, you simply *know*. It's a difficult thing to describe and it's not as exciting as reporting a word-for-word conversation. But in some ways it's more profound. You get a very distinct sense of tapping into or receiving knowledge that didn't exist for you before. It's not something you can scientifically measure or validate. I only know that communications from my guides are clearly coming from someplace outside of myself, as opposed to imagination and dreams which just as clearly come from my own mind. The difference is perceptible, if not measurable.

Looking back, I can see the experience at the end of Gateway of knowing my career issues would work out all right as being an obvious example of spiritual guidance. Still, at the time I didn't have any sense of being "directed" to do anything in particular. Nor did I find myself able to conduct conversations with any guide except occasionally. In fact, although I intermittently got other senses of knowing, I didn't connect any of them to receiving spiritual guidance until I attended a Guidelines program specifically designed to put you in contact with your guides. As I've said, Guidelines has become a favorite that I've repeated because of the profound sense of connection to guidance I get from it.

At my first Guidelines I met the guide who was my main source of direction for quite a while. In Click, I finally found a guide I could actually talk to . . . well, communicate with.

The reset exercises in TMI's graduate programs bring you to F-10, F-12, F-15, and F-21.[69] F-10 has never been much of anything for me. Every time I went into that state, I got the same visual: an old-fashioned Victorian train station, very similar to the train station at the beginning of the movie *Murder on the Orient Express*. I would always be standing on the platform beside the train, and sometimes I could vaguely see other shadowy beings in the distance. But that was it. Nothing happened, nothing moved, nobody talked to me. It was always just me standing alone on the platform, feeling utterly dorky and inept.

At this Guidelines, however, I'd had enough of that. We were doing the reset exercise for F-12 and, when I made the intermediary stop at F-10 on the way to F-12, there was that stupid train station one more time. I remember asking in total exasperation, "What's with this dumb train station where nothing ever happens? What's the point of this?"

---

[69]At TMI a graduate program is any residential program after Gateway. Everyone starts with Gateway; thereafter they attend graduate programs of their choice.

At which point, I literally *heard* an equally exasperated voice boom at me: "Well, get on the train, dummy!"

I can remember feeling absolutely astonished, but the first thing out of my (mental) mouth was, "I can't get on the train. I don't have a ticket."

Even more exasperated, the voice boomed again: "Well, hold out your hand and manifest one!"

Sure enough, I held out my nonphysical (astral) hand, and there was a ticket there, neatly labeled as "Ticket to F-12."[70] And when I turned around, there was a kindly looking white-haired train conductor waiting patiently for me to board the train's steps. I handed him the ticket, got on the train, found a seat by a wide picture window . . . and the train pulled out of the station and took me to F-12.

Interestingly, when I got off the train at F-12, the conductor followed me. He then unzipped his body like he might a wetsuit and emerged as an "energy" being, just a golden glow vaguely bipedal in form. And then he introduced himself with that unpronounceable name that I shortened to Click. "Nice to meet you at last," was his first comment. Click then told me that he'd be guiding me throughout my week at Guidelines if that was all right with me—an offer I eagerly accepted.

It should be clear by now that spirit guides don't always necessarily behave in ways that are obviously, uh, *spiritual*. When a whap upside the head with a two-by-four is appropriate, guides—at least *my* guides—have no hesitation in applying said incentives. I should also point out that spirit guides can sometimes have a somewhat strange sense of humor. They definitely have their own personalities and peculiarities.[71]

Participants at Guidelines nominally spend the week hanging out in

---

[70]Yet another point to remember is that once I get to F-10 or F-12, I have the very distinct sense of not being there in the body. Instead, I'm in an energy body that I can modify simply by willing it. Most of the time, I don't bother to manifest any particular body on the focus levels. But occasionally it's helpful to have a hand or something. In these cases, I simply set an intention to having a hand or whatever—and there it is. This is yet another barrier to scientific validation of these states—how do you measure or even detect an astral body? Appendix B discusses the concepts of astral, psychic, and spiritual bodies.

[71]My friend Charles once asked if it worried me that all my various spirit guides seemed to come from the stand-up comic section of the Guides-R-Us store. No, it doesn't bother me particularly. Somehow, that seems an appropriate source of guides for me.

F-21. Would it surprise you a whole lot if I told you I spent practically no time during my first Guidelines program in F-21? No, I thought not.[72]

One of the other nifty things about the Guidelines program is that you are loaned a hand-held cassette recorder for your use during the week and you're encouraged to take verbal notes of the various program exercises, literally narrating your experience while it is happening. As it turns out, with just a bit of practice, this isn't as hard as it sounds.

The result of all this is that I came home with a tape recording of my meeting with my main panel of guides. Here's how it happened. As usual, I was sitting up in my CHEC unit at TMI, with the headphones on, while the exercises were broadcast both over the headphones and over the speakers within the CHEC unit. As a result of this setup, occasionally on my tape recordings you can hear, very faintly in the background, the verbal directions on the exercise.

In my tape of one particular session early in the week, if you listen closely, you can hear Bob Monroe's voice saying something to the effect of, "Now ask your guide to take you on a tour of your total self." And dutifully you can also hear my voice repeat that request. I'd just met up with Click, and I said, "Okay, Click, it's time for a tour of my total self." Whereupon I literally felt my right hand—my nonphysical *astral* hand—being grabbed and jerked upward, while the answer I got was, "Oh, forget about what Bob says. We've got much more important things to do. Come with me!"

With Click's assistance I was guided, not to F-21 where we were supposed to go, but to Focus 39. I even protested: "I'm not supposed to be here! I don't know how to get so high. I don't know how to go to F-39!"

Click answered, "Don't worry, kid. It's okay. You're with me."

In this visit, my first beyond F-21, I found the F-39 level extremely bright, and very hard to maintain, even with Click hanging onto me. It was so bright and white I could barely see anything and I kept having to do breathing exercises to pump my energy levels up high enough to

---

[72]I think one of the reasons I tend to repeat Guidelines is that I keep hoping that sometime I'll attend it and actually do the exercises as directed. To this day I still can't do the "phasing" exercises from that program. When those are played during the program, I'm always off doing something else at the direction of my guides. Presumably what they're directing me to do is more important to my spiritual development than learning how to go to "Phase A" and "Phase B." Or maybe my guides are just being perverse.

maintain that state. Furthermore, although I could vaguely see a panel of judgelike beings, I could barely understand that they were trying to communicate with me. All sounds came through as static-filled and distorted. I couldn't quite figure out what they were saying. Click, in fact, had to translate for me.

Eventually, we worked out an arrangement where I would learn how to go to F-29, which was, apparently, the lowest focus level my panel of guides could visit. But that too was an extremely difficult level for me to visit or maintain at that time. So Click was appointed my "translator" or "intermediary" guide. He could talk to the panel and relay their advice, input, and assistance. Similarly, he could pass along my requests for help until I was sufficiently developed to meet with them.

For the rest of that Guidelines program, I spent all my focus-time with Click. Virtually none of that time was spent doing the official program exercises. It reached the point where Bob Monroe's voice speaking in my ears started to distract me, so I turned the volume down until I could barely hear the verbal instructions coming over the headphones. I concentrated all my attention on Click—my personal guide.

And he had a *lot* to tell me. In fact, I went home from that program with a virtual "honey-do" list of things that I was supposed to accomplish, not to mention a two-year deadline to get them all done. Among those tasks were things like:

- I was to leave my highly paid and now-comfortable techie-nerd career and find something more life-enriching to do.

- I was to move away from my beloved San Diego, where I'd lived for nearly 20 years and where I'd always expected to live until I died, and move somewhere "east."

- I was to continue my efforts in the focus levels, making a daily practice of meditation and contemplation.

There were other items on the list too, but these three were the biggies. These were the ones that I had absolutely no idea how to accomplish. What would I do if I left my career and started something brand new? I'd been working in the computer industry for more than 20 years. What would I do? How would I earn a living if I wasn't doing that?

Yet . . . while I loved the company—my earlier career squabbles having settled out quite nicely—and the people I worked with, my clients were less good for my mental health. I had contracts with the intelligence community and the Department of Defense. I was providing my clients with technology that would be used in ways that I deeply disapproved of. Although I had no special beef with any particular person—I quite liked my clients, in fact, on a personal basis—I had deep personal qualms about continuing to do this work for those particular organizations. In other words, I realized that my job was eating at my soul.

Click basically told me that couldn't go on. I had to stop it—and quickly too.

But what about leaving San Diego? I truly *loved* the area. From the first moment I'd set foot in that beautiful city, I'd felt at home there, in a way I'd never experienced anyplace else. I'd never given serious thought about moving away. Heck, I'd been in my house for more than 17 years, far longer than I'd ever lived anywhere in my entire life! Just the thought of having to winnow all the stuff accumulated over all those years in order to pack up and move practically gave me hives.

And where would I go? Especially, where would I go that was "east." I disliked the east coast, especially the area around Washington, D.C. It had all the bad traffic and high prices of San Diego, and with terrible weather to boot. Yet if I was moving east, I felt I needed to be close enough to the D.C. area to be able to regularly visit a friend who was seriously ill with a long-term, fatal disease. And while I'd spent nearly ten years living in upstate New York and New England, I no longer thought I could handle really cold winters. Two decades of San Diego's glorious weather had made me into an all-star weather wimp.

And financially, how would I manage? Granted, almost anyplace else was cheaper to live in than San Diego, but what would I do, where would I go, and how would I pay for it?

Serious questions, all. And with a two-year deadline, I didn't have a lot of time to figure out the answers. But the fascinating thing that only occurred to me when I was deep in the process of doing all those tasks, is that *not once* did I question that I had to do them. *Not once* did I seriously consider blowing off the list of tasks Click gave me to do. I'd been directed to give up my career, give up my home and friends and support system, and move someplace else—unspecified—to do something else—also unspecified—with no safety net to catch me if I screwed up, and no support system to prop me up if things started to go wrong.

Yet I never considered not doing any of those things.

My friends thought I was crazy. They tried to talk me out of it. They got mad at me. They resented the apparent ease (which wasn't at all easy!) with which I abandoned 20 years of friendship. I went through a deep mourning period not only for the friends I was leaving behind, but also for the beautiful city that had been my home. San Diego was home to me in a way I knew I'd never recapture once I left.

Yet I still knew I had to go. I didn't know where, or how, or even why. I simply had to leave. Click told me so, and I believed and trusted him. Like Dorothy following the Good Witch's advice, I simply followed the yellow brick road, with no real idea where it would take me.

I didn't, however, accomplish the move in two years. I completed my last task from that Guidelines in 20 months, four months ahead of the deadline. I settled in North Carolina and into a new, completely different life.

One increasingly popular way to interpret the latest cosmological theories is that our universe isn't a universe at all. Or rather, it's not a solitary universe, but rather a *multiverse.*

Perhaps ten years ago, physicists realized that some really difficult problems in physics could be explained if we had a universe with ten dimensions instead of four.[73] Inhabiting these ten dimensions would be cosmic *strings*, essentially *one*-dimensional lines with a thinness about the same as the nucleus of an atom—or smaller. Despite their extreme narrowness, they might extend for millions and millions of light-years in length.

String theory claims that the universe is really 10-dimensional and that it's made up of such 10-dimensional strings that vibrate in ways that generate the effects of subatomic particles. Essentially, in this perspective, a particular particle, say a proton, is nothing more than a specific

---

[73]Initially, different theories posited different numbers of dimensions, up to 16 or more. But, using the argument that simpler is better, the total finally settled on—at least in this regard—is ten because that appears to be the minimum number that explains how things work and because the equations that define a multidimensional universe are only fully mathematically consistent in ten dimensions.

vibrational mode of a tiny multidimensional string.[74] When it first started to be accepted, physicists hailed it as perhaps being the grand unified theory they'd been searching for because for the first time it provided a framework for unifying gravitation with quantum theory.

Science fiction writers use the concept of a multidimensional universe when they hypothesize something like "warp drive" (from *Star Trek*) or "hyperspace drive" as a way of getting past the travel limitation of the speed of light.[75] If you could step outside our three-dimensional space into a fourth or fifth spatial dimension, you might find that you could literally step across the gap and re-enter three-dimensional space someplace light-years away. Let me explain.

A one-dimensional surface is a straight line. You can go forward or backward on that line, but nowhere else. A two-dimensional surface crosses that straight line with another one. It's a flat sheet. You can move back and forth, as before, but you can also move from side to side. A three-dimensional surface adds the dimension of height to that sheet. Now we have something solid, like a cube or a sphere. You can go back and forth, side to side, and up and down. In most physics classes these days, you're also taught there is a fourth dimension, and that dimension is that of time. But time isn't like the three spatial dimensions. You can't go in any direction except forward in time.

Once we get above three spatial dimensions, it becomes hard to picture more in your mind. At best, the greatest thinkers of our time can, with effort, think in perhaps four dimensions. No one, even Einstein, can adequately envision five- or six-dimensional space. This difficulty may have something to do with the structure of the brain. Remember that the cerebral cortex is little more than a flat sheet? Sure, it's crumpled up so it'll fit into the relatively small space of the skull, but if you uncrumple it, it becomes a flat sheet, only a few neurons thick.

The thing is, it's pretty easy to project multidimensional objects onto a space that has one less dimension. For example, if you have a three-

---

[74]Protons (and other subatomic particles) have gone from being conceived of as tiny little balls of matter to "frozen energy" states to clouds of probability wave functions and now to vibrational states of a cosmic string. It's a fascinating series of changes in perspective.

[75]But of course, such science fiction concepts were around long before string theory was developed. It's not uncommon for science fiction writers to postulate things that eventually turn out to be not far from reality.

dimensional object, you can use perspective and beautifully portray it on a two-dimensional flat canvas to the point where it looks almost real. Since the cerebral cortex is basically flat, it can easily envision three-dimensional spaces. But anything more is really difficult to do.

Suppose you live in a two-dimensional world, a flat plane, and some obnoxious three-dimensional property developer decides to build a vertical flagpole smack in the middle of your yard. What would that flagpole look like to you? Well, all you'd see is the projection of that pole onto your flat yard. If the pole is very thin, it might look like a small round circle. The thinner the pole is, the smaller that circle would be. You can't see how tall the flagpole is—you're a two-dimensional being and you don't know the concept of "height." You can't even see if the flagpole digs deep into your yard—again, as a two-dimensional being, you don't what "depth" is either. You just have this sudden round thing messing up your yard. If the flagpole is very thin and if it's erected exactly vertical (perpendicular to the plane of your world), the circle in your yard gets very tiny, no matter how tall the pole might be in three-dimensional space. In fact, if the pole gets thin enough, that obnoxious circle simply disappears completely. You can't even tell it's there.

That's the way the multidimensional universe is. We can perceive three spatial dimensions and one time dimension. The other six dimensions, at least from the perspective of our four-dimensional space-time, are so tiny as to be all but nonexistent for everyday considerations.[76]

But, as the notion was developed further, it was quickly realized that something was drastically wrong. Instead of a single set of equations that explained everything, there were *several* sets of equations—five in all—that all appeared to be equally valid for string theory. But string theory couldn't be the ultimate truth, the Holy Grail of physics, if there were all these different—and generally incompatible—mathematical expressions of it. After more than a century of fruitless searching, suddenly having not one, but *five* grand unified theories was such an embarrassment of riches that physicists immediately suspected that none of them could be the truth.

Enter membrane theory or M-theory. M-theory adds one more dimension, making an 11-dimensional entity. It can be shown that the various

---

[76]The ten dimensions represent nine spatial dimensions similar to our normal three, plus the unique time dimension. So the extra six are all spatial dimensions.

mathematical expressions of the previous 10-dimensional string theories are all different ways of reducing the 11-dimensional membrane into 10-dimensional universes.

In other words, all the string theory representations are merely different ways of expressing the same thing!

What a relief. Of course, no one knows much about the equations that dominate M-theory. But I can give you a rough understanding of what it means.

Imagine that our 10-dimensional universe is represented by a flat sheet. In M-theory, there are an infinite number of these flat sheets, distributed throughout the extra dimension, like sheets of paper stacked together. Each sheet is a separate universe. Each sheet has neighboring universes on either side of it separated by a tiny gap.

Theoretically, it might be possible to step outside the sheet that represents our universe and step into another one. It may be possible even to find, or even build, wormholes between the universes. It may be possible to fold our universe, as you would fold a piece of paper to bring opposite edges together so you could literally step from one side of the universe to another in zero time.

The problem with that is that there is no guarantee that the laws of physics would be the same in any other universe. It is a different *universe*, you see, not just a different galaxy or a different place in our own universe. Such essential characteristics as the values for fundamental constants, and even fundamental aspects of physics, chemistry, and biology might be quite different in some other universe.

So how does this correlate to the concept of spirit guides? If we suppose that our universe is a 10- or 11-dimensional multiverse, beings that may exist in four or five or more spatial dimensions (as opposed to our three-dimensional selves) might be normally imperceptible. Just as with that two-dimensional homeowner and the three-dimensional flagpole, beings of higher dimensionality than our own might be nearly impossible to detect on our plane. If going into an altered state allows us to lift out of our three-dimensional "Flatland," we might then become aware of a larger community of beings around us, and might also be able to communicate with them.

Or it might be even more profound. We think of ourselves as inhabiting a three-dimensional space. (I'm ignoring the time dimension for this.) But what if we are *also* beings of a higher dimensionality? Perhaps entering an altered state is merely a way of accessing the other dimensions of our own selves. In that case, issues such as multiple lives—each of which might be separate projections onto different aspects of a three-dimensional space, or perhaps sometimes onto different combinations of different three spatial dimensions—survival after death, and communicating both with the dead and with spiritual beings would all be possible.

Physicists claim that the extra six spatial dimensions of 10-dimensional space are extremely tiny and therefore can contain nothing substantial. But remember that flagpole in that two-dimensional yard? From the two-dimensional homeowner's point of view, that flagpole indeed was so small as to be all but undetectable. But to someone who has a larger view of the universe, the flagpole stretched quite a distance above and below the plane of our oblivious homeowner. Perhaps those extra six spatial dimensions are like that. Perhaps altered states provide us with a mechanism to step outside our local plane and see the universe the way it *really* is.

This is little more than speculation, to be sure. But it is intriguing . . . and it might even be correct.

Clearly, that first Guidelines program had a profound effect on me. It quite literally changed everything external about my life—where I lived, what I did, who I was around. Yet the far more important changes were internal, not external. The greater realization I had was that I really am connected to spiritual guidance all the time—even when I don't know that I am. A large part of my conversations with Click included a mini-review of big events in my life and the subtle, unnoticed help and guidance I'd gotten during those periods. That review also clarified that my seemingly erratic path through life had actually been a straight line directly to where I was at that moment. It had all more or less been planned in advance; I was simply following the script.

But the concept of simply walking a prescribed path through life was difficult for me to swallow. I'm a true American in that I don't like other people telling me what to do. I don't cotton to the notion of following some prearranged path through life. To me, my life had been simply what happened. To realize at this late date that life isn't just "what happens" but that *everything* has been a step in a larger master plan—even all the failures and disappointments and losses . . . well, that's something I found very hard to swallow. If my life were that well-planned in advance, how come I didn't plan it well enough not to have such losses and failures?

It all came down to one classic question: why *do* bad things happen to basically good people?

So here again was another big blow to my belief system. As long as I was sure that we were independent beings with no ultimate goal other than to collect the most trinkets and no ultimate life plan other than to live as long as possible, then a bad thing happening to a good person was simply a case of random chance at work. There was no real need to explain it or justify it. It was a shame, it was too bad, and it was just the way things happened to work out.

However, if each person—if *I*—had an overall life plan that guided me from birth to death, then the only way I could understand the bad things that happened was to accept that the bad things were planned too. If promotions and successes and joys were preplanned, so too, were failures and disasters and sorrows.

But . . . *why?*

How could I possibly justify a life plan that had me losing nearly my whole family one by one starting in my teens? How could I justify a life plan that had me, over and over again, caring deeply about those I was doomed to lose? How could I justify life plans that dumped on some people big time, and let others lead a virtual charmed life? How could I justify life plans where all too often the wicked walked away from their sins unscathed while their innocent victims suffered mightily?

Where was the *sense* in all that?

All those apparent contradictions made a ton of sense, if only I accepted the scientific, rational view that our lives are the results of more or less random chance. I'd gotten through my whole life with that belief, and it worked for me. You learned the basic principles of how the world works. You learned what the danger signs were to possible risks. You did what you could to take precautions to avoid those risks. And if disaster struck anyway, well, sometimes you just got unlucky. There simply was nothing to explain away in terms of why bad things sometimes happened as long as I stuck to that scientific, rational belief system.

But if I accepted my experiential truth that there was an invisible guiding hand throughout my life, that complacent understanding of the world had to go. It meant I had to come to terms with the reality of concepts of Good and Evil. I had to understand why both those could exist in a world supposedly guided by spiritual forces. I had to address the concept of free will too. If our lives were indeed planned and scripted, do we indeed have the ability to choose? Are we simply puppets? Or independent beings? How can you resolve free will with a life plan directed by spiritual guides?

Most of all, I had to think seriously about my concept of God.

13

Tangled in Time

I need to revisit my experience at the remote viewing practicum for just a moment and talk about one other event that happened there. In this program, as you recall, I learned how to remote view and that I truly am capable of perceiving things far beyond my five physical senses. The double-blind experiment was a resounding success with odds, in our program alone, of about 50,000 to one against the results being a result of chance. Still, it was that Thursday, the final full day of the program, when the foundations of my entire scientific belief system shattered.

At the Thursday morning gathering right after breakfast all of us program participants randomly drew a sealed manila envelope, each having three pieces of information on the label. One of the data items was a person's name. The second data item was a city. The third data item was a date. In my case, I drew the name of Betsy in a small town in California I'd never heard of. And the date was some eight months prior to the current date.

We were directed to go to our CHEC units, and to use our new remote viewing skills first to diagnose the person noted on the front of our envelopes by remote viewing their physical, mental, and emotional bodies. Furthermore, we were to focus on the specific two-week period noted on the front of the envelope, in my case the previous April. Then we were to try to heal that person using whatever healing techniques we chose. Finally, we were to bring our still-sealed envelopes back to the meeting room.

I was very dubious about this particular task. I didn't have much experience trying to heal anyone. Sammy was my one stellar success story, and he'd died only a few weeks before. The standard TMI healing technique involved creating a "golden energy dolphin" which we could then send into the patient's energy body. Supposedly, we didn't have to know exactly what was wrong or how to correct it; we only had to perceive what areas of the person needed healing and direct the dolphin to do whatever was necessary to heal that area.

It was a technique I'd used only a few times (having joined TMI's Dolphin Energy Club only a few weeks before attending the program on remote viewing), and I wasn't very comfortable with that process.[77] Still, I was willing to give it a shot. I'd discovered that I generally was an average remote viewer, if only due to lack of regular, long-term practice, so I didn't have any particular expectations of success on this exercise.

But when I did the initial phase of the exercise and tried to diagnose what was wrong with Betsy, I realized that I was definitely getting some interesting information. Betsy, I sensed, had breast cancer. But it seemed to have spread beyond her breast into her lymph nodes near her right shoulder. I could feel a darkness there that felt "wrong" in some odd way. However, it also seemed to me that Betsy's real problem wasn't the cancer, even though it had metastasized. The real issue seemed more in her emotional body; she seemed to be experiencing a tremendous amount of pain, and frustration from that pain had led her into a deep depression. I even got an image of Betsy as a middle-aged woman, a little heavy, but deeply sad and aged beyond her years from that pain and depression.

The results of that diagnostic effort were so vivid to me that I was surprised. I didn't have any real faith that my conclusions were correct, but when the exercise turned to the healing phase, I dutifully sent out

---

[77]As a matter of fact, even now I rarely use the golden energy dolphin technique for healing. It simply isn't a technique that resonates with me.

my golden dolphin into Betsy's physical, emotional, and mental bodies and directed it to heal those areas that needed attention. But right at the end of the exercise, for reasons I couldn't explain and that were definitely opposite to the directions on the exercise, I instructed the dolphin to stay with her rather than returning to me. I then sent a mental message to Betsy that I was leaving a golden energy dolphin with her to continue assisting her through the following weeks.[78]

When the exercise was over I took my sealed envelope down to the meeting room and, under Skip's eyes, opened it. Inside were two pieces of paper. The first was a copy of a request Betsy had made to TMI's Dolphin Energy Club, explaining that she'd been diagnosed with breast cancer, and that it had recently metastasized to her left shoulder and lymph nodes.[79] But, she added, her real issue was that she was experiencing a lot of pain, and that pain and the isolation caused by her treatments, caused her to feel constantly depressed.

My jaw dropped when I read this description. By anyone's measure, my diagnosis had been exactly on target! No matter what else was in the envelope, I figured my session with Betsy had been a success.

But then I turned to the second sheet of paper. This was a report Betsy had written on the results of her healing session. She reported that she felt better, much cheerier, and that her friends and her doctor had all noticed her change in attitude. All that seemed reasonable . . . until I came to the final sentence in her report. "I feel as if I still have a golden energy dolphin inside me, helping me heal."

What?

I almost staggered, and had to sit down to assimilate that sentence. As far as I knew, leaving the dolphin with her had been my impulse. I'd certainly never heard of anyone else associated with TMI doing that. But then again, maybe it was normal for other healers to do that. I calmed myself and decided a little more investigation was in order before I started panicking.

Over lunch I wandered over to the laboratory building where I knew Shirley Bliley had her office. Shirley is a sweetheart and is the person

---

[78]I should mention that you can manifest as many golden energy dolphins as you like. So, leaving that dolphin with Betsy in no way limited me in healing anyone else at any time.

[79]Remember my near-constant dyslexia when in altered states. I often confuse left and right when I'm in those states.

who runs the Dolphin Energy Club (DEC) for TMI.[80] She collects the requests that people make and assigns the requests to teams of several DEC healers. She then collects reports from both the healers and the patients and distributes a summary several times a year to everyone.

I decided I would ask Shirley about leaving the dolphin with the patient, specifically whether this was a common practice that I'd simply stumbled upon. I described what I had done in my healing session, including leaving the dolphin in place with Betsy.

"Oh," she said, "that's very clever."

"Is that something that a lot of people do when they're doing DEC healing?" I asked.

"No," she said. "I've never heard of anyone doing that before."

I had much to consider as I returned to the program. Apparently my ad hoc style of healing was unique in Shirley's experience—and if anyone would know about a healing technique it would be her since she coordinated the entire healing program at TMI. Furthermore, I'd indeed correctly viewed Betsy's condition as it had been eight months earlier. Somehow, that didn't seem difficult to swallow. If I could remote view at all, why couldn't I remote view the past and diagnose someone's condition in the past? It stretched the boundaries of my sense of space-time reality, but didn't break my notion of physical truth.

But the dolphin I left inside her—something that apparently only I could have done—made my head spin. Because, you see, she'd written her report on her perceptions of her healing session and dated it *April 17.* I hadn't done the healing until mid-December of the same year. Apparently . . . somehow . . . I'd managed to not only *view* the past, but also to *change* the past. And I had documented evidence to support that change.

All of a sudden, everything I thought I knew about physical reality crashed around my ears. If the past wasn't fixed, if it was instead mutable, what else wasn't fixed? What had happened to "time's arrow"—that physical understanding that unlike all spatial dimensions, the time dimension only flows in one direction, from the past to the future? And how could causality still be true if you can go back into the past and *change* the causes? What

---

[80]Interestingly, DEC is the only healing organization I've ever heard of that charges the healers a fee rather than the patients! Healers pay a modest annual fee to help cover the costs of running the program, while those who request healing pay nothing. The only request of the patients is that they report on any results they perceive from the healing efforts.

is the cause and what is the effect, if causes—i.e., my healing session—can occur after effects—i.e., Betsy's sensing the dolphin I left inside her?

If attending the Gateway program had made me feel as if I'd stumbled down the proverbial rabbit hole, attending the remote viewing program made it clear that the rabbit hole was more like a wormhole into a wholly different universe, one in which the easy, comforting rules of physics I'd lived by my entire life no longer applied.

In fact, I realized that this one exercise made clear that *everything* I thought I'd learned in physics was fundamentally wrong. Believe me, it wasn't a comforting feeling.

Of all the events I've experienced since I began my journey, this one event has undermined my scientific world view more than almost any other. It is a very clear violation of "time's arrow" and implies that you can go back and forth in time and cause physical changes to the world *in the past* that are reflected (and documented) *in the present*.

This is extraordinary—and highly disturbing to someone who was rigorously trained in physics. All science is built on the concept that events have causes, which happen *before* events. You simply can't go back and change the causes after the fact. In fact, you can't go back at all . . . or can you?

To clarify why this is important, consider the case of a person who has constructed a time machine that can go backward or forward in time. Suppose he goes back into the past and kills his own grandfather, his father's father, *before his father has been born*. That means that his father will never exist. But if his father never existed, how could *he* have been born to build the time machine? If he doesn't exist, then he can't possibly build a time machine and go back to kill his grandfather, which means that his father indeed will be born, and so will he, which means he *can* build a time machine and go back and kill his grandfather . . .

You see the point. Apart from the obvious ethical issues of patricide this example raises, it also is what gives physicists migraines when considering the concept of violating time's arrow. If you can go back into the past and change the past, then you create unending paradoxes that have no solution. Science fiction writers since H. G. Wells have come up with all kinds of creative solutions for this dilemma, but none have really solid scientific foundations—until recently.

As it turns out, in the past ten years or so, physicists have started to realize that maybe it *would* be possible to go back and forth in time. Maybe time's arrow isn't as universally forward-pointing as we all thought.

Of course, moving *forward* in time is well-accepted by physicists—it has even been demonstrated many times. Once Einstein published his theory of special relativity, it soon became clear that leaping forward into the future is perfectly feasible. Let me explain.

Special relativity notes that when an object moves relative to you, the clocks on that object also appear to run slower than your clocks. The degree of slowness is related to how fast they're moving. At the speed of light, the traveler's clocks stop. But moving only fast enough to, say, orbit the Earth is sufficient to slow clocks a perceptible amount, especially if the experiment is conducted for a long enough time period. NASA has repeatedly confirmed that time dilation occurs in the slowing of the high-precision clocks carried by astronauts on orbital and moon missions. Other experiments with cosmic rays have also validated this effect, which is is called "time dilation" because the interval between ticks of a clock dilates or stretches in the traveling clock. An example may help clarify this.

Suppose you have two objects, Red and Blue, one traveling past the other. Red looks at Blue's clock, compares it to his own, and claims, "Your clock is running slow, Blue!" But if they're traveling at a steady velocity, then when Blue looks at Red's clock, Blue thinks it's Red's clock that is running slow! How can each of them perceive the other's clocks as running slow?

As long as both Red and Blue are traveling at a constant velocity, changing neither speed nor direction, they are each traveling in an *inertial* frame of reference. Einstein's theory states that there is no preferential inertial frame. From Blue's perspective, he's standing still while Red is traveling by him, thus Red's clock must be the one running slow. But from Red's perspective, Red is the one standing still while Blue whizzes by in the opposite direction, so it's Blue's clock that is slow. Both Red and Blue's perspectives are equally true if each is in an inertial frame of reference.[81] Meanwhile, to some outside observer, Green, traveling at a still

---

[81]An inertial frame of reference means that each is moving at a constant speed *and in a straight line* with respect to distant stars, the "fixed stars." If either is changing their speed or their direction (or both), they're in an accelerating frame of reference and this discussion no longer applies.

different velocity (again however, without changing either Green's speed or direction), *both* Red and Blue are traveling, and *both* of them have clocks that run slow, though not necessarily by the same amount![82]

The only way you can determine a preferential frame of reference, according to Einstein, is if there is *acceleration* involved in the motion. But acceleration is a very specific term in physics. Yes, it refers to changes in speed; either slowing down or speeding up are called "acceleration" in physics. But in physics, acceleration refers to *any* change in velocity— either a change in speed *or* a change in direction of motion, or changes in both. Even if you travel at a constant rate of 50 miles an hour, if you turn the steering wheel a slight amount to go around a curve, you've accelerated your car in the physics sense of the word.

This explains the famous "twin paradox," in which one of two twins, each 20 years old, is sent off in a rocket ship that moves at a constant rate of speed of, for example, 97 percent of the speed of light for five years according to the on-board clock. The traveling twin has therefore aged from 20 years to 25 years. He returns to Earth, again at a constant rate of 97 percent of the speed of light, which of course takes him another five years. When he lands at the vastly changed space port, he is therefore 30 years old according to his clock—and he looks exactly as a 30-year-old would look. Once he lands, he is greeted by his twin brother. But the twin brother, who stayed at home and whose clocks were not affected by the Einstein's time dilation is *not* 30 years old. If the traveling twin moved at 97 percent of the speed of light, the stay-at-home twin's clocks ticked *four times* faster than the traveling twin. When they meet, the traveler is 30 years old, but his twin brother has aged 40 years instead of ten and is now 60 years old!

---

[82]Suppose you're Green. You see Red moving east at 40 mph and Blue moving east at 60 mph. Red sees Blue moving east at 20 mph (the difference between their two speeds). Blue sees Red moving *west* at 20 mph. (Because Blue is moving east faster than Red is, it looks to Blue as if Red is going in the opposite direction.) Red claims Blue's clock is slow by a factor dependent on the 20 mph speed difference. Blue claims Red's clock is slow by the same 20 mph speed difference factor. But to Green, Red's clock is slow by an amount determined by the 40 mph speed Green observes Red traveling, and Blue's clock is slow by an amount determined by the 60 mph speed Green observes Blue traveling. I should also note that Red and Blue *each* think *Green's* clock is slow by the same amounts that Green thinks their clocks are slow! Thus, no one's clock agrees with anyone else's clock.

Think about this for just a moment. Both twins start off the same age. One twin travels at a very high velocity, and the other doesn't. Einstein claimed that you shouldn't be able to distinguish between any two inertial frames and that the clocks in each such frame look equally slow to each other. But the fact remains that when the twins meet, one of them is 30 years old, and the other is twice that age. Where's the consistency in that? It's a paradox, right? And paradoxes are absolute anathema to scientists.

There's a subtle error in this analysis that you may not have caught. The inability to set a preferential frame of reference only applies to *inertial* frames of reference, those traveling at a constant velocity and with no acceleration. But that's not the case here. If the twin moves off in one direction at a particular velocity and then returns, somewhere along the way he *had* to have changed at least his direction of motion even if he never changed his speed. In other words, he did not occupy an inertial frame of reference at all because his velocity—which includes both his speed and his direction of motion—had to have changed on his trip.[83] Therefore, we can easily distinguish which twin traveled and which twin stayed at home, and it's perfectly reasonable to allow them to come together with one being twice the age of the other.[84]

Looking at this example in another way, there's a very real sense in which the traveling twin has gone through a time machine. In some sense, his ten-year trip took him 40 years into the future. He didn't have to spend 40 years getting there as his stay-at-home brother did. He only had to spend ten years. Of course, the drawback is that once he's moved into the future, there's no way for him to go back to the past. Time travel in this classic sense is one-way only. It moves in the direction of time's arrow from past to future and that's all.

So there appears to be at least one really solid mechanism for traveling in time, at least in the direction of the future. You can't come back, but you can project yourself forward. Note one key element of such a time travel scheme: Because you can never come back in time, you can never send *information* backward in time. Therefore you can never affect

---

[83]Remember that even going in a circle *changes your direction of motion* and therefore is an acceleration. So no matter how the traveling twin travels out and back, *if he returns to his starting point, he* must *have accelerated at some point on his journey.*

[84]Well, at least it's reasonable to physicists.

the past in any way. Once you've moved forward, you're part of the future time stream. You might have skipped ahead a little, but you're still moving with the general flow of time. You haven't done anything really obnoxious to the concepts of cause and effect.

Recently, however, new theories of the cosmos have opened up new physically correct ideas for how true time travel might be accomplished. Various physicists have come up with at least half a dozen ways to move backward and forward in time—to construct a true time machine. Those methods may not be practical from today's engineering standpoint, but they open the door a crack to understand how time travel might be possible.

I'm not going to go into the details of how these various time machines would work, but a quick run-down of the possibilities should make clear that these ideas are probably not something you're going to see on sale at your local discount store any time soon.[85]

W. H. Van Stockum's time machine, proposed in the 1930s, starts with an infinitely long cylinder that spins at a rate near the speed of light. Such a cylinder, it turns out, would drag the fabric of space-time along with it. If you hop a ride on that cylinder, you'd literally go backwards in time after one complete revolution. The faster the cylinder spins, the farther back in time you'd go. Of course, it's impossible to build an infinite anything, much less spin it at near the speed of light. And the centrifugal forces on the cylinder if it spun that fast would rip it apart if it were constructed of any known material. But conceptually, there's no reason in physics such a machine would not work if it could be built.

About ten years later, Kurt Gödel came up with another time machine idea. Instead of rotating an infinite cylinder, he suggested that the universe itself is rotating. In his conception, you can travel backwards in time simply by taking a rocket ship around the entire circumference of the universe. There is a gotcha in this idea, unfortunately. Gödel estimated that the universe had to rotate once every 70 billion years or so, and that the minimum radius of the universe for time travel to occur is 16 billion light-years. Since your rocket ship has to travel at just under the speed of light for time travel to occur, that implies it's going to take you

---

[85]I'm indebted to Michio Kaku's wonderful book *Parallel Worlds* for some of this discussion of various time machines. I strongly recommend his book for anyone interested in this subject.

more than 100 billion years to make that complete circuit.[86] Of course, your local space-ship clocks won't register that kind of time interval, but if you only achieve that same 97 percent of the speed of light that the traveling twin did, your perceived elapsed time will still be about 25 billion years—nearly twice the total age of the universe since the Big Bang. Be sure to pack a good lunch!

In the 1980s more ideas for physically possible (or at least not physically impossible) time machines arose. Physicist Kip Thorne came up with a notion that was used as the basis for Carl Sagan's novel *Contact*. Thorne's machine involved building two spheres, each having an inner and outer shell, and connecting those two spheres with wormholes in the middle so that one end of the wormhole is inside one sphere and the other end is inside the other sphere.[87] You put one of the spheres in a rocket ship and send it traveling wherever you want to go at near light-speed and wait till it arrives. Notice that the clocks on that spaceship are running slower than your stay-at-home clocks. Theoretically, if you then jump into the wormhole back on Earth, you would be sucked through it to the rocket—and equally, you'd be sucked backwards in time to the rocket ship's time as well. To get home in this machine, you simply jump back into the wormhole at the rocket ship end and you'd be sucked back home. That vast, sucking sound you hear is thus a time traveler swooshing in and out of our space and time.

One problem with this time machine is that the wormhole has to be made out of negative energy. Negative energy is what keeps the wormhole open long enough for the traveler to jump through it. Now this energy is known to exist, though it's incredibly rare. One way to make it, in very tiny quantities, is to put two large, uncharged metallic plates very close together, not quite touching. If conditions are just right, the two plates

---

[86]Technically, since 16 billion light-years is the *radius* of the universe, the *circumference*, the distance you'd have to travel, is more than six times that, or about 100 billion light-years, since the circumference of a circle is 2π times the radius, or about 6.28 times the radius.

[87]A "wormhole" in space-time is a theoretical passage between two universes. It is as if a worm burrows out of our universe and into a neighboring universe. Wormholes are popular in science fiction as a way of traveling the vast distances of space, but since none have ever been confirmed experimentally, no one knows if they really exist. Also, it's not clear if, in trying to travel through the wormhole from our space to another, you would survive the attempt.

are attracted to each other and a tiny amount of negative energy is created. This is called the Casimir effect. Remember, in the discussion of quantum mechanics, a constant sea of virtual particles are constantly created and annihilated before they can be explicitly detected? Well, the Casimir effect is one reason physicists believe this to be true. While the creation of negative energy might seem to be a violation of physics' beloved law of the conservation of energy, the fact is that because it's a very brief violation, it "doesn't count."

There is one other little "gotcha" in Thorne's time machine: Those spheres have to be constructed out of negative *matter* and they have to contain enough negative *energy* to hold the wormholes open.

Negative matter is not antimatter, something that has been found, although in extremely small quantities. The particles that comprise antimatter—electrons and protons—have opposite charges to those of ordinary matter, so protons have a negative charge and electrons have a positive charge. When an atom of antimatter encounters an atom of ordinary matter, they instantly annihilate each other.

Negative matter is matter that has an opposite *gravitational* response than ordinary matter. In other words, it is *repulsed* by a normal gravitational field rather than attracted by it. In the case of negative matter, what goes up not only does not come down, it goes up . . . and up . . . and up forever. No one has ever seen any trace of negative matter so it's an entirely theoretical concept. Furthermore, it's not clear how we could detect it, even if it exists. And then, it's hard to understand how we'd either collect enough of it to construct a person-sized time machine, or how we'd build anything out of it that didn't immediately fly off into outer space. However, I was trained in physics, not in engineering, so I'm going to leave the construction details for someone else to deal with.

One more time machine concept makes use of colliding *strings*. As I explained in the last chapter, in trying to understand the Big Bang that started things off, cosmologists realized that our four-dimensional spacetime reality actually appears to be 10-dimensional instead. J. Richard Gott III in the 1990s realized this new cosmological perspective opened the door to a new way to travel in time.

If two of these cosmic strings were to collide, it might be possible to travel into the past by simply circling the colliding strings. In the example I mentioned before, of a two-dimensional being finding a three-dimensional mast in his yard, this would be the equivalent of finding two such masts colliding with the collision point being in the plane of the yard.[88] Then our intrepid homeowner could move into the past simply by moving in a circle around that collision point. To make the time machine, we only need to find (or make) a couple of these multidimensional colliding strings, and move around the point of collision where they intersect our usual space-time.

J. R. Gott III computed that for this time machine to work, the strings must each be traveling just short of light-speed, within a few ten-millionths of a percent of light-speed, in fact. And they must be incredibly massive, on the order of ten million billion tons of mass for every centimeter (about 4/10 of an inch) of length!

Still, this is a time machine that doesn't require negative energy or negative mass, and that doesn't require moving faster than light. In comparison to other approaches, it's relatively simple. Of course, finding two appropriate cosmic strings and getting them to collide at just the right time so you can circle them is a bit of a problem, but again . . . it's all in the engineering details.

There are other conceptual ideas for a time machine, and some of them may eventually become practical. But the problem with all of them is that if they work, they raise serious issues about the fundamental nature of time and how it relates to space.

Physicists often view time as a river. Rivers flow, generally, in one direction only. As long as time flows in one direction only, there's no problem. It's only if you attempt to go back into the past, get caught in a swirl or an eddy in the river of time—and especially if you go back into the past and *change* it—that conceptual paradoxes and other difficulties arise.

All of which brings me back to Betsy and the inexplicable experience of healing her in December, yet having her report the effects of that healing the previous April. Somehow, I apparently executed a major violation of time's arrow, and managed not only to *view* the past (to diagnose her condition), but also to *change* the past (resulting in her documented

---

[88]It's not necessary for both of these masts to be perfectly perpendicular to the yard. They can be at angles to the vertical, but since they each only intersect the yard at infinitesimally small points, it can be tricky for the two-dimensional homeowner to find and identify the correct point to circle.

experience of my healing efforts). Isn't that simply impossible in modern physics? As we've seen, apparently not.

The equations that give us our understanding of the universe don't appear to rule out the possibility of time travel, even time travel into the past. And there are two schools of thought about that. Traditionally, scientists have believed that whatever is not explicitly demanded by the laws of physics does not exist. In some sense, that's the materialist position.

But a new view is arising. If the fundamental fabric of the universe is really nothing more than vibrational modes in 10-dimensional strings and probability wave functions that assess the probabilities of all possible fates, it may well be that the correct way to view possible events is instead that anything not explicitly forbidden *must* exist. If probability wave functions extend to the entire scope of the universe throughout all of space and time—and they do—even events that are only infinitesimally possible must *somewhere* occur. It corresponds to the old saying among physicists that if you wait long enough anything that's *possible* to happen *will* eventually happen.[89]

In other words, if something *can* exist, it *must* exist.

The laws of physics as we currently understand them appear to permit time travel, into both the past and the future. Therefore, by this reasoning, time travel *must* be possible. Our understanding of physics is such that to accomplish it we believe it requires enormous speeds, vast masses, exotic energies and materials, or possible rips in the fabric of space-time. It's not clear how one person, using only mind and intentionality, can possibly accomplish time travel in any real sense.

But . . . it's not forbidden by physics. And if it's not forbidden . . .

---

[89]This also corresponds to a common shorthand comment that in physics, there are only three possible numbers: zero, one, and infinity. Something might not exist at all, which corresponds to zero. Or it might exist only once, which corresponds to one. But if it exists more than once, it *must* exist an infinite number of times.

14

Beyond the Pale

During the months I was planning and preparing to begin a new life away from San Diego, I found that something fundamental had changed within me. It was as if I had accepted a challenge and now was going through a rigorous training program designed to allow me to succeed at that goal. Of course, I didn't really have any idea what the "goal" was. But it quickly became clear to me that something interesting was happening to my views of the world—or rather, my views of the universe.

One change was that I was now strongly connected to spiritual guidance on a nearly daily basis. Not that they told me what to do—no, that would be too easy. Nor did they have a lot to say about mundane day-to-day issues such as where I should move, what I should do to earn a living, or anything of that sort. That mostly was left up to me to figure out on my own. Instead, I was guided to start a training program in spirituality and philosophy—subjects that had never been high on my personal priority list until then. I was a physics major, after all, and most physics majors are not known for their in-depth reading in philosophy and theology.

Another of the obvious changes in my life at this time was that my ability to go to higher focus levels increased dramatically. It was almost as if my willingness to accept extreme guidance that flew in the face of all practicalities was a test to see if I was ready for more. Once I'd passed that test and was fully committed to my new path, I was granted much more access to those higher realms.

In my meditation sessions at home, I still only had Hemi-Sync tones that supported access to F-21 as the highest levels. But now, with just the slightest nudge, I could easily access F-27. It didn't take much to send me flying.

And then, the week before the fateful Lifeline program where I retrieved the Beagle lander, my friend Deb called me on the phone. She had been to Starlines about a month before, and wanted to know if I'd like her to try to guide me to that ultimate focus level, F-49.

I immediately thought that was a wonderful idea. I knew virtually nothing about the upper focus levels, except F-32 and that aborted visit to F-39 where I'd had trouble maintaining that elevated state. But that had been a long time before, and I was much more experienced at holding high focus levels now than before. I was sure I could get at least part of the way to F-49 with Deb supporting me. I hadn't paid all that much attention to the descriptions of the official cosmology of the levels. I just knew that if going to F-32 was good, going to F-49 must be even better.

So, with no real preparation, Deb and I began our "tripping" session over the phone. By this time I was very good at going into altered states very quickly and soon found myself in an advanced meditative state. With her supporting me with energy work, I soon found myself moving upward. First, a stop at F-32, but I didn't—actually wouldn't—stay long there. Then we moved up to F-34 and F-35, the place that Bob Monroe had described as the "I-There" or the "Gathering." I liked that area a lot, but we were headed higher. We moved up to F-42, and then, in a final energy push, she sent me on up to F-49.

And I was awestruck.

My sense of this level was simply amazing. It felt as if I stood directly before the Eye of God. After a suggestion from Deb, I actually moved into the Eye—and if I'd been awestruck before, this was even more amazing. For those brief moments, God and I were One.

I didn't want to leave.

I wanted to stay at that level, reveling in the sense of Divine Love that permeated being One with God. But I couldn't maintain that level of energy forever, and eventually (meaning after about five or ten minutes),

I made my way back to where Deb waited. I'd been only semicoherent in describing what I'd experienced while I was in F-49, and now words didn't come any easier. I had no words to describe the sense of humility, awe, and wonder that accompanied visiting F-49 for that first time.

I should point out that a few days later I went off to Lifeline, where almost the first thing I experienced was the disturbing soul retrieval on the crashed Beagle lander, as described earlier. And within a week after that, I was heavily entangled in the traumatic kundalini awakening. Coincidence? I don't think so. I'm not quite sure which of these were causes and which were effects, but clearly having three major psychic and spiritual shocks virtually simultaneously was not a coincidence.

Once the kundalini energy was back under control, a process that took about two months, I realized that I was now able to command vastly greater energies than ever before. And a side effect of that was that I found that it was fairly straightforward to hit F-49 whenever I was doing a phone session with Deb. Mostly we didn't bother going that high, but we could do so if we wanted. That period lasted about six months until a group of TMI graduates decided to sponsor a joint effort to go beyond F-49.

A few words need to be said here about F-49. As appendix A makes clear, the focus levels are arranged in seven groups of seven levels each, for a total of 49 levels. In the "Miranon" cosmology, these are the only levels that are "knowns."[90] Although that cosmology acknowledges the existence of higher levels than F-49, it says nothing about any organizational structure corresponding to those far levels.

TMI's Starlines program is the only one that directly addresses these very high levels. It includes exercises to focus levels starting at F-34 and F-35, then eventually moves up to F-49. A final exercise offers the opportunity—if the participant is both ready and willing—to go beyond F-49 to whatever levels he or she can reach.

I hadn't yet been to Starlines when this group meditation exercise was announced. The plan for the exercise was that virtually all participants in all the various e-mail loops of TMI folks were to simultaneously go into altered states, meet at a common, specified location on F-27, and

---

[90]Before his death, Bob Monroe connected with a nonphysical entity he called "Miranon," who acted as his guide to the nonphysical and presented Monroe with a map of the focus levels from C-1 consciousness to the highest level that Miranon could access, F-49.

then use their group energy to catapult themselves upward as high and far as they could go.

It was a fun idea, and Deb and I had gotten pretty good at going to higher levels just between the two of us. We talked about wanting to participate and see how high we could go. So it probably shouldn't have been a surprise when, about a week before the specified group meditation, we found ourselves moving through a BWIC.

The first stop dropped us off at a focus level somewhere in the F-70s. Unusually for me, I didn't have an exact idea of which level we were on, I only knew it was somewhere in the 70s.[91] My sense of this particular focus level was that this area was a type of "upgrade center." Just as F-27 includes a "healing center" in which traumas and problems from a physical life can be treated and healed, the focus levels in this range were also devoted to improving your spiritual state—except that to get here and be worked on, those previous C-1 issues had to already have been healed. The center here was more for upgrading than healing.

After a brief stop here, and a little work done on me by those beings on that level, we stepped back into the BWIC for another stop.

It was a joyous, totally wild ride . . . and I ended up being dumped out in a focus level I didn't recognize. I asked where I was, and immediately had a sense of knowing that I was on F-112. I almost immediately felt a powerful energy flow similar to the kundalini flow I'd felt many months before, but it was both more powerful and more serene. Deb, also an energy worker, decided to work on my heart chakra and almost instantly I felt a huge increase in the "swirl rate" of my chakras—all of them, actually, not just the heart chakra—and it startled me.

I realized that I could feel myself splitting into two self-aware entities—a physical body and an etheric body. I was in both places and in neither at the same time. Then as I looked closer, I realized I wasn't split

---

[91]There's an interesting side note about knowing where you are. Some people, Deb included, almost never know what focus level they're on. Others, like me, almost always know where they are. In my case, if I don't know what level I'm on, I simply have to ask, "what level am I on?" and I get an immediate answer. It seems similar to the ability some people have to physically navigate with ease, and may in fact be a variation on that. Certainly, my sense of where I am geographically when I'm in C-1 is strong, and I very rarely get lost; Deb can barely navigate to the end of her own driveway without getting disoriented. So there may be an association between navigational skills in the "real world" and navigational skills when in focus. Or maybe not.

into only two, but that all my various energy bodies were separating . . . and there were far more than the seven or so described in standard New Age energetic literature. Those seven appeared to be those available in the focus levels below F-49 levels, but above those levels there seemed to be hundreds, thousands . . . millions?? . . . of energy bodies. It felt as if I could be simultaneously in all of them, yet all of them were still separate at the same time. It's a difficult thing to explain.

Throughout this, my heart chakra could feel the constant link from energy body to energy body, and the flow of energy was quite powerful. The chakra literally ached from containing the flow.

The strain of maintaining this ultra-high focus level was extreme, and we rapidly tired and returned to C-1. But in thinking about this experience after the fact, I noted that I felt in some way significantly changed or enhanced in some permanent way. The only real way to describe it was that there was some type of heightened awareness or sensitivity I couldn't at that moment define in words.

But a week later, things really got strange. The session, again with Deb, was of such importance that I described it in detail in my journal. This is the relevant excerpt from that journal entry:

We were met by a giant ball, much larger than any previous one. We went inside the ball and hung on, as it moved into a BWIC of enormous size. Great fun rolling and bouncing down the BWIC, but then I steered us out of the ball, and along a very dark series of side tunnels, more normally sized. Kept bouncing and rolling along those, but I was clearly leading us somewhere specific: "Take second left, now third upward branch, now turn left, etc." Eventually we were deposited in a very dark place, quite hard to see. [There was a] slight red glow and we were surrounded by dark, angular beings/ things with sharp jagged tops, like extremely sharp mountains. It was very difficult to see, but after a short while my [astral] hand was taken by one of the beings, and I was led inside (holding Deb's [astral] hand so she followed.)

Inside it was slightly brighter, but not much, still very dark and murky. I could see my hand and it was more like a dark scaly, leathery fin—reminded me in shape of the *Creature from the Black Lagoon's* hand. I could also see more of the creatures who ringed us, and under most circumstances they would be extremely frighten-ing—practically Satanic in appearance and very ferocious looking. But the feeling radiating from them was one of serious intent of purpose. These people were devoted to improving themselves spiritually—a little reminiscent of Tibet's (pre-China) dedication to religion over economics. I sensed they were very good people. There was no fear, no trepidation, no concern at all. I just waited to see what would happen next.

I gradually understood that this was some type of ritual demonstration or initiation or something of that sort, and a little later understood that I was to bring light to this very dim place. (I understood that their visual system operates in the infrared, which is why it seemed so dark and reddish to me.)

Deb then commented that my face was beginning to break open vertically, down the middle of my face—and a bright light was shining forth. I actively split it, much like shedding a skin, only the skin looked like these people—not human, and let my energy body shine out. Deb started funneling energy into me as a steadying force, and I could feel the heart energy of all those around us focusing in on me. It was like being a prism or a lens, focusing the energy upward to the domed roof, and forming a huge glowing ball. We worked on that ball quite a while, then Deb pointed out I was splitting again, this time at the heart chakra. Almost simultaneously, I said I was starting to generate heart energy into the ball to shower over everyone.

I suddenly realized it was time for us to go elsewhere, so Deb and I left with their thanks, leaving the glowing ball of heart energy— which still didn't seem to illuminate the room.

We stepped back into the BWIC and started moving upward at a tremendous pace. Deb commented a couple times that we were making huge strides, going great distances. I could tell that again there was someplace specific we were headed. For me, it felt like the pull of Home drawing me closer and closer. I didn't say anything about that until after Deb commented, "You know how you keep saying you feel like you're from someplace else? I think we're heading for that someplace else." And that's exactly what it felt like.

And then we were there. I faced a humongous, intensely bright golden wall of energy that was part of me and yet not part of me. Deb, who was not on the same level, made a suggestion about somehow tuning to that, and I said, no . . . it was like being laser light— coherent light in which all the photons are both the same and yet not the same. I was "cohering" to the giant wall of energy in some manner I couldn't explain. It felt as if I literally merged with the wall, became the wall, was no longer separate from it as I'd been for so long. A totally awesome experience, filled with satisfaction and love.

There was no "me" there was no "other" it was just one. I was the Wall and the Wall was me; there was no separation between me/It.

The Wall was not really energy exactly—it was more pure Thought. As if energy doesn't exist until Thought makes it so. It's the closest I've ever come to being in the Source of everything—even more than the Mind of God in that focus level F-49 experience. Relatively speaking, that Mind of God seemed petty and small compared to this Wall. As if that were the Mind of God for our tiny universe, but the Wall is the Thought that Sources all universes.

The Wall also was massively interdimensional, wrapping the entire universe within one small piece and extending far beyond four-dimensional space-time. While the Wall and I were One, I seemed to get the message, "You must do more."

More what, exactly?

Deb suddenly felt her own energy body warping and twisting as if it were multidimensional too, and I commented that she was right. Her "flat" (i.e., four-dimensional energy body) was popping upwards, expanding and unfurling some of its other dimensions to become more true to her true self. Her description of what she was feeling was very similar to the sensations I'd had at F-70-something last week: not exactly comfortable, not exactly uncomfortable, not exactly painful, not exactly not painful . . . just really strange.

While I was watching over her unfolding, I had a sudden sense that this was a very high Focus level—somewhere around F-253. I have no idea why that suddenly came to me, other than I think I had the stray thought, "I wonder where I am."

I sensed that Deb had about as much as she could tolerate at the moment, so I stepped away from the wall very regretfully, dropped back to her focus level, and formed a protective shield around her. After a moment, we stepped back into the BWIC.

We ended up in the same dark place as we started, except this time I could see everything perfectly. It was as clear as day. Apparently my visual system had been attuned to the different frequency ranges. I realized that those who greeted us had a gift for Deb, and suggested she accept it. She did so with great gratitude and it lodged strongly in her heart chakra.

We stepped out of this place and dropped quickly back to C-1. Or what passes these days for C-1 for each of us!

In discussing this with Deb afterwards, a couple things became clear. First was that the experience on the dark world was a test of readiness for us. Had we reacted with either fear or loathing or concern or anything other than total love and acceptance—from both of us—because of the dark, threatening appearance of the people there, and the darkness of the world, we would never have gone farther.

It also strongly reminded me of my experience with F-13. I explained to Deb that the way I resolved my dread in visiting F-13 was just to go there and deliberately give copiously exactly what I thought was being taken from me unwillingly before: love energy. In the Dark World, I did much the same thing, becoming a huge emitter of love energy, drawing from Deb's reserves, and reflecting back the energy they broadcast at me to make a huge glowing ball of love that transformed into an umbrella, showering it down on all those present. That was the right answer, it appears, and that was what gave me permission to go on to the Golden Wall.

It's like the song says: "Love is the answer to it all."

As last time, when done, I could again see my own aura around my hand. But where on Saturday [the time of the visit to F-112] I could see only one clear auric level, this time I could see at least five to seven levels. And the outermost one, the one that pulsed with power, was dark, almost a rich inky indigo—the darkest blue you can imagine and still distinguish any hint of blue. I'm not sure it's a "usual" auric level because it seems quite different from the other levels. Somewhat different in shape, but definitely different in power and in quality.

I am still seeing fainter traces of aura around my hand this morning.

When scientists speak of a grand unified theory (GUT) or a theory of everything (TOE), they don't really mean *everything*. Such folks are almost always physicists of one breed or another, either quantum physicists or cosmologists. In either case, what they really are talking about is a theory that unites all the major concepts in physics—that brings into alignment gravity and electromagnetism and all the other fundamental forces of physics. That is the holy grail of physics, and so far, the best candidate appears at the moment to be membrane theory, as discussed earlier.

Calling such a theory a theory of *everything* embodies the underlying presumption on the part of physicists that physics is *the* fundamental science, and all other sciences in this view are mere derivations. Understand physics, they claim, and you can—theoretically, anyway—derive all other aspects of the universe.

But there is a problem with that perspective. Moving from quantum physics to chemistry isn't a total impossibility, for instance, though it's difficult to imagine that someone who knew absolutely nothing about chemistry could derive *a priori* the characteristics of such anomalous compounds as, say, water. But, chemistry seems easy enough compared to the task of deriving the properties of biology, the science of life. How do we go from subatomic particles to living systems? And even if we could derive the concepts of biology, how could that help us in understanding mind, the science of psychology?

You see, that's the problem with the current concept of a grand unified theory—it's really only a grand unified theory of *physics* and doesn't at all begin to explain how we go from physics to chemistry to biology to psychology. It unifies nothing except that one single science.

One ambitious scientist doesn't take such a limited view of a unification theory. Dr. Ervin Laszlo is renowned in Europe, the recipient of numerous international prizes including the prestigious Japan Peace Prize, and has spent much of his life trying to understand how systems work. He aspires to create a unified theory that truly unites *all* the key sciences, including:

- Cosmology, the physics of the extremely large: solar systems, galaxies, and the entire universe

- Quantum physics, the physics of the extremely small: atoms and subatomic particles

- Biology, the science of living systems

- Psychology, especially the study of consciousness and mind, the most difficult topic and one that is barely defined, much less understood.

Clearly, this is a far more daunting task than merely uniting all of physics! So what led Laszlo on this quest to achieve far more than others aspire to?[92]

---

[92]Much of this chapter draws on Ervin Laszlo's two books on his Akashic field theory, the highly readable *Science and the Akashic Field: An Integral Theory of Everything*, and the more detailed (and more technical) presentation in *The Connectivity Hypothesis: Foundations of an Integral Science of Quantum, Cosmos, Life, and Consciousness*. I strongly recommend both of these books to the interested reader. Details of both books are in the suggested reading list.

First, you should understand that while physicists claim to be close to understanding everything, the reality is that cracks in both quantum physics and cosmology are appearing in the form of experimental results that don't quite fit in with any of the prevailing theories. Physics, more than any other science, rests totally on experimental results. In the late 1800s the prevailing theory of a universal ether and understanding of Newtonian mechanics (the classical comprehension of how objects move and interact) and Maxwellian electromagnetic theory famously caused scientists to claim that "all had been discovered" and that the rest of physics was merely a matter of "mopping up" by explaining the few remaining phenomena that hadn't yet drawn scientific attention.

Unfortunately, the famous Michelson-Morley experiments had already been performed.[93] Its anomalous results were the thin edge of a crack in the fundamentals of physics that resulted in Einstein replacing Newtonian mechanics with relativistic mechanics and the development of the weirdness of quantum physics.

Ervin Laszlo noticed that not only does today's physics have some difficult things to explain, there are more than a few similarly "anomalous" experimental results in biology and consciousness experiments too. Unlike many other scientists who prefer to ignore such results, or assume that they'll be explained later, or assume the experimenters are fraudulent or simply mistaken, Laszlo seeks to bring such experimental results into the realm of his theory. What are these cracks in current understanding? Let's review the basic problems in each of these areas.

Cosmological Conundrums

1. A Universe as Flat as a Pancake

Modern physics has united space and time in relativistic theory into a "space-time continuum" with a shape that reflects gravitational impact. But in physics, the continuum itself is assumed to have an underlying curvature. In other words, space is assumed to be curved even in the absence of matter. The presence of any mass of matter such as a sun is

---

[93]The Michelson-Morley experiments attempted to demonstrate the presence of the "ether" by trying to measure the difference in the speed of light based on whether light was moving with or against the flow of this substance. In complete contradiction to all predictions, they detected no differences in the speed of light no matter what direction they looked.

sufficient to deform space-time; the issue here is the curve of space-time in locations where there is no matter present to deform it.

Much research by astronomers and cosmologists has been directed to figuring out if space-time has the curve of a sphere (i.e., an enclosed, limited universe) or a saddle (i.e., an open, unbounded universe). The results have surprised everyone in that the continuum, over very large distances and to quite high precision, appears to be absolutely flat rather than measurably curved. Unfortunately, to explain such flatness requires that the Big Bang that initiated the universe some 14 billion or so years ago must have been, in Laszlo's words, "staggeringly fine tuned"—implying that the amount of matter in the universe had to be preset to a factor of 10^9 or one-billionth. A change in the total amount of matter by a factor of one-billionth either more or less would result in a space-time that was perceptibly curved. Having a universe so unremittingly flat is extremely difficult to explain away.

2. Where's the Mass?

A lot of the universe's mass appears to be missing. The mass in the universe does not account for the strength of gravity detected. Granted, not all cosmological matter is detectable with telescopes, if for no other reason that the only matter we can easily see is that which is hot enough to glow, or which is close enough to a glowing object, like a star, to reflect some of that object's glow—for example, planets. Still, even adding in a substantial allowance for such nondetectable matter, scientists still can't make the equations balance. There's way too much gravity and not nearly enough matter to explain it.

3. When Gravity Goes Bad

Gravity is a trusted force. We rely on it. Gravitation is an attractive force, the *pull* of two masses toward each other. The closer the two objects are, the harder the pull and the faster they tend to approach each other. Thus, an object falling toward the Earth picks up speed as it falls, moving faster and faster as it approaches. Similarly, an object thrown into the air moves slower and slower as it moves away from the Earth. Gravity doesn't *push* objects. It pulls—or does it? Unfortunately, a mounting body of evidence indicates that galaxies actually *accelerate* as they move farther apart. This is the exact opposite of what one would expect, and implies there's some type of negative gravity operating. Clearly, something is amiss with our understanding of this basic force.

4. Fine Tuning the Fine Tuning

One extremely difficult issue for physicists to explain is why various fundamental constants of the universe have exactly the values they do. In some cases the values are exquisitely finely tuned to make life as we know it possible. Such fundamental constants define the specific qualities of elementary particles, how many such particles there are, and how those particles interact. In addition, universal constants repeatedly define recurring harmonic ratios that are extremely hard to justify on the basis of random events. If those values varied by extremely tiny amounts, chemistry—and, as a result, life—would not be possible. The most common explanation for how the universe could be so highly tuned derives from membrane theory, discussed earlier, and presumes that there are many universes and that we happen to live in *this* universe simply because those constants are so finely tuned. But that explanation is weak, at best. It doesn't really explain anything.

5. A Horizon Too Far

No matter in what direction astronomers look, the universe seems more or less the same. That implies that the same forces act pretty much everywhere and in all directions—and that is a problem. It is as if all parts of the universe are responding to similar conditions, yet in one direction we see light from galaxies that took about 14 billion years to arrive here, while in the opposite direction we see light from other galaxies that also took 14 billion years to arrive. That implies that those two extreme parts of the universe are about 28 billion light-years apart. But if the universe is 14 billion years old, light traveling from one side of the universe to the other would need double the length of time the entire universe has existed to go from one side to the other. Yet we seem to detect strong correlations between events at either end of the universe. How can objects so dizzyingly far apart correlate their development to the degree they apparently do?

Quantum Quandaries

1. Entanglement Is Snarled Up

Quantum physics, in its study of the characteristics of the world of the very small, produced the concept of entanglement. Although glibly talked about and presented, it is extremely poorly understood. There appears to be no real reason why elementary particles become entangled, and only a limited understanding of how they do so. In fact, most of the problems within quantum physics are directly associated with the weirdness of entanglement.

2. The Unreality of Quantum Reality

A key characteristic of quantum physics is that nothing is really real until it is measured or observed. In a very real sense, elementary particles are nowhere and have no characteristics until they are observed. They are simultaneously both nowhere and everywhere. Quantum particles apparently do not really exist, but merely have a *potential* existence until they are measured or observed. Laszlo uses the brilliant metaphor that an observer literally fishes the quantum particle out of a sea of potential particles, at which point the quantum becomes "real." But the fisherman is blind to which potential quantum reality he is pulling on until it's out of that sea of potentiality. The particle itself appears to choose which possible state it will be in.

3. The Uncertainty of Knowledge

In the 1920s Heisenberg's uncertainty principle set the cat among the pigeons in physics. This principle states that it is impossible to simultaneously know all aspects of any quantum particle. If we know position to a high degree of accuracy, we cannot know the particle's precise speed of motion. If we know its speed of motion accurately, we cannot simultaneously know its exact position.[94] The act of observing one characteristic destroys all possibility of knowing the other. This is now so well known in physics that it's taken as a given, but why should this be so? What is it about the act of observing or measuring something that causes knowledge of a complementary quality to become unknowable? What impact does observation or measurement have on a particle—and why?

---

[94]If we give up perfect precision, we can know both position and speed of the particle. It's just that the combined uncertainty of both measurements has a minimum value—there's a minimum level of "fuzziness" in measurements that is mandated by the uncertainty principle. For example, as the precision of our measurement of a particle's position improves and the error in that position measurement decreases toward zero—i.e., we have more and more exact knowledge of that particle's location—the error in measuring its speed has to get larger. If we know the position of the particle exactly, with zero error, the error in any speed measurement has to approach infinity, which implies no knowledge at all of how fast it's going. But if we're willing to settle for less precision in location, we can know quite a bit about the particle's speed.

4. The Sociability of Quanta

If two quantum particles become entangled, they stay entangled, even if they later are separated by vast distances. Thus, when the fisherman (using Laszlo's earlier metaphor) fishes one of the two particles out of the sea of quantum potentials, that particle is free to choose its states. But once that happens and that particle is observed, its entangled twin particle can no longer choose its state freely. It must always choose a complementary state to that of the directly observed twin particle. More puzzling is the fact that this entanglement can be extended to all particles in a complete experimental setup, such that if one particle is measured—and thus moves from "potential" state to a "real" state—then *all* particles in the system similarly become real—even if the experiment to measure them is not carried out! Now, that's just weird.

Biological Bafflements

1. Coherent Organisms

To the astonishment of nearly everyone, biological systems are not exempt from the same unifying characteristics that seem to mark the worlds of the extremely small and extremely large. While much of an organism behaves with classical predictability, certain aspects of whole organisms exhibit behaviors that are strongly reminiscent of the same weirdness that entangled quantum particles display. This has become such a well-defined reality that a new field of "quantum biology" has appeared to try to understand how macro-scale organisms can exhibit quantum behaviors.

Complete organisms, ranging from cells to organs to animals to groups of animals, demonstrate that their behaviors and reactions are coherent to an inexplicable degree. This means that all parts of the organism—whether cell or complete animal—are correlated to every other part, virtually instantaneously and certainly much faster than electrochemical signals can travel from part to part.

Adaptability is an essential feature of a living system. It must stay in dynamic equilibrium with its environment, responding rapidly and precisely to changes in the outside world. This is accomplished by a constant symphony of chemical manufacture and destruction, with hormones, proteins, enzymes, RNA and DNA, among many other compounds, constantly created and destroyed in response to current needs of the organism. So being adaptable to sudden changes in the environment clearly has strong survival advantages—but how does it work when organisms respond faster than their parts can receive information about the necessary changes?

And consider this: Cells in an animal are constantly dying and regenerating. The rate of replacement of cells varies quite a bit, with skin cells lasting only a couple of weeks while bone cells might last two or three months. It's a truism, in fact, that virtually every cell in your body is replaced every seven years. But if this is so, how is that coherence maintained within the organism?

2. Genetic Enigmas

Another issue for modern biologists is the problem of understanding inheritance. Textbooks traditionally assure students that all is understood with the concept of inheritance. Genes, consisting of molecules of DNA, define the basic blueprints of the body, and those genes are what are passed from one generation to the next. The Human Genome Project already has succeeded in mapping all 25,000-odd genes within the human species (and we're busy mapping the genomes of other species too). With the assurance that they really do know what they're doing, molecular biologists thus feel free to tinker with the construction of DNA and have begun to change that genome in an attempt to remake it according to our image of what it should be.

The only problem is that this image of certainty doesn't match the biological reality. Darwinists claim that the only thing that affects the inheritance process from generation to generation is the correct transmission of genetic information; events that simply change the overall body of the organism do not, in this view, modify the inheritance of the following generation. Unfortunately, there is now firm biological proof that organisms can in fact change their DNA in response to environmental factors, and can, to at least some degree, control the genetic characteristics their offspring inherits. Lamarck, it seems, was more correct than previously believed—and Darwin not nearly as correct as is commonly preached.

Consciousness Conundrums

1. The Connected Consciousness

Traditionally, science views inputs to the conscious mind as limited to normal sensory channels—sight, sound, touch, taste, smell, and so on. Communications with consciousness beyond that have been treated as myth, delusion, or even hoax. Yet current consciousness researchers, including psychologists, biologists, and psychologists, have discovered a rich collection of connections that cannot be explained by standard five-sensory modalities. These are called "transpersonal" connections. The evidence for them is overwhelming. They have been demonstrated under laboratory conditions with odds ranging from millions to one, to billions to one, so only those with totally closed minds refuse to accept their reality.[95]

But because of this bias by traditional science, transpersonal effects are labeled paranormal rather than normal. In fact, the only thing paranormal about these connections is that we don't yet have scientific explanations for how they work. Just to cite a few of these demonstrable effects:

- The ability of native tribes to communicate well outside of sensory range, both within the tribe and across tribes and cultures.

- The ability of people to transfer images and impressions; this is particularly demonstrable when there is a close emotional tie between the people.

- The universality of certain images and archetypes across virtually all cultures and all civilizations in all eras.

- The ability of one person to affect the physical body and brain of another person, even when physically remote to them; this is nonlocal healing.

This collection of problems in quantum physics, cosmology, biology, and consciousness research inspired Ervin Laszlo to attempt to construct a theory that could explain *all* of these anomalies with a single theory. The result is his Akashic field theory—possibly the best potential explanation for all the cited enigmas. Laszlo's wonderful and highly readable book *Science and the Akashic Field* revisits each of the puzzles presented earlier in cosmology, quantum physics, biology, and consciousness to dis-

---

[95]See Dean Radin's wonderful book, *The Conscious Universe*, for in-depth, highly detailed documentation of the studies that demonstrate these effects.

cuss how his theory of an Akashic field can explain how and why each of these effects occurs.[96] But here, I'm concerned primarily about the puzzles of consciousness and other paranormal phenomena, so I will focus on them.

Akashic Field Theory

Laszlo hypothesizes that to explain all the previously described puzzles (and more), some mechanism in the universe must be able to link particles and organisms throughout space and time at speeds far beyond the speed of light. There must be some type of *information* field in the universe that contains information about all events and all particles in the universe at all times.

In other words, in a very real, scientific sense, the universe is truly One. We are not separate beings. Nor are we separate objects. Instead, we are all part of the same information field, just a localized cluster of data.

This field appears to act not only as a carrier of current information, but also as a *memory* for the overall universe. In other words, the ancient cultural tradition that there are records in which all details of our lives are stored—the legendary *Akashic Records*—would not only be true, Laszlo even knows where they are.[97]

The Akashic records, in fact, are contained in the underlying structure of the universe itself, in an ever-present *Akashic field* that permeates the entire universe and contains memories of everything that happens everywhere through all of time. Laszlo even named the field the Akashic

---

[96]If you want a somewhat more technical presentation of his theory, I strongly recommend Laszlo's book *The Connectivity Hypothesis*. Written at a higher technical and mathematical level, it nonetheless is also very readable.

[97]In the Hindu tradition, the Akashic records contain a memory of everything you've experienced throughout your life. At the end of life, you are given a chance to review those records. In traditions that include the concepts of karma and reincarnation, the Akashic records determine whether your overall karmic burden is of "good karma" or "bad karma." A preponderance of good karma would result in your next life being one of greater spiritual accomplishment and success. A preponderance of bad karma would result in a life that is at a lower spiritual level—perhaps even that of an animal. In TMI tradition, the Akashic records are generally found on F-27, which is the level at which you plan your following life based on the spiritual lessons you still need to master.

field in tribute to the similarity of characteristics between the field and the legendary Akashic records.

That's too much information to store, you might complain. But remember the earlier discussion of holographic memories and the huge quantity of information that can be stored in them? As you'll see below, the density of the Akashic field is such that we would not run out of "memory" space for the entire possible lifetime of the universe.

The Akashic field theory begins with a few premises based on current findings across all fields. Laszlo bases his theory on simple premises:

1. The universe is filled with energy even in a "vacuum."

2. This energy is the virtual energy of the cosmos.

3. Universal forces and constants arise from the interaction of these virtual energies and the "real" particles and systems of particles in space-time.

The first premise is well understood in contemporary physics. Einstein's theory of general relativity implies that space—even a physical vacuum—has certain physical qualities, one of which is that it is composed of energy. This energy, present everywhere all the time, is called the zero-point energy or ZPE, originally noted by Max Planck. The amount of ZPE is, in Laszlo's word, "staggering." Current best estimates are that the energy contained in each cubic meter is about 10^{93} kg/cubic meter![98] This is 10^{80} (or the number one followed by 80 zeros) times the energy density of an atomic nucleus!

The second premise refers to the continual creation and annihilation of virtual particles that goes on throughout the cosmos, everywhere, all the time. The particles are called "virtual" because they appear and

---

[98]If you're not comfortable with the metric system, don't worry. Since I'm only presenting general orders of magnitude, you can safely substitute "pounds/cubic yard" for "kilograms/cubic meter" without any real loss of accuracy. A cubic meter is larger than a cubic yard by about 30 percent and a kilogram is about two pounds (specifically, 2.2 pounds make 1 kilogram). Neither conversion factor makes much difference in such a general discussion, so feel free to use English units if you prefer.

disappear so quickly that they cannot be either observed or measured. Again, there appears to be strong theoretical support for this premise in current cosmological theories.

The third premise comes from some of the most advanced theories in physics today. It appears that interactions among particles within the physical universe are carried out or "mediated" by a combination of real particles and these virtual particles that cannot be seen or measured. For example, electrical interactions—the electrical field—appear to be implemented by way of virtual photons, which affect magnetic fields too. Gravitational interactions are apparently implemented by virtual "gravitons," and so on.

Remember that gravity, electrical fields, and magnetic fields are all *vector* fields. They all have not only a strength, but a direction. For example, the gravitational field of the Earth has a specific value, and points in the direction of the center of the Earth. A magnetic field has similar strength and direction, which is why the compass needle always points to the north magnetic pole, and so on. In fact, all known fundamental forces in physics take the form of vector fields.

Interestingly, several current contenders for a cosmological GUTs presume there must also be another type of field present, universal, but *not* having a direction. This field is a *scalar* field, scalars being simple numbers with no direction associated with them. Laszlo's Akashic field theory hypothesizes that universal scalar field to be an Akashic field of scalar—nondirectional—potentials that permeates everyplace in the universe.

So why is that important?

One major reason why is that waves that travel through scalar fields, unlike those traveling through vector fields (such as electromagnetic waves, or light) *are not subject to the limitation of the speed of light.* In other words, there is no theoretical limit to how quickly radiation in a scalar field can travel because the vibrations in a scalar field are not perpendicular (transverse) to the direction of motion. A scalar field wave doesn't look like a water wave, wiggling from side to side as it propagates lengthwise, the way light waves and all electromagnetic radiation do. Instead, propagation of waves in a scalar field is along the direction of motion (longitudinal).

The most familiar longitudinal wave is sound, which is created when a vibrating object alternately compresses and expands a pocket of air. Sound travels through the air by radiating that compression/expansion out along the direction the sound wave travels, finally reaching your eardrum. The variation in air pressure forces your eardrum to wiggle in and out in rhythm with the air's compression and expansion. Those physical wiggles are then detected and translated by your nervous system into the sound of a beautiful song—or the cacophony of traffic noise.[99]

In recent times scientists have realized that in very special circumstances it's quite possible for sound to travel through certain materials at speeds that are faster than the speed of light. In fact, the speed of longitudinal waves is actually proportional to the mass density of the medium through which they propagate. Thus, to make longitudinal waves (like sound) go very fast, all you need is an extremely dense medium for them to travel through.

Recall, however, that "mass" and "energy" are the same thing—Einstein demonstrated that a century ago with his famous $E=mc^2$ relation: energy equals mass times the square of the speed of light—a constant. Thus, the speed of a longitudinal wave in the cosmic energy field is proportional to the energy density of that field.

Now go back and look again at what that energy density is: 10^{93} kg/cubic meter. Or, in joules (and applying a factor of the square of the speed of light to convert kilograms, a mass measurement, into joules, an energy measurement) the energy density of open space in a vacuum is on the order of 10^{104} joules/cubic meter!

That number is a one followed by 104 zeros, or 100 million trillion trillion trillion trillion trillion trillion trillion trillion. It is so mind-bogglingly large it's literally inconceivable except in the abstract.

By hypothesizing an Akashic field that is both universal and scalar in nature, Laszlo offers a legitimate, scientific explanation for how apparently impossible things can happen—and can happen virtually instantaneously everywhere.

Consider, for example, the estimated size of the entire physical universe. If we assume the universe was created about 14 or 15 billion years ago, the largest size the universe could have expanded into since that time is 15 billion light-years—the distance light travels in 15 billion years—in

---

[99]Thus, it is legitimate to claim that if a tree falls in a forest and there's no one there to hear it, it makes no sound. The air will still be compressed and expanded as before, but until there's an observer to convert that variation in pressure into the perception of sound, the sound itself does not exist.

all directions.[100] Call it 30 billion light years across from one extreme to the other. Certainly that's a huge size, right? And, if you remember, it raises the question of how both ends of the universe can apparently correlate to each other, given that light cannot possibly transmit information from one side to the other in the 15 billion years the universe has existed.

But compare that total span of the universe to the energy density of the universe to get a perspective on how big the universe *really* is. A light year is approximately 10^{13} meters (a one followed by 13 zeros). So in 30 billion years, light could travel 30 billion times that distance. This total distance is approximately three followed by 23 zeros:

300,000,000,000,000,000,000,000 meters

But compare that admittedly huge number to the energy density of a *single cubic meter* of empty space:

100,000,000,000,000,000,000,000,000,000,000,000,000,000,000,00
0,000,000,000,000,000,000,000,000,000,000,000,000,000,000,000,
000 joules/cubic meter

You think the "vacuum" of space is dense with energy? It seems that way, doesn't it? In fact, it makes the universe itself seem kind of small. More importantly, however, with that type of energy density—and thus mass density, it seems clear that a universal scalar field would have no trouble traveling at virtually instantaneous speeds. It also should be obvious that the phenomenon of entanglement, at least of quantum particles, can be understood—at least conceptually—in the presence of a scalar field with the potential to transmit information virtually instantly anywhere in the universe.

Furthermore, if information is stored in the Akashic field holographically, it means that all parts of the scalar field could contain the entire set of Akashic records for the entire universe. Thus, it isn't even really a matter of how fast information can be transmitted in this field. *The information is already there!*

---

[100]One way to envision the Big Bang's inflation is to imagine the inflation of a balloon. If the universe is on the surface of the balloon, there is no location in the universe that is the "center" of the explosion, yet all parts of the universe are expanding away from all other parts. While this makes a convenient way to envision the apparently contradictory features of an explosion with no center that expands in all directions, it also violates the experimental results that the universe has no curvature and is perfectly flat to the greatest precision we can measure—which implies that we're most likely *not* on the surface of a sphere. Cosmologists don't have *all* the answers, you know.

If Laszlo's Akashic field theory is correct, paranormal abilities, remote viewing, telepathy, and accessing information outside of local space and local time merely becomes a process of "reading" or "interpreting" the holographic Akashic information field in our local corner of the universe. This also implies that *anyone* has the potential to "be psychic" because that same information is local to all of us. It's a matter of learning how to do it and practicing it until you get it right. And visiting the far reaches of the focus levels may indeed be the best—perhaps the *only*—way to directly perceive the unity that an Akashic information field implies.

There are a lot of interesting aspects to my visit to the far reaches of F-253, not least of which is the permanent change it has generated in me. Describing that change is difficult to put into words, but I can offer one specific, apparently permanent result that directly impacts my C-1 life: I am apparently unable to watch the movie *What the Bleep Do We Know!?* Let me explain.

That movie was a surprise hit independent film that hung around in movie theaters for months and months before it finally came out on DVD. If you haven't seen it, I do recommend it; I've heard it's very good. I say that in spite of the fact that I've at least nominally seen it three times. Or rather, I've sat in front of screens where it was playing three times.

The first occasion in which I supposedly saw the film was the morning after my visit to the Golden Wall on F-253. I didn't really know what the movie was supposed to be about, but I'd heard it was good, and someone who knew I was a physics major in college had told me I definitely needed to go see it. The morning after the Golden Wall session, I noticed in the paper that there was a super-cheap showing at 10 A.M. only. So, on an impulse, I decided that was the showing I had to go to.

I knew I wasn't totally grounded at the time; more than 12 hours after that particular session I felt like I was floating around somewhere around F-27 rather than being firmly planted in C-1.[101]

---

[101]I'm not all that good at grounding myself sometimes, especially when I've gone to very high focus levels or had extreme experiences while in focus. If anything, my ability to ground myself is getting worse, not better. In fact, I often spend much of my so-called "waking conscious" life in focus levels other than C-1. I've had enough practice at it that I'm pretty functional in the C-1 world as long as I'm in F-27 or lower—with the exception that my sense of direction dissolves. Given my normal excellent sense of where I am, if I start making wrong turns or getting lost when I'm driving, it's a sure sign that I'm not exactly in

I paid my money, found a good seat, and pretty soon the lights dimmed. And within moments, the opening animation sequence started. That animation sequence, with the swooshy blue tubes and dips and swirls, is virtually identical to the imagery I get when in a BWIC transitioning to levels well beyond F-49. Within seconds, I was off in the realms of the upper focus regions.

Every so often I would drift down to a level within arm's reach of C-1 and would become aware of what was on the screen . . . and within moments there would be another swooshy blue animation sequence or swooshy camera work—and I'd be catapulted back up to the upper focus levels again.

So of the entire movie, I think I actually *saw* a total of perhaps ten to 15 minutes of what was on the screen.

Hmmm. I chalked that up to a new "lesson learned": don't go to the movies when you're not well grounded.

Several months later, I'd just completed my move to North Carolina, and a friend from San Diego came to visit me and see my new home. She had never seen *What the Bleep Do We Know!?* and wanted to do so, and it was still playing in the local theaters. I hesitated, remembering my previous experience, then relaxed. After all, I was deeply mired in the process of unpacking and settling into my new house. I hadn't had the chance to do any serious meditation for weeks, and all that physical unpacking and moving and such certainly had me firmly grounded in C-1. I was sure it wouldn't be a problem this time.

So we went to see *What the Bleep Do We Know!?* Within moments, that same swooshy blue animation sequence had pushed me out into the upper focus realms just as before. If anything, I saw even less of the movie this second time than I had the first time. Hours after we'd arrived home, I was still *way* out there. Well after midnight I had to call my friend Deb in Toronto to ask her to talk me down.

I didn't try to see the movie again until it came out on DVD. I bought a copy, determined this time to actually watch it all the way through. I

C-1. And if I'm floating on any level above F-27, people around me definitely notice that I'm more than a bit "spacey." If I'm with any of my North Carolina friends when I'm "out there," they simply explain away any of my weirdities by pointing out, "She's from California." Confused and wary waiters or sales clerks immediately relax and nod knowingly. In the South, I've found that explanation is a universally accepted excuse for virtually any strange behavior.

had a couple of friends over, we all parked in my den, and I put on the DVD.

Sure enough, within moments I was not only "out there," but *way* out there. Again, I actually perceived only moments out of the entire film. I haven't bothered to try to watch it since then.

I did, however, talk to Dr. Darlene Miller, Director of Programs at TMI, to see if anyone else had the same reaction to the animation sequences, and she told me that no one else had reported anything like that. Apparently I accidentally, but deeply, encoded the animation as a cue to go into upper focus levels, so every time I view the movie, that conditioned response is activated.

So what's the point of all this? I think there are a couple of key issues. First, the sense of what it feels like to be in these extremely high focus levels is one of universal connection. At levels above F-27, and even more so at levels above F-49, you have no doubt that everything in the universe is connected to everything else. There is no such thing as "us" and "them" or even "me" and "other." Everything is truly One.

And while my experience may seem to be unique to me, if you talk to almost anyone who has done some serious exploring of upper focus levels, they all say the same thing. There is a sense of love. Of acceptance. Of peace. And, most of all, a sense of Oneness with everything else. Not just oneness with other people or other countries or even other animals. But oneness with *everything*—the rocks; the stars; the hydrogen atoms floating between galaxies. It's not just the entire world that is included in a grain of sand—it's the entire universe. This sense of universal connection is entirely consistent with the oneness implicit in Laszlo's Akashic field theory.

Actually, my sense is that our universe is encoded in that "Mind of God" sense I got in F-49. When beyond that state, it feels more like our universe is only a tiny mote and you have access to the oneness of *all* universes. Accessing these extreme focus levels takes me back to my days of wanting to be an astronaut. Except now, I don't need a billion-dollar rocket ship to go exploring. I can do it right here, any time I want. I can visit worlds I never knew existed.

Are these perceptions real? I honestly don't know. Nor do I see any way to validate them for centuries if not millennia. Until we have the technology to literally take our physical bodies out among the stars, there's no way to tell if I'm hallucinating or perceiving reality. All I can do is point out that my perceptions of things much closer in time and space *can* be validated, and have been. And these distant wanderings feel exactly the same to me in terms of how I get the information and what receiving it feels like.

But if I accept that in F-12 I have access to physical places beyond the reach of my five physical senses, and that in F-15 I have access to times beyond the here-and-now, is it so impossible to consider that perhaps there are ways to be one with literally everything else in the universe? Isn't that the definition of having God inside you? Or of being One with All? Every major religious tradition has that sense of oneness and con-nectedness as the ultimate truth. And while I would have scoffed at such a sense several years ago, now I can no longer doubt its reality because experiencing such connection, such universal love, completely changes your life. It's impossible to fully describe it or explain it to someone else. It's simply something you have to experience for yourself.

Laszlo's Akashic field theory provides the most credible and com-plete scientific explanation I've been able to find for my travels through altered states of consciousness. My experiences in remote viewing, heal-ing, perceiving energy and spirit beings, accessing information outside our normal time, using my intentionality to change aspects of the physi-cal world, and so on—all those become believable and perhaps even rea-sonable if Laszlo is correct. If—somehow—the mind can connect with and even manipulate the Akashic information field, if the information in that field is stored holographically (i.e., all information stored in all parts of the field), then the mysterious, amazing, *impossible* events I've experienced don't seem quite so impossible after all.

But even if Laszlo is wrong, I have to admit I'm glad I started off on this journey. It hasn't always been comfortable or easy; changing your life and your fundamental belief system to the extent that I've changed mine is never easy. Sometimes it's been harder than I could ever have imagined, and sometimes it's been more than a little scary. I've grown accustomed to overt violations of my deepest beliefs about how the world works. I'm sure even more difficult challenges lie ahead. It's been a wild, crazy, and often downright weird journey of the mind, of the spirit, of the heart—but I wouldn't have missed it for the world.

15

I Knew What I Had to Do and Began

One day you finally knew what you had to do, and began . . .
— from "The Journey" by Mary Oliver

My journey of the spirit continues. I'm still seeking to understand how such strange things can happen to a person who began this trip as a staunch materialist. I'm still struggling to overcome both disbelief and the desire to believe too easily, as I try to come to some type of equilibrium between what I know from direct personal experience and what I thought I knew from schoolbooks and the opinions of others.

It's not an easy path. But while investigating and researching this book, I realized that science and mysticism may at last be on a converging set of tracks, rather than the diverging ones they've been following for centuries. It isn't that the mystics have changed their views of the world. Instead, science is at last beginning to lose just a tiny bit of the arrogance that insisted that cold materialism was the *only* way to understand the universe.

But as I was finishing this book, I realized I have one more story I need to tell, one more experience to share with you. My wonderful friend Charles died about a month ago as I write this. He'd had ALS, Lou Gehrig's disease, for three years, and had been formally diagnosed more than two and a half years. ALS is a killer. In some senses it's the exact opposite of Alzheimer's.

In Alzheimer's, the cognitive neurons in the brain are killed (for reasons not yet understood). The result is that over the course of months and years, victims of Alzheimer's gradually lose more and more of their abilities to remember, to reason, and to understand their world. Their bodies are still comparatively hale and hearty—they can live in this state for many years. My own grandmother suffered from Alzheimer's (long before it was called that) from the time I was in elementary school. She finally died during my senior year in college, but her mind had completely gone many years before. The horrifying thing about Alzheimer's is that while the cognitive functions are deteriorating, the victims can literally *feel* themselves losing their minds. In my grandmother's case, this was especially heartbreaking because she always prided herself on her intellect, and with good reason. It's a truly horrible way to die, horrible for the victim, and horrible for all the family and friends.

ALS is equally horrible but in the opposite way. ALS destroys not the cognitive neurons, but the motor neurons—the nerves that control the muscles in the body. The ALS victim generally shows little or no cognitive impairment.[102] They're as smart and rational and logical as they ever were. They still have full sensations in their bodies. But as their bodies slowly lose the ability to move, they become cognitively aware people trapped inside immobile, nonfunctional bodies.

In Charles's case, it started with his hands, then moved to his arms and legs. After about a year, having broken several bones and suffered numerous nasty falls as his legs started to betray him, he was in a wheelchair full time. From there he progressed to a motorized wheelchair, voice-activated computer and mouse systems, and breathing assistance because his diaphragm and chest muscles could no longer adequately pump air in and out of his lungs.

---

[102]Stephen Hawking, the brilliant British physicist, is a classic example of someone whose ALS disease has almost totally paralyzed his body but who remains brilliant and aware intellectually. He's also an exceptional case. Diagnosed with ALS in his 20s, he has lived with the disease for many decades. The average time from diagnosis to death here in the U.S., I'm told, is about 18 to 24 months.

Through all this, Charles was intelligent, rational, and fully aware of what he was losing. He and his incredibly brave wife, Mary, faced trauma after trauma as each loss of function meant another little piece of him had died.

In spite of his Ph.D. in physics, Charles was incredibly psychic and, unlike me, had been his entire life. He was one of the very few people I could discuss my bizarre experiences with openly and honestly. It is unfortunate that by the time I was deeply into this new journey, he was unable for reasons of schedule and, later, health, to do the types of programs I was doing at TMI. But I shared my experiences with him and Mary as much as I could, bringing them CDs and tapes so they could experience these altered states of consciousness too. Charles even joined TMI's Dolphin Energy Club as a healer, and continued his efforts to help other people almost until the very end. He got good at going into various altered states on his own—an essential skill once he lost the use of his hands to manipulate tape and CD players.

He asked me to check in on him on the focus levels on occasion, and each time he did so, I was able to find him and let him know where he was, and how his spirit was progressing. He'd also specifically asked me if I would monitor his death process, and once he was gone, report back to Mary how he was and how he was faring. I agreed to do so, of course.

As the end neared in early December 2005, Mary called me to come back and visit quickly because time was clearly very short. I drove up to the D.C. area to say my final goodbye. By this time, Charles was under hospice care, though the medical prognosis, barring any particular infection or accident, was that he might live as long as another four to six months. In fact, on my previous visit not long before Thanksgiving, he and Mary and I had talked about that. He had expressed then the hope that he would hang on until February, and Mary and I both saw no immediate reason why he shouldn't be able to do so, barring infection or accident.

But he had gotten an infection which would have been minor in anyone who had chest muscles strong enough to enable him to cough, and that illness had been exacerbated by other events that also wouldn't have affected anyone healthier. And now it seemed he'd decided he no longer needed to hang on until February. He was ready to go now.

As I reported to Mary when I first arrived at his house, I did a meditative session just before I left home and found that at least 95 percent of

Charles had already crossed over, with only a tiny piece of him hanging onto life with great tenacity. When I went into the bedroom to say my farewell to him, I could see that was true. He was barely clinging to life. When he was able to speak, he was openly and clearly asking for assistance in moving from the land of the living to a spiritual plane. Despite these clear requests, everything he said was rational, lucid, and cogent. He wasn't delusional. He wasn't drugged out. He understood everything said to him. He obviously was perfectly rational, though he had difficulty forcing enough air through his vocal cords to enable him to speak understandably.

He and I said our farewells. He was hardly able to talk, but I played a couple of Hemi-Sync meditations for him at his request.[103] I sat next to him and meditated with him as they played.[104]

In my meditation, I had an image of the piece of him still clinging desperately to life, as a boy, perhaps nine or ten years old. If you remember the folk tale about the little Dutch boy with his finger in the dyke, you'll have a pretty good approximation of the impression I got. This stout little boy was absolutely convinced that if he ever took his finger out of the dyke, something disastrous would happen. He was stubborn, very strong-willed, and totally determined that he had to save the day and keep his grip on life by keeping his finger firmly plugging that hole. Disaster simply wasn't going to be allowed, not on *his* watch!

When I relayed that description to Mary, she immediately recognized that as one piece of Charles's persona—a part of him she was quite

---

[103]TMI has an extraordinary series of tapes called the "Going Home" series designed with the help of Dr. Elizabeth Kübler-Ross. I had given these tapes to him about three weeks before because it was clear even then that he was beginning the final stages of preparing for death. These tapes are designed for those who are mortally ill to assist them in experiencing a peaceful and serene death process. There are two albums, one for the person dying to help them come to terms with their death, and one for the family, friends, and caregivers to help them accept and support the person dying, with love and understanding. I cannot speak highly enough about these tapes. They're simply superb.

[104]I did have to warn him that the tapes from Going Home had verbal guidance spoken by Bob Monroe on them. Charles didn't particularly like the sound of Bob Monroe's voice, and he made a face that clearly expressed an irritated, "Well, if that's what I have to put up with, I suppose I'll have to suffer through it." He might have been knocking at death's door, but he still had his own opinions about things.

familiar with but that I had never before encountered. I told her that I was trying to get the little boy to trust me, but he was very suspicious and very worried that bad things would happen if he let go. Meanwhile, however, I described to Mary that I'd found the rest of Charles's spirit on a much higher focus level, and it brought immediate tears in her eyes. Though these details had surprised me, in her eyes, they were what she would have expected him to want to do.

I stayed in the D.C. area for a couple of days, but the house was growing very crowded as more and more family arrived from all over the country to say their final farewells. On Saturday, after one last farewell to Charles and Mary, I drove home, promising to keep working with him on the spiritual plane.

I continued to do long meditation sessions with Charles all Saturday afternoon and evening, and all day Sunday. In each case, I felt the little boy was beginning to trust me more and more, but not nearly enough to let go of that dyke.

Early Monday morning, I made another attempt. I went into a meditative state and connected with the little boy again.[105] This time, I had a brilliant idea. I asked him if he wanted to see where the rest of Charles's spirit was. He said he did, but that he couldn't take his finger out of the dyke. I then suggested that I help him build a temporary patch over the dyke hole, something that would allow him to leave just long enough to check out where Charles was hanging out, but that he could take off when he wanted to come back. He agreed, and I manifested some hammers and nails along with some big boards, which we used to cover that tiny finger hole. The patch was impressive in size, but it still worried the little boy. What if it started leaking, he asked. Maybe he shouldn't go with me after all . . .

But I had an answer to that too. I held out my hand and manifested a device that looked like a large remote control with a big red button and a light on it. This was a "leak detector," I told him. If the patch started leaking, the red light would start blinking and he could push the red button and he'd immediately return right here to take care of it.

With that reassuring him, he clutched the remote control in one hand, and took my hand in his other, and I gently guided him up to F-25 where the rest of Charles's spirit waited. As soon as he got there, the other

---

[105]I was using one of the Going Home tapes for all these meditation sessions to help keep me on track. These tapes have Hemi-Sync tones that support you visiting focus levels F22 through F27.

aspects of Charles's personality greeted him with joy, love, and thanksgiving. The little boy was embraced and welcomed with great love and celebration.

I didn't feel the need to stay with him for long but just before I left, I told the little boy that he now had a choice to make. If he decided he needed to go back and put his finger in the dyke again—in other words, if he wanted to cling to life just a little longer—all he had to do was push that red button on his leak detector and he'd immediately return there. If, on the other hand, he decided he wanted to stay here permanently with the rest of Charles's spirit, all he had to do was to drop the device and it would disappear and he could stay right there, surrounded by love and welcome.

With that, I left that focus level, not sure what decision the little boy would make. It took perhaps another ten minutes or so for me to come out of the meditative session and back to C-1 consciousness, and as usual, I noted the time I opened my eyes and ended the session. It was 9:04 A.M. according to the digital clock on my cable TV box. I felt that for the first time, I'd made real progress in soothing the fears of that little-boy piece of Charles's spirit. And, unlike the previous couple of days, I didn't feel a need to do another session on him for a while.

About noon, I got a call from Mary. Charles had passed away. Specifically, he took his last breath at 8:55 A.M., approximately one or two minutes after I'd left that little boy on F-25. Apparently, the little boy had dropped the device almost as soon as I left.

I told Mary about my morning meditation, and she and I shared a few tears over the phone. I told her I'd do a session with Charles later that day to make sure he was well and happy on the other side. We hung up, both a little numb, but both relieved that Charles's last ordeal with ALS, a disease that robbed him of many things, was finally over.

As the numbness wore off that afternoon, I was absolutely thunderstruck at what I'd apparently done. Yes, I'd done soul retrievals before. Yes, I'd become very comfortable talking about death, understanding spiritual existence, and yes, I'd become completely convinced that our existence does *not* stop merely because our physical bodies do. But I'd never before actually assisted someone to cross over spiritually. I'd never taken their hand and guided them into the afterlife and helped them achieve the perspective they needed to choose for themselves whether to cling to physical reality or let it go.

I'd never helped anyone die.

Late that evening, when I had a chance to regain a little calmness, I fulfilled the final promise I'd made Charles. Several months before he'd asked me if, once he died, I would find him on the spiritual plane and reassure Mary that he was all right. I went into a meditative session and went back to visit the whole Charles, still happily puttering away on F-25. And there he gave me two messages, one for one of his daughters, and one for Mary. I passed those along to them as my final gift to them from their beloved Charles.

And then I realized the date. The previous summer, in July, a friend and I had attended a seminar given by Robert Bruce in Charlottesville. I found Robert Bruce's energy techniques very powerful, to the point that, despite sitting upright in a straight chair in a classroom setting, I was able to easily access focus levels of F-35 and above, and a number of times during that week was way out in the F-100s. And this was without any Hemi-Sync support, nor the support of friends pushing me upward with energy surges.

I came out of one of those classroom sessions, however, with a specific date highlighted as a "death day"—and that date was the exact day Charles died, five months later. Though I never told Mary about that prediction for obvious reasons—for one thing, I wasn't totally sure to whom the date applied—I did tell the friend who was at the seminar with me and one other person, neither of whom knew Charles or Mary. And I documented it in my notes for the seminar.

I suppose I should view this story as just one more step down this path I'm taking. Several times I've discussed it with my guides to understand why I was given this role to play in Charles's death. Dying was something Charles apparently needed help with. Dying, transitioning from a physical existence to a spiritual one, can be very scary, even when you fully understand that things are better on the other side.

But I too gained from that experience. It's taught me that I need to work on my own tendency to cling to life beyond all rationality. I need to be willing to give up the things that I have now—the "trinkets" that include physical life itself—in order to gain the greater spiritual existence that waits. Life here in the physical isn't the be-all and end-all of anything. At best, it's a single classroom in a lifetime of coursework. But to graduate and go on to the really fun courses, you have to be willing to let go of your seat in this classroom in order to progress to the next one.

There is a teaching I ran across several years ago that has always stayed with me:

> Since only Death is certain
> And the Time of Death is totally unknown,
> How should I live my life today?

The essence of this teaching is to bring to light the reality that death is truly the only certainty in life—even above taxes. And since none of us know exactly when we are to die, it's important to both be prepared to die at any time and also to live our lives to the utmost now. Which raises the final question of the teaching, what specifically should you do *today*, knowing that death may arrive at any moment?

It's a fascinating and challenging way to live your life because it forces you to prioritize your actions, to do those things that bring you both great satisfaction and joy and also to accomplish those things that you want to complete before you transition to a spiritual existence.

But . . . what if the time of death is not "totally unknown"? What if you know, more or less, when you are to die? And possibly how you will die? How does that change what you do today? Or does it?

I have learned much from two friends in this regard. One is a man whose answer to such a question is two-fold: You must live as if you are going to die tomorrow, and you must plan your life as if you are going to live forever. (I should note here that he's highly analytical, and spent his career as a hugely successful stock analyst.) So his response to this question is to live fully in each and every day, wringing every drop of sweetness and joy out of it you can, but also to assume that you'll live forever more, and make sure all your i's are dotted and your t's are crossed, particularly financially (given his particular forte).

I find that advice excellent in some respects, and perhaps a little less excellent in others.

My other friend was Charles. At the end of his life he was a quadriplegic, his breathing was severely affected by the disease, and his life had narrowed to a very tight focus. There was little he could actually *do* in his final days; he merely was waiting—and often praying—for death to take him.

In the two and a half years from the time Charles was diagnosed until his death, he spent much of his time preparing himself for his departure. ALS is always fatal, so for all those months he knew he would die very soon, though he did not, of course, know exactly when "very soon" would be. In some ways, rather than preparing himself to live forever, as my first friend proposes, he prepared himself to die now. All his plans—will, health directives, etc.—were in place to ensure that his wife and children were protected as best he could manage. But his concentration and focus was on preparing himself spiritually for death rather than on preparing himself to live fully now.

This also seems an excellent model to me. He always was highly aware of the spiritual realms, and had no problem with death itself, but only with dying.

Death isn't hard. But sometimes *dying* is hard indeed. It broke my heart to see Charles struggle so with his dying process, and I deeply admire the courage with which he faced it every moment, not to mention the courage with which his wife and family faced it as they watched him die over and over again in tiny steps.

But neither of these answers, as admirable as they are, really addresses my particular question: *What if you know exactly when—and how—you are to die? What do you do? How do you live* now *if that time and date of death is near?*

Some time ago I attended a Guidelines program at TMI. As I've mentioned before, Guidelines is my favorite TMI program because of the depth of insight I get about my life. I go to it expecting to come home with yet another list of "honey-do" tasks for me to accomplish over the next months. On the Monday of this particular program[106] my journal notes that I experienced an increasing sense of grief. I found myself—for absolutely no reason at all—growing sadder and sadder. I knew I was deeply grieving for something; I simply had no idea what it was I was mourning. In fact, I was convinced that someone close to me had experienced a death. Since I knew a good friend had a very ill and very dear dog, I wondered if the dog might have died. But the level of grief I felt seemed excessive for the death of a dog that all of us knew would die soon.

I understood that grief on Tuesday.

Over the course of several meditations on Tuesday, I realized I was seeing an image of my own death. By mid-afternoon Tuesday, I had the complete information on how—and approximately when—I would die. And, as ever at Guidelines, I also received instructions as to how I should respond to this particular death scenario.

---

[106] All the week-long TMI programs begin Saturday evening and end Thursday evening, with only breakfast, goodbyes, and departures scheduled for Friday morning.

Clearly, this gave rise to a number of questions. First, was this vision real, or was it my imagination gone wild? Second, if it was a real look at my future, *why* was I being shown it? What purpose did that serve? Third, was there any way I could validate this image?

Over the next days I completely abandoned the exercises in the program. When we were sent to our CHEC units to do an exercise, I simply laid the headphones to one side and spent the time doing my own meditations and prayers as I tried to determine whether the vision was real, and if so, when it would happen, and why I was shown my death.

I got answers to "when" and "why" at the program. I was being shown this, my guides told me, for several reasons. One was that I had to become accustomed to the specific manner in which I would die so that when the time came I could respond appropriately. Thus, I should expect to experience this vision over and over again until I became used to it and could get past it to understand the death experience I would have. Indeed, for months after that program, I fairly regularly got this or a very similar vision of my death. Occasional details varied, but not by much.

As for when I would experience that death, I got a general time frame at the program. I also now more fully understood exactly why I had been guided to leave Southern California and move to North Carolina and saw how that direction had brought me to the point where my destiny could be accomplished.

All of which led to the question, what exactly was it I was supposed to learn from this information? What was it I was supposed to do between now and then to get ready for my death? That answer too came at Guidelines: I was to learn how to forgive anyone and anything involved in my death—especially myself.

Dying sometimes isn't only hard, it's incredibly challenging. Could I do this? Could I offer heart-felt forgiveness? It seemed an impossible task even as I understood it was what I had to do.

I left Guidelines at the end of that week literally in a state of psychic shock. It took days and days for me to drop back to anything like normal C-1 waking reality. It wasn't something I felt I could talk about with anyone at first, but I had a friend who was waiting for me to tell him all about my Guidelines experience as I generally did after my programs there. What on earth could I say about the week when virtually my entire program had been overwhelmed by this one single vision?

Mostly I talked around the issue. I had a key question that I did not get an answer to at the program. *How could I validate this information as real and not merely imagination gone wild? How could I confirm it, short of waiting to see if it happened?* Over the course of an afternoon's conversation, I tried to figure out a way to ask those questions without revealing what kind of guidance I'd gotten that required me to have those answers. I simply wasn't ready to talk about that—wasn't sure I *could* talk about it without dissolving into mush.

My friend has been on a deep spiritual path for many more years than I and is very wise. I'm sure it was clear to him that I was very troubled over *something* from the program, though he didn't know exactly what. So when I asked him if it was his experience that spirit guides ever lied, he answered very carefully. Watching his face, it was obvious he knew he was walking on very delicate ground. No, he answered, in his experience they never lied, but they did sometimes withhold information if it would not be to your benefit to know it at that moment in time.

Well, withholding information wasn't what my guides had done in this particular case, so that didn't enlighten me much.

After a few more minutes, I asked another question: How can you tell if what you experience as "guidance" is truly coming from your guides rather than your own imagination? Is there a way to determine that?

Again, he answered very carefully. He referred me to a wonderful book, *Inner Work*, by Robert A. Johnson, which included a set of four principles for validating inner guidance.

On the way home that day I swung by a bookstore and bought a copy of that book. I read through it very quickly, but focused on pages 94 through 96, which described how to determine a valid interpretation of an experience by questioning your interpretation of it in the following manner:

1. Does this simply repeat knowledge you already have?

2. Does this inflate your ego or seem self-congratulatory?

3. Does this shift any responsibility away from yourself?

4. Does this in any way contradict the long-term flow of your life?

A "yes" answer to any of those questions would be sufficient to question whether the experience was true spiritual guidance or ego-based imagination. Unfortunately, my answers to each of those questions was a vehement "no."

Did I know before this that I would die relatively young? Certainly not! Was this information that inflated my ego or in any way built me up? Not hardly. Would this shift any responsibility away from me? Far from it; I now bore the full responsibility to prepare myself for death *and* to be ready, willing, and able to offer heartfelt forgiveness in the process. And did this contradict the long-term flow of my life? Unfortunately, that also was a no. At the program, my guides clearly showed me visions of exactly how my life had been building to this specific death virtually since birth. Not only did it fit into the long-term flow of my life, it was its natural culmination.

In other words, by every measure I could discover, this was a real, prophetic vision of my personal future.

I had much to deal with over the next weeks. It was hard for me to come to terms with such information. I had to "sit with it" a while to see if I could cope with the prospects now laid out in front of me.

But the most important and challenging task was to come to terms with death itself. To understand that no matter what my dying process might be, I still had to be conscious and aware of my own heart. I had to keep my wits about me, even at that most extreme moment, and be prepared to offer complete forgiveness.

If moving from California had been a daunting task, this prospect seemed far worse. In the months after reluctantly concluding that my vision was correct, I spent a lot of time researching forgiveness and practicing it on a daily basis. What did it mean to "forgive" someone? What did I really have to do? The vision of my death recurred nearly daily, along with gentle encouragement to continue walking this path and a sense of deep sorrow from my guides at having to put me through this challenge.

I was introduced to a new guide around this time, one who, I was assured, would be with me almost constantly until the very end. BT looks funny, almost like a cartoon blob, he has a pun-awful sense of humor that can make me laugh out loud in the middle of a meditative session, and he has less fashion sense than a color-blind six-year-old. Still, his constant presence with me has served as an always available warm hug and a reassuring shoulder to lean on. In my life, I've very rarely had anyone I could lean on in times of trouble, generally being the one others lean on instead. Having BT around has helped reassure me that I don't have to do things completely alone.

Within a few months of that Guidelines program, I had done enough spiritual work on myself that I felt I could honestly say that I was willing to embrace the death laid out for me. I did a series of deep, wrenching meditations in which I offered up forgiveness in advance to virtually everyone who I might possibly need to forgive, and eventually I found I could do so easily and comfortably.

Interestingly, the specific manner of my death is now an issue of total unimportance to me. I've internalized the truth that damage to the physical body does not in any way damage who I am, or change my real existence at all. I'm still me spiritually, psychically, and in all the ways that matter.

But in the process of accepting and even embracing the end of my physical life, I've developed my own philosophy of how I want to live my life *today*, knowing that death will come sooner than I may like. Many years ago Neil Diamond recorded a simple song that says, in effect, no matter who you are, life *always* is "done too soon." Whether you're Jesus Christ, Gandhi, Dr. Martin Luther King, Jr., Mother Teresa—or Hitler. We all want to live longer than we can.

So what do we do? What really matters in this life?

Here, then, is my advice to you, based on my journey that has no end and that leads someplace, though I don't know where. This is my answer to the question of *"How should I live my life today?"*

Love joyously each day.

Love generously, with your heart and mind and soul and body.

Love courageously, not counting the cost. Embrace love wherever you find it and however it manifests itself for you, whether it's returned or not, whether it's received graciously or rejected or even ignored. Loving is the important part, not being loved in return.

Love fully and with your whole heart, forgiving everyone you possibly can, even when you think they don't deserve to be forgiven. Most of all, forgive yourself, for most of the things you really need to forgive derive directly from your own thoughts, beliefs, and actions.

Live in love.

Namaste,[107]
Maureen Caudill
North Carolina

---

[107]Namaste is a Hindu word that translates roughly as, "the Spirit in me recognizes and honors the Spirit in you; we are One in that Spirit."

Afterword

So You Want to Be a Psychic

Guess what? You undoubtedly already *are* psychic. The trick is to learn how to access and use those psychic skills. Humans appear to be naturally psychic; it's part of our normal human inheritance. So how do you go about "discovering" what you really already know how to do?

As you know, my journey from skeptic to psychic began with my attendance at a program at The Monroe Institute in Faber, Virginia.[108] A number of similar paths might have been equally effective. But this one I know from personal experience, and this is the technology I've seen perform miracles for friends and clients, so this is what I recommend.

You can get started with TMI's Hemi-Sync technology in several ways. You can purchase a set of CDs from either a local dealer in Monroe Products or directly from their website. I recommend the "Gateway Experience" CDs, which come in six "Waves." Each Wave consists of three CDs, each with two separate exercises, for more than six hours

---

[108]The Monroe Institute, 365 Roberts Mountain Road, Faber, VA, 22938; 1-866-881-3440 or 434-361-1252; website: www.monroeinstitute.org. TMI products are available at the separate catalogue website: www.hemi-sync.com.

of individual exercises. The Waves build on each other, so initially you must use them in sequential order, starting with Wave I and working your way up to Wave VI.

Other taped meditations can also be helpful, though they vary quite a bit in efficacy. I found John Edward's series of tapes "Developing Your Own Psychic Powers" particularly useful. And Robert Bruce's book, *Astral Dynamics*, is a true gem for understanding life energy and learning how to manipulate it. His website, www.astraldynamics.com, is another excellent source of information on working with subtle energies and out-of-body experiences. If you can find a seminar he's giving on his New Energy Ways system, I highly recommend taking it.

For a quick, guided introduction to Hemi-Sync meditation with an experienced and TMI-accredited facilitator to help you, consider attending a weekend Gateway Outreach Excursion workshop. I'm located in North Carolina and mostly do workshops in that region of the country, but there are accredited Gateway Outreach Excursion trainers all over the world. The TMI website—www.monroeinstitute.org—lists the currently accredited trainers under Non-Residential Programs. Accredited trainers are also almost always dealers for Monroe Products, so you can ask your local trainer for guidance in choosing appropriate Hemi-Sync titles (there are more than a hundred different choices) to meet your specific needs or situation.

In addition to the Gateway Outreach workshops, I also offer other Hemi-Sync based programs and workshops. My website is www.MaureenCaudill.net. You'll find a listing there for the Gateway Outreach Excursion and other workshops I currently have scheduled.

Gateway Outreach Excursion workshops run two full days, usually Saturday and Sunday, and are highly experiential; you spend most of the workshop in altered states of consciousness, learning to access these states for personal enrichment and development and also for practical everyday skills in problem-solving, attention, memory recall, and the like. They serve as excellent introductions to Gateway Voyage, and participants in a Gateway Outreach receive a substantial discount if they later sign up for the residential Gateway Voyage program.

If you have a week to spare and can afford to travel, consider attending the full six-day Gateway Voyage residential program either at TMI itself, or at one of the various satellite locations around the world where the full program is offered. The Gateway Voyage is a residential program, generally running from Saturday afternoon to Friday morning.

Check the TMI website under Residential Programs or call their office for schedule and locations.

I highly recommend any or all of these steps.

But the most important key to developing and accessing your own psychic abilities is the belief that you have them. Like any human skill, you must practice them and use them regularly to fully develop them. You'll undoubtedly find you're better at some skills than others. Perhaps you're very good at precognition but can't remote view consistently worth beans. Or perhaps you're an excellent psychic medium, but can't do more than the simplest psychokinetic tasks. You can only find out if you work to develop your skills and see how well you progress.

You also must learn to pay attention to the subtle signs your growing psychic skills provide you because, as I hope you've noticed, psychic messages tend to be nonverbal ones, and they are often metaphorical and symbolic. Only rarely are they explicitly verbal. Books of dream symbols and general archetypes can provide a certain amount of guidance on the meanings of those symbols, but remember that your own mind has its personal symbolic language that you have to learn to interpret.

For example, I often have exploration sessions over the telephone with a friend who lives in Canada. I realized long ago that when I see a tree, she generally sees a UFO. But the function, meaning, and messages of my tree are virtually identical to those of her UFO. Thus, the message is the same, although the symbols and metaphors in which it is couched are vastly different in the two cases and are very specific to each of us. Only practice and experience learning your own internal sets of symbols can truly guide you in understanding the messages you receive.

In addition to believing in your own abilities and paying attention to subtle signs, it's important that you also surround yourself with others who, at a minimum, do not actively discourage your efforts. In other words, you have to open your mind to new possibilities and new communities of people so you can expand your personal horizons and access new potentialities. This isn't always easy to do because it means breaking down some significant barriers in your own belief system.

If you've been paying attention to the story of my journey, you will have noted that breaking down barriers is not always comfortable or easy in any respect: physically, emotionally, mentally, or especially spiritually. Sometimes it means your entire philosophy of life must change. Sometimes it only strengthens the philosophy you already have. Be aware that starting off on a journey like this may cause you to reexamine old beliefs and abandon some of them for greater, more inclusive new ones. And occasionally, as I have found, it may mean ripping out entire world views and replacing them with brand new ones. Personally, I think that's a wonderful thing. But I just want to remind you that I never said it was going to be easy!

Thus, if you truly want to develop your psychic skills, my suggestion is the same as the apocryphal answer to the question of how to get to Carnegie Hall: Practice, practice, practice.

Appendix A

Putting Focus Levels in Focus

As mentioned earlier, before his death, Bob Monroe connected with a nonphysical entity he called "Miranon," who acted as his guide to the nonphysical and presented Monroe with a map of the focus levels from C-1 consciousness to the highest level that Miranon could access, F-49. Understanding this hierarchy of levels will help in gaining a perspective on my experiences in altered states of consciousness.

I freely admit that when I was first exposed to this cosmology, I mentally snickered. This was too strange to be believed. However, as time has passed and as my own experiences with the focus levels expanded, I have discovered that in many ways this organizational structure of the focus levels seems, at the very least, to be consistent with those experiences. So I present it here as a way of organizing and thinking about those experiences.

Miranon divided the focus levels from C-1 to F-49 into seven sets of seven levels. Each set of seven levels represents a progression followed by an ascension to the next set of seven levels. Table 1 gives the basic layout of the level hierarchy.

Table 1. The Hierarchy of the Focus Levels

Group	Focus Levels	Domain
I	C-1 to F-7	Plant consciousness
II	F-8 to F-14	Animal consciousness
III	F-15 to F-21	Human consciousness
IV	F-22 to F-28	Bridge states between physical and nonphysical life; levels entered at death
V	F-29 to F-35	Lowest nonphysical life realm; spiritual realm
VI	F-36 to F-42	Middle nonphysical life realm; spiritual realm
VII	F-43 to F-49	Highest nonphysical life realm; spiritual realm

I should note here that these general groupings are not meant to imply, for example, that animals are *always* restricted to levels F-8 through F-14. That simply isn't the case in my experience. I have encountered a number of animals, not all of them domesticated pets, on various focus levels as high as F-27. My cat Sammy, for example, now resides in F-27, as do many other pets of friends and family. Some wild animals can also be found at that level too.

Within each of the groups of levels, you can only ascend to the next set of levels on a permanent basis if you're willing to transform your level of consciousness. At the bridge states—Group IV—a choice is made whether to return to the lower levels—Groups I through III—or whether to transform into a spiritual-only being. If the latter decision is made, that person or entity can no longer incarnate as a human being. The decision to progress past F-28 implies a decision to stay as a spiritual being only, with no further physical incarnations.

Nor do these basic groupings imply that it's impossible for humans to visit any level above F-28. Instead, the labels on these groups as being plant or animal or whatever, merely imply that these levels are the *typical* locations in which these types of consciousness may be found. Individuals may spend their time at focus levels higher or lower than these areas.

This is particularly true when you consider C-1 consciousness. Many, if not most, people spend virtually *all* their waking time in C-1. They—we—are awake and alert pretty much all the time. They don't meditate, and except for an occasional daydream or brief periods of woolgathering, are constantly focused on the here-and-now. This does not imply that such people are spiritually at the same level as a broccoli! Nor is it necessarily true that very religious people spend all their conscious time in the nonphysical levels. Some do, but many more do not. That has nothing to do with their personal faith or religiosity.

Within each of these sets of seven, colors are associated with the individual focus levels in a repeating pattern. These colors tend to be reported by substantial numbers of people experiencing these levels, *but not all*. In addition, each level within the set is associated with a particular type of theme and these too are repeated. For example, the middle—fourth—levels of each set of seven are the levels of Love energy where access to love and heart energy in all its forms is easiest.

Table 2 presents a summary of the colors and major domains of each level within the groups. The colors are not quite the same as the visible spectrum—red-orange-yellow-green-blue-indigo-violet—nor are they quite the same as those commonly associated with the major chakras.

Table 2. Resonance of Levels within Each Group

Focus Level w/in Group	Focus Levels	Color	Domain or Theme
1	C-1, F-8, F-15, F-22, F-29, F-36, F-43	Blue	Security; pulsing
2	F-2, F-9, F-16, F-23, F-30, F-37, F-44	Red	Outer Reality; mirror image of Security level; sensory awareness
3	F-3, F-10, F-17, F-24, F-31, F-38, F-45	Yellow	Inner Reality; expanding consciousness
4	F-4, F-11, F-18, F-25, F-32, F-39, F-46	Rose	Love; openness to realities beyond current level
5	F-5, F-12, F-19, F-26, F-33, F-40, F-47	Green	Healing; complementary to level 6; awareness of next reality
6	F-6, F-13, F-20, F-27, F-34, F-41, F-48	Purple	Ascension; greater understanding of next reality; complementary to level 5
7	F-7, F-14, F-21, F-28, F-35, F-42, F-49	White	Wholeness; total awareness and understanding across this set of 7 levels

In essence, as you scale the hierarchy of focus level groups you revisit the same seven domains again and again, each time at a deeper or more profound level, and each time increasing your overall spiritual awareness.

For example, as you go up the grouping hierarchy, from Group I to Group VII, each return to the Love level provides greater and greater opportunities to understand and access that power. Thus, the heart energy in, say, Group III, F-18, is useful for worldly healing of both physical and psychological issues. But the heart energy of F-32 is more of a spiritual heart energy. And the heart energy of F-46 is more akin to divine love.

Within the hierarchy of seven levels, the first three levels, Security, Outer Reality, and Inner Reality, are *horizontal* levels; they neither ascend nor descend. The fourth level, the Heart level, is both ascending and descending; it comprises a vertical axis. The fifth and sixth levels, Healing and Ascension, twine around the fourth level, with the fifth level being a descending level and the sixth level being a complementary ascending level. Finally, the seventh level, Wholeness, touches all others; it is fully ascendant; it is from this level that one ascends into the next group of seven. Often, significant changes in consciousness are required to transition from the seventh level of one group to the first level of the next higher group.

One way of viewing a tour of these focus levels is that of traveling a rising spiral, where each turn of the spiral brings you back to the same concepts as the previous turn, but at a substantially more profound level.

Miranon actually provided a slightly different perspective of these levels to Bob Monroe when this cosmology was originally described. In Miranon's description, each group of seven can be viewed as two intersecting braids surrounded by a circle. The first three levels of any group, Security, Outer Reality, and Inner Reality, constitute a braid moving in the horizontal direction with Security and Outer Reality coiling around the Inner Reality strand. The second three levels of the group, Love, Healing, and Ascension, constitute a similar braid, with Ascension and Healing twining around the Love strand. The seventh level, Wholeness, provides a circle that encloses the intersecting horizontal and vertical strands, yielding a figure that looks like a cross enclosed in a circle. This complex figure looks much like a Celtic knot.

Remember that this organization of the focus levels is merely that: an organizational structure to help in understanding how the various levels relate to each other. It also can help make sense of the differences in the types of experiences that are reported on the different levels.

Table 3 may also help clarify these levels more specifically, particularly with respect to the experiences described previously. In this table, the general TMI description is in regular type, and descriptions that are specific to my personal experiences in the levels are in *italic*. Groups of focus levels are shaded to help distinguish them.

Table 3. The Individual Focus Levels above C-1 Consciousness

Focus Level	Focus Description	Level	Description
F-2	Outer Reality state	F-26	Healing state; belief territory
F-3	Inner Reality state; state of synchronized right and left brain hemispheres.	F-27	Reception center, the Park, Healing center, Akashic records, Earth core F-27, etc.
F-4	Love state	F-28	Wholeness state
F-5	Healing state	F-29	Security state
F-6	Ascension state	F-30	Outer Reality state
F-7	Wholeness state	F-31	Inner Reality state
F-8	Security state	F-32	Love state; *love energy world, initiating life state*
F-9	Outer Reality state	F-33	Healing state
F-10	Inner Reality state; mind awake/body asleep	F-34	Ascension state; I-There state
F-11	Love state; access channel for hypnogogic auto-suggestions	F-35	Wholeness state; I-There state
F-12	Healing state; expanded awareness; clairvoyance, etc.	F-36	Security state
F-13	Ascension state; *machine reception area and machine ascension state*	F-37	Outer Reality state
F-14	Wholeness state	F-38	Inner Reality state
F-15	Security state; state of no time; the Void; *Library; subset of personal Akashic records*	F-39	Love state; *Mushroom café*
F-16	Outer Reality state	F-40	Healing state
F-17	Inner Reality state	F-41	Ascension state
F-18	Love and heart energy state; *excellent healing state*	F-42	Wholeness state, I-There clusters; *Map Room for I-There clusters*
F-19	Healing state	F-43	Security state
F-20	Ascension state	F-44	Outer Reality state
F-21	Wholeness state; bridge state; OBEs	F-45	Inner Reality state
F-22	Security state; coma, OBE, dreams, etc.	F-46	Love state
F-23	Outer Reality state; after-death state (temporary)	F-47	Healing state
F-24	Inner Reality state; belief territory	F-48	Ascension state
F-25	Love state; belief territory	F-49	Wholeness state; *Mind of God*

This cosmology of course has no real scientific merit. Its source—channeled communication from a spirit guide—is far from validated, and it has little or no correlation to scientific data.

Still, from an experiential perspective, this organizational structure provides a useful and consistent perspective on the altered states of consciousness from F-10 through F-49. This basic structure seems correct to me; it is consistent with my experiences.

Appendix B

The View from the Other Side

It isn't only science that has something to say about the types of experiences I've had. Traditional lore, from shamanic literature to Eastern healing philosophies, all have opinions, concepts, and ideas that are relevant to these events. In particular, three key nonscientific concepts—at least, nonscientific in the Western tradition of science—strike me as accurately describing some parts of what I've experienced. These key concepts are the ideas of multiple energy bodies, the human aura, and the notion of chakras and *chi*. As it turns out, scientists are beginning to be able to detect some parts of these "subtle" energies, so it seems fitting to begin the discussion reviewing what these are.[109]

---

[109]There are many excellent books on Eastern medicine, chakras, and auras, but much of this discussion derives from one of the best and clearest authors I've found, Cyndi Dale's various titles on Chakra Healing (*New Chakra Healing: Activate Your 32 Energy Centers, New Chakra Healing: The Revolutionary 32-Center Energy System,* and *Advanced Chakra Healing*). All are strongly recommended, but do peruse the other titles in the suggested reading list's Healing and Energy Work sections for other suggestions.

Energy Bodies

According to Eastern thought, we each have more than one body. The obvious one that we see all the time is the *physical body*. This body is the only one officially acknowledged by Western science, which often treats it as a machine. But in the Eastern tradition, at least three other bodies make up a human being, and these bodies are definitely not machine-like. These bodies are not physical, nor are they detectable with most current technology. Instead they are *energy* bodies—and, in these traditions, these energy bodies are where we really live. The energy that they are made up of is a "subtle" energy or a life energy.

The first of these energy bodies is sometimes called the *astral* body. It is that part of us that goes on out-of-body excursions, and resides in the realms of F-27 and below. In Robert Bruce's excellent book, *Astral Dynamics*, he suggests that when we fall asleep, the energy bodies separate from the physical body, thus allowing out-of-body, or astral travel, to occur.[110] The trick in learning to go out-of-body, according to Bruce, is not in learning how to separate from the physical body, but rather in learning how to *remember* what the astral body does when it's separated.[111]

Once the astral body is separated, a second split occurs from that body to a *psychic* body. This body, composed of even more highly vibrating subtle energy, can travel to higher focus levels—in the F-30s and F-40s. The psychic body is much more highly connected spiritually and psychically. Again, according to Robert Bruce, this second split happens very often, but we usually don't recall what the psychic body does when it has separated from the astral and physical bodies.

---

[110]See suggested reading list for details.

[111]Robert Bruce has probably done more hands-on investigation of out-of-body experiences than anyone else currently alive. Like Robert Monroe, his intense curiosity has led him to develop an extensive series of practical, learnable techniques for going out-of-body and remembering what happens. In his opinion, the "forgetting" problem of out-of-body experiences arises because the physical brain can only record one memory sequence, and normally that's the sequence of the physical body—which stayed asleep in bed the whole night. His books offer techniques for training yourself to remember instead the memories of the astral body, which may have been roaming all over the neighborhood while the physical body slept peacefully. With practice, you may also learn to remember what the psychic body does at night, though this is harder for most people to do. See Bruce's book, *Mastering Astral Projection* for a 90-day course in learning to go out-of-body.

One final energy body is the *spiritual* body. The spiritual body is the realm of mystics and deeply advanced people. It resides in the far focus levels of the high F-40s and beyond F-49.

These three energy bodies plus the single physical body comprise our total selves. In this tradition, although the physical body may perish, the energy bodies cannot perish. They connect us to our past and future lives, and it is in these bodies that the stuff resides that makes us who we really are on a mental, emotional, and spiritual level.

Another view of multiple energy bodies is that we have a "mental" body, and "emotional" body, and a "spiritual" body. The Monroe Institute's healing program addresses healing through each of those, as well as addressing issues in the physical body. If there is a problem in either the emotional or the mental body, then the physical body will in some way reflect that problem. Thus, someone who is frightened of public speaking but who is facing such an ordeal, might have breathing difficulties as the emotional body generates actual physical problems.

From perspectives such as this it is easy to see that attacking only the physical symptoms of a problem does not necessarily fix the causes of the problem. Western medicine might fix the physical symptoms, but the problem would be likely to recur until the emotional body's issues were dealt with.

Since these energy bodies, whether you consider them as astral, psychic, and spiritual or mental, emotional, and spiritual, connect us to *all* our other lives, and problems that are not resolved in one life can sometimes show up as symptoms in another. Many people who experience past life regressions discover the reasons for their current life's physical and emotional ailments in events that happened in some other life. For example, a person who was hanged in one life might in a current life, experience throat or breathing problems. The Eastern tradition insists that if such a person can embrace the *original* problem in the previous life, the symptoms in *this* life will go away. And for some people, that does seem to work.

Chakras

Chakras also are fundamental to understanding Eastern medical traditions.[112] This begins with the assumption that the body has a subtle

---

[112]Chakra is pronounced "shock-rah."

energy that flows through it, which Chinese medicine calls *chi* or *qi*. This subtle energy flows through a set of energy channels much as blood runs through veins. These energy channels run to and from a set of energy centers located throughout the body. It is in these energy centers that our physical bodies connect with our spiritual selves.

Traditionally, there are seven main energy centers within the limits of the physical body and another five main energy centers that connect outside the physical body but within the overall energy field. In addition to these 12 main energy centers, there are dozens of minor chakras. But a quick review of these main ones will give you a sense of what they are.[113]

A chakra may be visualized as a vortex—a kind of miniature energy whirlpool that generally is approximately horizontal, with the widest part of the whirlpool farthest away from the body. The first six of the seven main chakras actually are double connected vortexes, with the narrowest parts meeting approximately at the spine, and the two wide ends in front and back of the body. The seventh chakra is a vertical whirlpool rather than horizontal.

The chakras serve multiple purposes in the body. They record memories both from the current lifetime and from other lives. They store beliefs, feelings, hopes, and dreams. They regulate various physical systems, with each chakra having a specific set of systems to oversee. They also are the communications points for our various energy bodies, the physical, mental, emotional, and spiritual aspects of ourselves. This last characteristic is important because it implies that each chakra has specific physical, psychic, and intuitive ways of communicating with us. Thus, a problem in the energy center of one chakra can be communicated to you as a physical symptom, as bad dreams, or as psychic messages—or any combination of these.

The seven most commonly discussed chakras literally run the length of the spine. The first chakra is right at the end of the tailbone and is often called the root chakra. This chakra is where the kundalini energy resides before it is awakened. It is the most grounded of the chakras, connecting to passions, sexuality, genitals, and the like.

---

[113]I recommend any of Cyndi Dale's books on chakra healing for anyone interested in this subject. The discussion that follows is based on her work. Her books provide a wealth of information based on long-term experience and study of using chakra energies to heal. See the suggested reading for several titles.

The second chakra is the center for creativity and it's located just below the navel in the lower abdomen. In women, it's the place where life energy is stored. It is deeply connected to the reproductive system in women, along with the intestines and lower digestive system.

The third chakra is the power chakra, located just below the sternum in the solar plexus or stomach area. This chakra controls judgments, opinions, and beliefs. It is particularly important for men, who seem to use it as a source of decisions. It controls the stomach and the organs in that part of the body.

The fourth chakra is the heart chakra, located right at the level of the heart, and it is the center of love, being in the middle between the life-giving love of the sexual chakras and the divine love of the psychic chakras. This chakra controls the heart, relationships, love, and compassion.

The fifth chakra is the communications chakra, located in the throat, approximately where the larynx is. This chakra allows us to express ourselves and also controls issues of self-responsibility. This chakra also allows our souls to express their needs and wants—think of things like Freudian slips.

The sixth chakra is the third eye chakra, located in the middle of the brow between the two eyes. This chakra seems deeply involved in perception, including seeing auras (discussed below), remote viewing, clairvoyance, and the like. It is linked to the hormonal system, particularly the pituitary gland and regulates hormones and endocrine releases.

The seventh chakra is vertical, rising upward from the top of the head. It is the "crown" chakra and it connects to both the pineal gland in the brain and the cerebral cortex. It also is involved in regulating the immune system and such varied psychological issues as learning disorders, neuroses, and psychoses. This is our direct link to the divine and the spiritual world. People with powerful crown chakras tend to be very psychic and often extremely spiritual in nature.

In addition to these seven major in-body chakras, five more connect to our energy bodies. These additional chakras are less involved with the physical body than with connecting the physical to the spiritual. These chakras also have their own roles.

The eighth chakra is located just above the top of the head and appears as a flat spinning disk. Cyndi Dale considers this chakra the portal in and out of current space-time. People focusing on the eighth chakra often have images of other worlds, and may also find their Akashic records— the records of everything we've seen and done in our lives. In Monroe terms this chakra seems to have elements of F-15—the sense of being outside of space and time—and especially F-27—which is where people generally find their Akashic records stored.

The ninth chakra is the soul chakra and it is located as a vortex just above the eighth chakra. Cyndi Dale considers this chakra the home of the "genes" of the soul. This is the part of us that transmits information from lifetime to lifetime.

The tenth chakra, the grounding chakra, is located just under our feet and connects us to the earth. It brings earth energy into the physical and energy bodies, and emits wastes, hurts, and other damages to the earth. In some sense, you can think of the tenth chakra as a set of lungs, breathing in good, clean energy and breathing out waste products and stale, used energy.

The eleventh chakra actually consists of a set of vortexes in the palms of each hand and in the soles of the feet. This chakra proves a mechanism for absorbing the raw energy that the various physical and energetic bodies need.[114] It's a bit like an energetic digestive tract, taking in energy in a raw form and converting it into a form usable by the body.

Finally, the twelfth chakra is a complete secondary chakra system consisting of some 32 separate points scattered all over the body. Many of these are associated with various organs such as the spleen, liver, gall bladder, and so on. Others are associated with physical structures like the arms, elbows, wrists, knees, and throat. This is the chakra that makes us human, linking our specific physical body to the primary chakra system—chakras one through 11—and to the various energy bodies that are part of us.

Auras

In the Eastern tradition, it is believed that all natural objects have an aura that surrounds them. In humans, these auras extend anywhere

---

[114]If you work with Robert Bruce's New Energy Ways (NEW), you'll notice he suggests doing a lot of energy work with your hands and feet. This is precisely because the chakras in the hands and feet are energy-absorbing chakras. His NEW system actually delves into functions of the minor chakras I don't describe here. But if you compare his work, based on decades of practical experience working with energy, and Cyndi Dale's presentation of major and minor chakras, you'll find close agreement in terms of which chakras do what.

from millimeters to feet in all directions. If you imagine your body as being surrounded by an energy body that looks a bit like a warped onion, with all its different layers, you get the idea. Some of these auric layers are very thin—only fractions of an inch wide. Some are quite thick, up to several feet wide. And some take a very experienced practitioner to discern.

The aura reflects your personal energy field, a field of subtle energy rather than familiar energies of science. All natural objects have an aura, but living objects, with their greater life-force energies, have bigger, brighter auras than nonliving objects.

Auras can be photographed in a couple of different ways. The more scientific method is that of Kirlian photography, developed by a pair of Soviet scientists in the 1930s. Basically, those being photographed place their hands on a metallic plate that has a mild current running through it. The photograph is then taken under special conditions, usually in a darkened room so the colors are very strong.[115] All kinds of experiments have been done with Kirlian photographs, including cutting a leaf in half, then taking a Kirlian photograph of the half-leaf. The resulting picture shows the aura of the *whole* leaf, rather than the half that was physically present on the plate.

If you go to a psychic fair these days, you'll often find a booth that does "aura photographs" for you, using a computer. In this case, you sit in a chair and put your hand on a plate of sensors. A digital camera feeds your image into the computer and the software of the computer combines inputs from the hand plate and the digital image to come up with a representation of the aura that corresponds with how a person would see it. Note that in this system, the camera does not directly perceive the auras. The software computes what the aura probably looks like based on the sensor information from the hand and adds that imagery to the digital photograph. Still, the best such computerized systems are checked repeatedly with experienced humans who can reliably perceive auras, and their reliability appears to be quite good.

Seeing auras yourself is really quite easy in concept, though it takes

---

[115]I have been told, but have no explicit documentation to verify it, that Kirlian photography is much easier to do successfully if using Polaroid types of cameras rather than usual 35-mm type photography. The process by which Polaroid cameras and film generate images is quite different from 35-mm image production, so perhaps there is some truth to this.

a fair amount of practice to perceive them easily and reliably under all conditions. I admit I'm not particularly good at viewing auras. I have to work hard to see them at all, and if the lighting conditions aren't right, I often can't see them. But when I do succeed, the appearance is unmistakable. They cannot be confused with afterimages—the common skeptical claim—or any other phenomenon.[116]

Even if you can't *see* an aura, it's not at all uncommon to *sense* one. Most people have had the experience of meeting someone who instantly "rubs them the wrong way" or who "puts out bad vibes." That person doesn't have to actually *do* anything for you to have this sense. In such cases, it's highly likely that you're picking up something in that person's aura on a subconscious level.[117] Similarly, there are people you're instantly attracted to, again for no obvious reason. An excellent example of that is the actress Sandra Bullock. She usually generates an instant sense of likeability, as do the Dalai Lama, Oprah Winfrey, and many other religious and popular figures. Only part of these people's attractiveness is based on their physical characteristics; much more is that their auras radiate positive, likeable qualities so strongly that virtually everyone can pick up on them.

Auras change from moment to moment in terms of both brightness and color, and those changes reflect your current mood, health, and other physical and psychological conditions. If you're feeling down or oppressed by life, your aura reflects that. If you're feeling upbeat and positive, that too shows up in your aura. If you're feeling physically ill, your aura will show that too. In fact, an expert practitioner—this may also mean someone with medical training—can look at a person's aura and diagnose

---

[116]An afterimage occurs when you stare at anything without shifting your eyes. If you do this long enough, the rods and cones in your retina get saturated and exhaust their ability to produce signals to send to the brain for interpretation. As a result, you find that you suddenly are seeing a complementary image instead of a true image. This is easiest to show with colors. If you stare hard at anything that is bright red long enough, you'll suddenly begin to see a yellow "shadow" image. And if you close your eyes, you'll still see that shadow image for a while. All this is merely a function of the cells in the retina exhausting their ability to produce signals for the brain.

[117]In fact, beginners may find that it's easier to see auras with their eyes closed rather than open! If you're having trouble seeing an aura, try looking at the person for a moment, then closing your eyes. You may surprise yourself and see it quite clearly.

medical and psychological conditions with astonishing accuracy. A surprising number of doctors and nurses use their abilities to sense auras to help them care for their patients. Often this is done surreptitiously, and sometimes even subconsciously, and generally primarily to guide them in determining what tests to run to determine a formal diagnosis rather than to explicitly diagnose a patient.

Some people's auras are fainter in brightness and/or paler in color than others. A pale or colorless aura may indicate a person who is physically ill or emotionally upset. The most vivid auras are often around those who are intensely spiritual and intensely connected to higher planes of existence.[118]

So how do you view an aura? Under ideal lighting conditions, the person you want to view should stand or sit quietly a few feet away and in front of a bland background. White or light beige backgrounds are very good, and even a black background works. But when you're first beginning to learn to view auras, avoid trying to view people against a colored or patterned background because the color of the background will make it much harder to correctly distinguish the colors of the aura.[119]

The person you're trying to view should also have a fair amount of bare skin visible. Auras can be seen through clothing, but they are sometimes muted in brightness. Also, the colors and patterns of clothes, like the colors and patterns in the background, can sometimes distort the colors of the aura and make it hard to reliably distinguish those colors. Often this means you're primarily viewing the aura around the

---

[118]Michael Talbot, author of the excellent *The Holographic Universe* (see the suggested reading list), has speculated that the concept of haloes derives from auras. Haloes are often depicted in images of holy people in a broad variety of religious traditions throughout the world, including Buddhism, Judaism, and Christianity. He suggests that people who are exceptionally holy have auras so strong and so bright that virtually everyone can see them. In a culture where the only exposed skin is usually the head and neck, an aura would be easiest to see in that part of the body. Thus, Jewish and Christian saints and other holy people literally would be seen by believers with a golden glow around their heads and shoulders. This golden glow then is presented in images as the familiar halo. It should be noted that images of the Buddha, from a culture where men are often bare from the waist up, typically have haloes that similarly surround the entire upper body of the Buddha.

[119]Since all living beings have auras, you can also practice viewing auras of pets or even houseplants.

head and shoulders rather than about the torso. Unless, of course, it's summertime!

So convince a friend to learn with you. Sit about eight or ten feet apart with each of you in front of a light, bland background. Ideally, you want the overall lighting in the room to be fairly dim, perhaps with the primary light source coming from the side. First, be sure you note where the shadows fall on the background. You don't want to confuse shadows with the aura.

Begin by focusing your eyes just over the person's shoulder, perhaps by looking at where the neck meets the shoulder. Gradually, shift your focus to just behind the person rather than right at their neck and shoulder. Now shift your focus farther back, then farther, until your eyes are focused on infinity. This takes some practice to do because your eyes have been trained since birth to *focus* and what you're trying to do is to *unfocus* them.

If you keep this unfocused state long enough you will start to see a glow around the person's head. This is where most everyone instantly loses their image of the aura because your natural instinct will be to shift your attention to focus your eyes on the glow. Don't do it! Instead, keep your eyes unfocused and observe the glow only with your peripheral vision.

When most people initially start to see the aura, they don't see colors. Instead, they see only a gray or silvery glow. This is because when you're doing it right, you're viewing the aura on the edges of your visual field. In this part of the retina, you have many more rods (black and white sensors) than cones (color sensors), so you don't perceive color very well in that part of your visual field. On the other hand, rods are much more light-sensitive than cones are, which is probably why they sense the aura more easily than cones.

The process of learning to see the aura in color is thus, at least in part, the process of learning how close to the center of your visual field—where more color-sensitive cones are—you can view them without losing the visual acuity of the rods in your retina. This simply takes practice.

When you see the aura, initially you may only see a single color. Again, with practice you can distinguish the layers of the aura. Experienced practitioners can see ten or more layers. With just a little practice, most people (even me!) can see anything from three to five layers, depending on circumstances.

The closest description to an aura is that it looks a lot like the corona of the sun during an eclipse. Often it's dynamic and flaring rather than static. It doesn't exactly match the outline of the body, but encapsulates the body in a shape that resembles an egg.

You can even feel a person's aura if you pay close attention. Here's another thing to try with your friend. Stand about six to ten feet apart, and decide which one will be the "feeler." Let's assume Mary is the feeler and Bob is the person whose aura will be felt. Bob should close his eyes and stand quietly while he imagines breathing in love energy with each inhalation, and breathing out negativity with each exhalation. Meanwhile, Mary should shake her hands a bit and rub them together to raise their energy levels. Then, holding her hands palm out in front of her, she very slowly approaches Bob from any direction—front, back, or side. At some stage, Mary's hands will start to tingle and perhaps even have a slight burning sensation similar to the pins-and-needles sensation you get when a foot has fallen asleep. If Bob is sensitive and paying attention, he may also be able to tell when Mary starts to feel his aura, even if he's blindfolded and Mary doesn't make a sound.

You can try this with a friend under different conditions. For example, you can practice deliberately feeding energy into your aura. Just imagine that the energy you're breathing in goes straight to the aura making it as bright and vibrant as possible. Or you can imagine putting up a wall between you and your friend, holding your aura inside the wall. If you pay attention to how far away the aura can be felt, you'll get a sense of just how dynamic the aura really is.

Auras reflect your emotional and physical state. Problems can be seen by experienced viewers as dark or misshapen areas in the aura. But auras can also reflect the connections people have with each other. It's not uncommon for two people who have deep emotional bonds to have auras that actually merge when they are standing even moderately close to each other. You can see this in Kirlian photographs of the hands of two lovers who are kissing when the photograph is taken. Their auras literally arc across, one to the other, merging into a single united shape. But this can happen even in those who are not actively kissing or even touching each other. If their emotional bond is strong enough, the connection between the two can be detected by almost anyone, no matter how discreetly they are behaving. Other people may not explicitly be able to see the auric fields, but they certainly react to it.

Karmic Considerations

Another key Eastern concept is that of reincarnation and karma. In Hinduism, reincarnation is treated as fact, and it is expected that the exact personality is reborn in a new body. This does not exactly match the sense of multiple lives that correlates with my experience, and does not match the multiple lives sense of TMI's cosmology. The difference is important.

In Buddhist and Hindu views, reincarnation in a new life is controlled by the *karma* you have amassed in current and previous ones. You can think of karma as a life plan that allows you to learn about different aspects of good and bad through incarnated existences. Since understanding all aspects of life is important for overall spiritual growth, everyone will have some lives at high levels of spiritual development and some at lower levels, including reincarnating as animals.

This, in fact, is one of the reasons Hindus tend to be vegetarians and have a profound respect for all living beings—you never know when the ant crossing your patio is the spirit of your great-uncle Oswald!

Karma transfers from life to life, but is a bit like a combination carrot and stick. Good karma generates the reward of a better life next time, even if good deeds don't profit you in this physical life. Bad karma generates the punishment of dropping down on the spiritual levels and reincarnating as a lower person or animal. Only by becoming an enlightened being—a Buddha figure—can you ever escape the constant cycle of birth-death-rebirth. You cycle again and again until you finally become so enlightened and so good that you have no further need to reincarnate. You've learned your lessons.

Contrast that concept with the experience most TMI folk have of multiple lives. The differences may seem subtle, but they are distinct. In the TMI view, at the end of life you move to F-27, to a life planning center. In this center you review your life and determine for yourself, with the aid of your guides, what aspects of spiritual growth you still need to work on. That information then allows you to select the circumstances of your next life to provide the environment that will allow you to work on those aspects of your spiritual development. This may mean that you choose to be born with a physical disability or that you plan a life filled with financial need or other sad circumstance. Or it may mean you plan a life with few obvious challenges, one that is "charmed" relative to the average person's.

Whatever that life plan is, however, it is specifically designed *by you* to enable you to work on the specific lessons that will most promote your spiritual development. It's not a payback or a punishment for having done poorly in some previous life. Instead, it's a carefully chosen environment that's designed to assist you in learning a specific set of spiritual lessons. Maybe you have to repeat a lesson if you didn't get it the first time, but it's not a karmic repetition or punishment as in Hinduism or Buddhism. It's merely another mechanism to allow you to progress on the spiritual plane.

Seeing Is Believing

Energy bodies, chakras, auras, and karma are well known and fully accepted in Eastern traditions. They're fundamental parts of Eastern medical science and Eastern belief systems. Unfortunately, here in the Western world, they're more often considered the realm of crackpots and charlatans than legitimate medical procedures and scientific theories.

However, scientific research is starting to confirm that there may indeed be something to all these concepts. Medical science is studying acupuncture, which manipulates the flow of subtle energy through the various chakras in the body, and discovering real physiological changes that result from genuine acupuncture treatments. A few maverick inventors are trying to construct detection devices that detect and image the subtle energy systems in a more direct way than the computerized "estimated" images of auras now available. And some medical practitioners are realizing that they've been making use of their own abilities to see chakras all along in helping them determine how their patients are really doing and what help they really need.

Glossary

The **bold** words in the glossary definitions are also found and defined within the glossary.

acceleration. In physics: any change in **velocity,** which means either a change in speed of motion or a change in the direction of motion from straight-line motion, or both. Thus, a satellite orbiting the Earth is undergoing constant acceleration because it is constantly changing its direction, even though its speed orbiting the Earth is constant.

activation function. In a **neuron,** the cell converts the net input signals it receives into an outgoing response signal. The relationship between the total input signal received and the strength of the output signal is the activation function for that cell. Typically the activation function has a minimum near-zero value and a maximum value, and a continuously increasing but not straight-line function between those two extremes.

Akashic record. A record of everything that has happened to you in your life. In Hindu and other Eastern traditions, the end of life is followed by a review of your Akashic records to determine the quality of your following life (*see also* **karma**). In TMI tradition, the complete Akashic records are generally found on F-27, though some records may be found in other focus levels. Akashic records, depending on tradition, may include everything that has happened in *all* your incarnate lives.

algorithm. In programming a computer, you need to know the sequence of steps the computer is supposed to perform to transform the input data to the desired output data. That sequence of steps is the algorithm. For example, to compute an average of a list of ten numbers, a simple algorithm might be a) set the result location to zero, b) for each of the ten numbers, retrieve the number and add it to the value in the result location, c) when all ten numbers are added together, divide the value in the result location by ten and put the answer back into the result location, d) stop.

alpha brainwaves. Those brainwaves that are approximately in the 7 **Hz** to 15 **Hz** frequency range. When alpha brainwaves are the predominant frequencies, the brain is generally in a light daydream or light trance state.

altered state (of consciousness). Any state of consciousness except the normal daytime awake-alert state. This includes the state of being asleep, being in a daydream state, being in a trance state, being in a coma, or any of a number of other conditions.

ALU. *See* **arithmetic logic unit.**

amplitude (of a wave). Waves are identified by their amplitude and their **frequency** or **wavelength.** Amplitude refers to the strength of the wave—the difference between the top of the wave and the bottom of the wave, or often, the difference between the top of the wave and the zero-point halfway between top and bottom.

analog. Variables and measurements which may take continuous values are analog variables. For example a standard analog watch may have a sweep second hand that moves smoothly around the dial. The seconds are thus measured in terms of continuous values from zero to 60 seconds, including fractional seconds. In the context of this book, **neural networks** are analog systems rather than **digital** ones.

analytical overlay, or **AOL (in remote viewing).** Refers to a common error that remote viewers make in which they detect a perception that reminds them of, say, an apple. Because they are reminded of an apple, all other perceptions are filtered by the thought that the object must therefore *be* an apple. To avoid this in remote viewing sessions, it's important to ask yourself or the viewer, if you are monitoring the session, *why* the perception reminds you of an apple. Is it because of color, shape, texture, flavor, scent, or some other characteristic? That brings the perception down to the most basic raw form and gives better overall accuracy.

android. An android in the strictest terms is a robotic system that is in the shape of a human being, even if only roughly. For example, in the *Star Wars* movies, the droid R2-D2 was not an android, but a robot. The protocol droid C-3PO, however, was an android because of his manlike shape. However, it's not uncommon to see the term applied to any intelligent robot that appears to behave in a humanlike way.

antimatter. In antimatter, the protons in the nucleus have a negative charge and the electrons around the nucleus have a positive charge. Antimatter particles and matter particles instantly annihilate each other if they come into contact.

AOL. *See* **analytical overlay.**

arithmetic logic unit, or **ALU.** In computers, generally the **central processing unit,** or **CPU,** is used for simple integer arithmetic and for logic functions. They typically have associated with them a separate chip that specializes in complex arithmetic functions, including noninteger arithmetic; e.g., decimals.

artificial intelligence. The attempt to make computers which behave with humanlike intelligence, even if over a very limited range of problems.

astral body. In Eastern traditions, one of the **energy bodies** associated with the physical body. During most **out-of-body experiences,** the astral body is the one that is doing the traveling. It appears to be associated with TMI **focus levels** below F-27. *See* appendix B, for a full discussion of energy bodies.

aura. The physical body is surrounded by a series of energy layers that can sometimes be seen by those who are practiced in the necessary skills to do so. The aura is layered, and changes constantly to reflect the mental, emotional, and physical state of the person. Traditionally, all natural objects have auras around them. *See* appendix B for details on this subject.

axon. The part of a **neuron** that transmits the neuron's signal to other neurons and cells. It transmits only a single signal, though the axon may branch to hundreds or thousands of other cells; all such cells receive the same outgoing signal from the axon.

Babel fish. From Douglas Adams's brilliant science fiction "trilogy" of books, *The Hitchhiker's Guide to the Galaxy*, the Babel fish is a fish that is put into the ear and thereafter can instantly translate any human or alien language into the native language of its host. It is such a mind-bogglingly fabulous idea that someone should try to invent one.

belief system territories (F-24 through F-26). In TMI's cosmology, focus levels F-24 through F-26 are the realms of the belief system territories. Those who die with strong beliefs about what the afterlife will be like will find a section of these focus levels in exactly that image. They then reside in these belief territories until their minds become more open to larger possibilities, at which point they are ready to transition to F-27 for further spiritual growth. *See* appendix A, for more details on the TMI Miranon cosmology.

beta brainwaves. Beta brainwaves are those approximately in the frequency range of 15 **Hz** to 35 **Hz**. When the brain is predominantly producing brainwaves in this frequency range, it is in the usual daytime awake-alert state.

Big Bang theory. The current, widely accepted theory that the beginning of the universe consisted of a Big Bang—a rapid inflation from a single point to the complete universe we see around us. Details of why this theory is so widely accepted by physicists is way beyond the scope of this book, but consider Michio Kaku's *Parallel Worlds* and Brian Greene's *The Fabric of the Cosmos*, both listed in the suggested reading list.

binaural beats. This phenomenon, discovered about a hundred years ago, refers to the ability of the brain to perceive frequencies that are outside the audible range of the human hearing system. Binaural beats are created when one frequency is heard by one ear and a slightly different frequency is heard by the other. In such circumstances, the brain actually perceives the beat frequency, or the difference between the two input sounds, rather than the input sounds themselves. This allows **Hemi-Sync** to make use of brainwave frequencies substantially outside the range of human hearing.

buckeyball water interdimensional chute, or **BWIC.** A term coined by the author and a friend to describe the sensation of traveling to focus levels beyond F-49.

BWIC. *See* **buckeyball water interdimensional chute.**

byte. In computers, the byte is a common unit of measurement of memory. It refers to one set of eight digital ones or zeros or eight bits. A digital representation of a byte might be 0100 0111. Each number in the byte can have only the value of one or zero, nothing else.

c. *See* **speed of light.**

C-1 consciousness. In TMI's terminology, C-1 consciousness refers to the normal awake-alert state. It can be thought of as a state in which **beta brainwaves** are predominant and the person is wide awake and alert to his or her surroundings.

Cartesian coordinate system. Named after René Descartes, the mathematician, this is one of the most common mathematical coordinate systems used. It refers to three straight-line axes that are all perpendicular to each other and that all intersect at a common zero-point.

Casimir effect. Named after the man who first documented it; a phenomenon in which two uncharged metal plates are positioned in parallel very close together. Under certain conditions, these plates will exhibit an attractive force between them and will generate a tiny amount of **negative energy.**

central processing unit, or **CPU.** In a computer, the semiconductor chip that interprets and executes instructions—the "smarts" of the computer.

cerebral cortex. The cerebral cortex is the most recently evolved part of the human brain. It is the wrinkled lump of brain cells that most people envision from pictures of the brain. However, when removed from the constraints of the skull and spread flat to eliminate the wrinkles, the structure of the cerebral cortex is actually similar to a very large thin sheet. The cerebral cortex is where many of the higher reasoning, memory, and language functions reside.

chakra. In Eastern traditions, chakras are vortexes of subtle energy at specific locations in the body. There are seven main chakras commonly discussed and located within the physical body, plus up to five other main chakras, and literally hundreds of minor chakras. *See* appendix B, for a discussion of chakras.

chi. In Eastern medical traditions, chi is the energy of life. *See* appendix B for a discussion of chi. *See also* **kundalini.**

clairaudience. The ability to hear things that are beyond your normal physical hearing range. This is related to **remote viewing.**

clairsentience. The ability to "touch" or "feel" objects that are beyond your normal physical sense of touch. This is related to **remote viewing.**

clairvoyance. The ability to see things that are beyond your physical range of view. This is closely related to **remote viewing.**

coherence. In biological systems, coherence refers to the ability of a whole organ, organism, or groups of organisms to behave or react as a single unit, often inexplicably, as when the reaction occurs faster than all parts of the organism (or group) can possibly have received information about the stimulus causing the reaction.

cones. In the eye, cones are the sensory cells in the retina of the eye that detect color. Cones are more prevalent in the center of your visual field than along the edges, so color perception is better there than in your peripheral vision.

conscious mind. In psychological terms, this is the part of the mind that we are aware of when we are awake and alert. Consciousness and the conscious mind are not well understood and are active areas of research across several scientific fields.

cosmology. A cosmology is a coherent theory of how the universe works, how it's put together and how it operates.

CPU. *See* **central processing unit.**

DEC. *See* **Dolphin Energy Club.**

delta brainwaves. Delta brainwaves are those that correspond to the deepest levels of sleep or the deepest trance states. When in a delta state, the predominant brainwave frequencies are in the 0.5 **Hz** to 4 **Hz** range.

dendrites. Dendrites are the parts of the **neuron** that connect with **axons** of other neurons or other input sources. They include electrochemical receptors to detect incoming signals from the **synapse** and pass those signals to the main body of the neuron.

digital. A digital device is one that operates in discrete numbers rather than continuous values. For example, television channels are digital numbers: 2, 3, 4, etc. There is no television channel labeled 3.44.

Dolphin Energy Club, or **DEC.** The Dolphin Energy Club is a function of The Monroe Institute in Faber, Virginia, that provides free healing services to anyone in need of help. Those who want to volunteer as a healer pay a small annual fee to help defray the cost of the program and intermittently are sent information about healing requests. The healers are encouraged to provide **remote healing** efforts for the person named in the request in any manner the healers wish. The Monroe Institute charges nothing to the prospective patients for these services; they request only that the recipient provide them with whatever feedback they can on the effect of the healing efforts.

double refraction. The double refraction effect is one in which a beam of light sent through crystals of specific types appear to be split into two separate beams. *See* chapter 16 for more details.

ECB. *See* **energy conversion box.**

electromagnetic wave. Light is now known to be a **transverse** electromagnetic wave comprised of an electrical portion, oscillating perpendicular to the direction of motion of the wave, and a magnetic portion, also perpendicular to the direction as well as perpendicular to the electrical portion. In terms of **Cartesian coordinates,** the electrical portion oscillates in the X-axis direction, the magnetic portion oscillates in the Y-axis direction, and the wave travels along the Z-axis. The color of light is determined by the **frequency** of this electromagnetic wave and the brightness of the light is determined by the **amplitude** of the wave.

emotional body. In Eastern and non-Western medical traditions, the emotional body is a map of your emotional state. Since emotions can affect your physical body, it is believed that emotionally derived problems can best be determined by viewing the emotional body, determining imbalances there, and correcting those imbalances.

energy bar. The energy bar is a device that in certain TMI altered state exercises you manifest out of **subtle energy.** Because it is manifested by you, you can change its form, character, capabilities, and all other aspects simply by changing your intentions about the energy bar.

energy being. In an altered state of consciousness, you often find yourself sensing the presence of other beings in those states. Some of those beings may be other people (for example, in an **out-of-body experience** you may encounter others who are similarly out of body). But some appear to be those who do not at the moment have a physical incarnation at all. Such beings are often called energy beings and sometimes "spirit beings" because they are comprised solely of energy rather than mass.

energy bodies. In non-Western traditions, we have one or more energy bodies. Depending on the tradition, these can be mental-emotional-spiritual bodies or astral-psychic-spirit bodies, and so forth. *See* appendix B for details.

energy conversion box, or **ECB.** As a part of the **preparatory process** for going into an **altered state of consciousness,** TMI instructs you to create and fill an energy conversion box with symbols of all the things that might distract you from your meditative session. You then close the lid of the box and imagine yourself turning your back on it and walking away. The ECB improves concentration and reduces distractions.

entanglement. A well-demonstrated but poorly understood phenomenon of **quantum physics,** entanglement refers to the fact that particles that are created under special circumstances appear to mirror each other forever or until the entanglement condition is broken. Measuring the physical characteristics of one of the entangled pair thereby conclusively tells you the exact characteristics of the other, no matter how far apart the two particles may be.

epigenetic. This refers to the biological fact that new structures appear in organisms during development that cannot be explained by structures present in the original egg.

ESP. *See* **extrasensory perception.**

excitatory signal. An excitatory signal is an input stimulus to a neuron that causes that neuron's overall activation level to increase—it arouses the neuron to produce a greater response signal.

explicate order. David Bohm postulates that the universe is a type of hologram in which the underlying truth is an implicate order that is analogous to the film of a hologram, and the everyday reality we perceive is nothing but the projection of the implicate order, or the equivalent of the image produced from the holographic film. The explicate order thus refers to that everyday world we perceive about us and, like the holographic image that you can view but not touch because it's not really there, has no true reality. *See also* **implicate order.**

extrasensory perception, or **ESP.** Psychologists use the term extrasensory perception to describe almost all psychic skills except the ability to manipulate matter, which is called **psychokinesis.**

fetch-execute-store cycle. In digital computers, the fundamental operational cycle is a process in which the next instruction is fetched from memory, that instruction is executed, and the results of the execution are stored back into memory. Contrast this with the brain's **stimulus-activation-response cycle.**

focus level. In The Monroe Institute's conception, different altered states of consciousness are called focus levels and have different characteristics. These focus levels are numbered rather than named to avoid as much cultural bias as possible. *See* appendix A for a description of the various focus levels.

free flow. A **Hemi-Sync** exercise in which the directions on the tape or CD guide you into a specific focus level, then no other directions are provided until the end of the exercise, when further verbal instructions bring you back to regular **C-1** waking consciousness.

Ganzfeld experiment. A Ganzfeld experiment in psychology is one of mild sensory deprivation. It is believed that such sensory deprivation enhances the mind's ability to perceive psychic information by removing distractions from the physical world.

golden energy dolphin. In TMI's **DEC** healing exercises, you manifest first an **energy bar** out of subtle energy, then you convert that energy bar to a golden energy dolphin, which you then use as a healing agent when you are trying to do **remote healing.**

grand unified theory, or **GUT.** In physics and cosmology, a grand unified theory provides a way of uniting all five fundamental forces of physics into one equation or set of related equations. This means uniting electricity, magnetism, gravity, and the weak and strong nuclear forces into a single whole. This is also called a **theory of everything.**

grounding. When working in **altered states of consciousness** you can become slightly disconnected from physical reality or slightly "spacey." Grounding exercises bring your consciousness back to physical reality. At the end of nearly all TMI tapes and CDs, special **beta** tones of frequencies are there for the sole purpose of grounding you and bringing you all the way back to an awake-alert state.

GUT. *See* **grand unified theory.**

Heisenberg uncertainty principle. Developed in the 1920s, this physics principle states that it's impossible to know exactly all aspects of a subatomic particle. Measurable quantities come in complementary pairs, and to measure one member of a pair precisely, is to give up all knowledge of the value of the other member. Thus, there is always a minimum level of uncertainty in all measurements. This value is extremely small, so for the ordinary scale of the world, it doesn't affect things. It only has an impact in the world of the subatomic scale.

Hemi-Sync. A registered trademark and patented technology of Monroe Products in Lovingston, Virginia, Hemi-Sync is a technology that safely and reliably guides even inexperienced people into **altered states of consciousness** through the use of **binaural beat** technology. *See* the discussion of Hemi-Sync in chapter 2 for details.

Hertz, or **Hz.** Hertz is a physics unit of measurement of frequency that stands for the number of cycles per second of any repeating object, such as a wave. It's the most commonly used unit of measurement for wave frequencies.

hologram. A hologram is an image produced by interference patterns caused by splitting a laser beam, reflecting one part of the beam off the object to be imaged, and then interfering that beam with the other beam. The interference pattern that results is stored on film. The image is reconstructed by taking the holographic film and passing another laser beam through it.

Hz. *See* **Hertz.**

implicate order. In David Bohm's theory of a holographic universe, the implicate order is the underlying holographic reality. The everyday world is merely the explicate order, the holographic image that is projected from an unfolding of the implicate order. *See also* **explicate order.**

inertial frame of reference. An inertial frame of reference in physics is any observer or object that is moving at a constant speed and in a straight line with respect to very distant stars—those that are so distant they don't appear to move with respect to Earth and are thus "fixed." If the observer changes either his rate of motion or his direction of motion, his frame of reference is not an inertial one because to do so he must have undergone some type of **acceleration.**

inhibitory signal. In a neuron, an incoming signal that tends to lower the neuron's overall activation or arousal state is an inhibitory signal; this in turn tends to lower the neuron's output signal.

karma. Karma is a life plan that allows you to learn about both good and bad aspects of existence through a series of incarnated lives. *See* appendix B for details.

Kirlian photography. Kirlian photography is a way of photographing the **auras** around humans and other natural objects. *See* appendix B for details.

kundalini. In Eastern tradition, the kundalini energy is a form of **chi** or life energy that lies at the base of the spine coiled like a snake. *See* appendix B for details.

kundalini awakening. A kundalini awakening occurs when the kundalini energy rises up through the body, coiling several times around the spine and rising over the head similar to a hooded cobra. If this happens spontaneously and without warning, the symptoms can be extremely uncomfortable.

longitudinal wave. A longitudinal wave is one where the vibrational pattern oscillates in the direction that the wave travels. For example, sound is a longitudinal wave.

materialism. Materialism claims that the only reality is the measurable physical reality of the body and measurable universe. It denies the existence of concepts like a soul, spirit, subtle energies, and the like.

Maxwell's equations. In a tremendous breakthrough in physics in the mid-1800s, James Clerk Maxwell formulated a series of four very simple equations that unified electricity and magnetism into a single electromagnetic whole. Maxwell's equations also support the wave theory of light and provide a mathematical formulation for the speed of light in a vacuum being always constant.

mechanics. In physics, mechanics is the study of how objects move.

membrane theory, or **M-theory.** In cosmology, membrane theory supposes that cosmic 10-dimensional **strings** reside in an overall 11-dimensional space. The equations that govern this 11-dimensional space are not yet known. However, using this formulation it can be shown that all of the separate mathematical formulations of 10-dimensional strings resolve to the same formulation in 11-dimensional M-theory space. Thus, M-theory is the current leading candidate for a **TOE.**

mental body. In non-Western traditions of healing, some ailments have mental causes rather than solely physical ones. Thus, healing the mental body is crucial to a genuinely complete healing of those ailments. *See* appendix B.

MetaMusic. MetaMusic is a registered trademark of Monroe Products of Lovingston, Virginia. It consists of music scores in which **Hemi-Sync** tones have been embedded. MetaMusic is very popular as an aid to relaxation, concentration, and meditation.

Michelson-Morely experiment. In the late 1800s, it was believed that if light is a wave, the wave must be traveling through some type of medium, just as ocean waves travel through water. The postulated medium was an "aether." The Michelson-Morely experiment attempted to confirm this by verifying that light traveled at different speeds through this aether depending on whether it moved with or against the flow of the aether itself. The results of this experiment were completely unexpected—and negative. Light travels at the same speed through space in all directions.

monism. In philosophical terms, monism is the belief that everything is one. It is contrasted with the dualist approach that insists that there are two separate entities, such as body and soul, or brain and mind. Many monists claim that there is only the body; this is the position of the materialist (*see also* **materialism**). An alternative monistic view is that there is nothing real about the physical world at all, and the only true reality is that of the spiritual realms; this belief system is that of the idealist.

monitor (in remote viewing). The monitor in a **remote viewing** session supervises the viewer, keeps track of how the viewer is doing, and asks questions designed to reduce the viewer's **analytical overlay** and other errors.

Monroespeak. This is a common, affectionate term for the jargon that is associated with The Monroe Institute. Founder Robert Monroe's acronyms, such as **REBAL** and **ECB,** along with basic terms such as **focus levels,** have migrated into common use at TMI.

morphogenetic field. Rupert Sheldrake, the British scientist, proposes that a universal morphogenetic field similar to a quantum probability wave function, sets probabilities that a particular type of system, such as a crystal or biological system, will coalesce into a particular physical form. *See* chapter 7 for a discussion of this theory.

M-theory. *See* **membrane theory.**

namaste. Pronounced na-mah-shtay, a Hindu expression that means, loosely translated, "The spirit in me recognizes and embraces the spirit in you."

negative energy. An extremely rare form of energy, negative energy has opposite properties as positive energy. It can be created briefly and in extremely tiny quantities through the **Casimir effect.**

negative matter. A postulated, but not yet demonstrated form of matter which reacts oppositely to gravitational fields. Whereas **antimatter** is opposite to regular matter in terms of charge, negative matter is opposite to both regular matter and antimatter in terms of gravitation. In other words, in the presence of a gravitational field, negative matter is repulsed rather than attracted to the object.

neural network. A neural network is an organized, highly interconnected collection of **neurons** that perform specific information processing functions.

neurocardiology. This scientific discipline is the study of the functions and operations of the neural cluster that resides in the heart.

neuron. Commonly called a brain cell, neurons exist throughout the body, with significant clusters in both the heart and the digestive system.

neurotransmitter. A neurotransmitter is any one of a variety of specific chemicals that either enhance or suppress the transmission of signals from **neuron** to neuron.

Newtonian mechanics. First presented by Sir Isaac Newton in the 1600s, Newtonian mechanics provides a solid and effective understanding of how objects move and interact in the everyday world. In the realm of the extremely fast, it breaks down and must be modified by **relativistic mechanics.** In the realm of the extremely small, it breaks down and must be replaced by **quantum mechanics.**

outbounder protocol. In remote viewing protocols, one popular methodology is to send a person to a random location, and have the remote viewer connect with that "outbounder" person and try to view whatever that person is observing. While it must be carefully done to ensure that only the outbounder knows the destination—and often not until after they leave the laboratory—such protocols are often extremely effective demonstrations of the validity of remote viewing.

out-of-body experience, or **OBE.** An out-of-body experience is one in which your physical body appears to be inert and asleep—such as from a sleep process or from anesthetic or severe physical trauma—but you have the perception of being able to travel throughout the world in your **astral body.**

paranormal. Anything that science can't really explain is often treated as being "paranormal" or outside the realm of normal reality. Once an explanation for the phenomenon is understood, that phenomenon moves from the paranormal to the normal. Thus, the paranormal consists of phenomena we can't yet explain scientifically.

parthenogenesis. In biology, parthenogenesis is a form of asexual reproduction.

photon. A quantized packet of light waves is called a photon. When light behaves like a particle, this is the particle.

pink noise. Pink noise is noise across the entire frequency range of human hearing, but modified to account for normal levels of hearing loss at high and low ends of that spectrum. *See also* **white noise.**

polarity. Of an electromagnetic wave: polarity of any transverse wave, such as light or ripples in water, is determined by the axis along which the vibration occurs. Electromagnetic waves can be polarized in any direction perpendicular to the direction of travel. Think of a disk with an arrow through it. The arrow points in the direction the light wave moves, but the electromagnetic fields can point in any radial direction on the disk. The specific direction that the electromagnetic fields vibrate in is that wave's polarity.

preparatory process. One step to going into an **altered state of consciousness** is a preparatory process. In Monroe tradition, this process consists of relaxing, making use of an **energy conversion box,** doing some **resonant tuning,** constructing a **REBAL,** and stating an affirmation. **Hemi-Sync** tones then guide you into the desired altered state.

probability wave function. In quantum mechanics physical matter isn't really a solid object. Instead, physical matter is nothing more than a mathematical function of probabilities that reflect the chances that a particular type of object would be measured at a particular location if the measurement were actually done. Until the object is observed, there is no object. Once it is observed, however, the probability wave function collapses into a single value and the object exists.

psychokinesis. This is the skill of manipulating physical matter solely through the mind and intentions. Spoon-bending is an example of a psychokinetic skill.

qi. *See* **chi.**

quantum mechanics. Quantum mechanics is the study of how objects interact in the realm of the very small—at subatomic scales.

REBAL. *See* **resonant energy balloon.**

refraction. When working with waves that move from one transmission medium to another, changes in the density of the medium changes the speed at which waves move. Thus, when light travels from water to air, the speed of motion of light changes, such that a ruler half-submerged endwise in a container of clear water appears to have a kink at the air-water boundary. This is due to the bending of the light waves as they go from water—a dense, low-speed medium—to air—a less dense, higher-speed medium.

Reiki. A non-Western healing tradition, Reiki is a form of energy and healing work that attempts to align and clear **chi** energy blockages in the body.

reincarnation. A part of many Eastern religious and philosophical traditions, reincarnation supposes that after death, your spirit is provided with another body for a new life. Depending on the specific tradition, some claim that the very same personality is reincarnated. Others claim that only the fundamental spiritual self returns with relatively little specific carryover into the next life. There is also a disagreement over whether past sins and successes are punished or rewarded, respectively, in following lives.

relativistic mechanics. Relativistic mechanics studies how objects traveling at very high speeds, approaching the **speed of light,** interact with each other.

remote viewing. Remote viewing is the skill of observing locations remote from your five physical senses. It can include **clairvoyance, clairaudience,** and **clairsentience.**

resonant energy balloon, or **REBAL.** A resonant energy balloon is part of The Monroe Institute **preparatory process.** It consists of imagining a flow of **subtle energy** or **chi** up through your body and out the top of your head, to cascade around you along all sides.

resonant tuning. Resonant tuning is part of The Monroe Institute **preparatory process.** It provides a method of breath control by having you breathe in slowly and deeply through your diaphragm, then exhale while vibrating your vocal cords in a sound.

rods. In the eye, the cells in the retina that are black-and-white light detectors are called rods because they have a rod-like shape. Rods are more sensitive to both motion and low levels of light than **cones** and they are also more prevalent along the edges of your visual field.

scalar. A scalar is any quantity that has only a magnitude associated with it, so it can be represented fully by a single number. For example, in physics, speed is a scalar quantity that reflects how fast you are going. But velocity in physics is a **vector** quantity because it means not only how fast you are going, but also in what direction you're moving.

soul retrieval. A soul retrieval is a rescue operation in which you identify a recently departed person who is "stuck" in the **focus levels** that correspond to recent deaths, and who seems unable to move past that level for further spiritual growth. Often, these people are those who die unexpectedly or suddenly and who have not had time before death to prepare themselves to die. To do the soul retrieval, you assist those persons to first recognize that they are dead, and to move with you to the higher focus levels so they can continue their spiritual growth.

space-time. In physics, the three physical dimensions plus one time dimension make up physical space-time continuum. Recent **cosmology** theories indicate that our universe may have up to ten total dimensions rather than only these four.

speed of light (in a vacuum), or **c.** This is a universal constant and is approximately equal to 186,000 miles per second.

spirit body. The spirit body is presumed in non-Western healing and religious traditions to be associated with the physical body but not limited to that location. *See* appendix B for a discussion of the spirit body and **energy bodies** in general.

spirit guide. A spirit guide is a spirit being who works with you on your spiritual development while you are alive. It is very similar in concept to a guardian angel. The spirit guide provides you with advice, counseling, support, and the like. You still have to do the work, however.

spoon-bending. Spoon-bending is an example of **psychokinesis,** the skill of manipulating physical matter with your mind.

spreading activation. A mechanism by which **neural networks** process information. Input stimulus generates activity within the **neurons** of the network which flows from the input side of the network to the output side; there it generates the network's overall response to the input stimulus.

Stargate program. The CIA, the military, and other Department of Defense organizations funded **remote viewing** programs for more than two decades as part of the intelligence-gathering efforts. One of the names under which these efforts operated was Stargate.

stimulus-activation-response cycle. Neural networks operate in a process of receiving a stimulus, becoming activated, and generating a response. Compare that process to the digital computer's **fetch-execute-store cycle** of operation.

string theory. String theory proposes that the fundamental elements that make up our universe are not probability wave functions or subatomic particles, but rather tiny, 10-dimensional vibrating strings. In the 1990s this was considered to be the most likely candidate for a **GUT** but when five separate mathematical formulations of string theory were discovered, it was realized that string theory is not general enough for that role. Recently the replacement for string theory is the 11-dimensional **membrane theory,** in which it can be demonstrated that the five formulations of string theory are five separate ways of describing the same thing.

strings. In cosmology, according to **string theory,** the universe's subatomic particles are nothing more than different vibrational modes of tiny, 10-dimensional strings.

subconscious mind. In psychology, the subconscious mind consists of mental activities below the level of awareness of the **conscious mind.** Dreams, for example, are posited to be generated in the subconscious and can only rise to our conscious awareness when the barriers between conscious and subconscious are lowered during sleep or other **altered states of consciousness.**

subtle energy. Subtle energy is supposed to be nonmaterial life energy in non-Western healing and religious traditions. *See* appendix B.

synapse. At the point where one **neuron** connects with another there exists a synapse or a synaptic junction. The **axon** of one neuron links to the **dendrite** of another at the synapse. The axon and dendrite do not actually touch. Instead **neurotransmitter** chemicals carry the signal across the synaptic gap from the axon to the receiving dendrite.

telepathy. Telepathy is the psychic skill of reading another person's thoughts.

theory of everything, or TOE. *See* **grand unified theory.**

theta brainwaves. Brainwaves that fall into the frequency range of about 4 **Hz** to about 7 **Hz** are theta brainwaves. When your brain is producing primarily theta brainwaves as the dominant frequency range, you are in a trance state or in a light sleep state.

time's arrow. Time's arrow is the analogy for the physics concept that we can only travel in one direction along the time dimension. That is, we can only move from the present to the future and cannot move from the present to the past. The analogy is that time flows like a river and we cannot move upstream.

TOE. *See* **theory of everything.**

transverse wave. A transverse wave oscillates in a direction perpendicular to the direction of motion of the wave. Light is a transverse electromagnetic wave, as are waves in the ocean, in that the water bobs up and down while the waves themselves move forward from ocean to shoreline.

two-slit interference experiment. The two-slit experiment conclusively proved that light must be a wave and not a particle because it demonstrated that light interferes with itself as it passes through two narrow slits. *See* chapter 9 for a discussion of this experiment.

vector. A vector quantity is any that has both a magnitude and a direction associated with it. For example, in physics, speed is a **scalar** quantity that reflects how fast you are going. But velocity in physics is a vector quantity because it means not only how fast you are going, but also in what direction you're moving.

velocity. In physics, velocity means not only how fast you are going, but also in what direction you're moving. It is a **vector** not a **scalar.**

wavelength. The wavelength of a wave is a measure of the distance from maximum value to the next maximum value of the wave's oscillation. In ocean waves, for example, it refers to the distance between crests of waves. It is generally inversely related to the **frequency** of the wave in that the faster the frequency the shorter the distance between wave crests.

wave-particle duality. Wave-particle duality is an expression for the fact that particles exhibit both the characteristics of waves and the characteristics of solid particles, depending on the specifics of how they are observed.

weighting value. In an artificial **neural network**—a simulation of a neural network—a separate weighting value is applied to each connection between **neurons.** If the weighting value is positive, that connection is an **excitatory** one. If the weighting value is negative, that connection is an **inhibitory** one.

white noise. White noise refers to noise that is random across the entire range of human hearing, with approximately equal noise volumes at each frequency level. *See also* **pink noise.**

wormhole. A wormhole is a postulated mechanism for moving outside of our physical universe and then returning to it in a different location. It is sometimes hypothesized that black holes may be openings to such wormholes. The idea is that if you could successfully traverse such a wormhole, you could travel nearly instantaneously to locations all over the universe.

zero-point energy, or **ZPE.** Zero-point energy is that energy that fills the vacuum of empty space where there is no matter or other outside source of energy. It's an active area of research for both cheap and abundant energy systems and for transportation drives for space travel, but is not well understood at this point.

ZPE. *See* **zero-point energy.**

Suggested Reading List

The titles suggested below are not intended to be all-inclusive—that would require a substantial library of works! But these are books and other material I found especially clear and useful in understanding the topics of this book and in facilitating my own journey into strangeness. The list is necessarily incomplete, but I believe these titles may assist you as well. They're organized by general topic, with some books falling under more than one topic.

Biology

Holland, John H., *Emergence: from Chaos to Order*, Helix Books, Addison-Wesley, Reading, Mass., 1998.

Johnson, George, *In the Palaces of Memory: How We Build the Worlds inside Our Heads*, Vintage Books, Random House, Inc., New York, 1991.

Lipton, Bruce, *The Biology of Belief: Unleashing the Power of Consciousness, Matter, and Miracles*, Mountain of Love/Elite Books, Santa Rosa, Calif., 2005.

Pearsall, Paul, *The Heart's Code: Tapping the Wisdom and Power of Our Heart Energy*, Broadway Books, New York, 1998.

Sheldrake, Rupert, *A New Science of Life: The Hypothesis of Morphic Resonance*, Park Street Press, Rochester, Vt., 1981, 1987, 1995.

———, *The Presence of the Past: Morphic Resonance and the Habits of Nature*, Park Street Press, Rochester, Vt., 1988, 1995.

———, *Seven Experiments That Could Change the World*, 2d ed., Park Street Press, Rochester, Vt., 2002.

Strassman, Rick, M.D., *DMT: The Spirit Molecule*, Park Street Press, Rochester, Vt., 2001.

Varela, Francisco J., editor, *Sleeping, Dreaming, and Dying: An Exploration of Consciousness with The Dalai Lama,* Wisdom Publications, Boston, Mass., 1997.

Channeling and Communicating with the Dead

Edward, John, *After Life: Answers from the Other Side,* Princess Books, New York, 2004.

———, *Crossing Over: The Stories behind the Stories,* Jodere Group, San Diego, 2001.

Mateu, Lysa, *Psychic Diaries: Connecting with Who You Are, Why You're Here, and What Lies Beyond,* Harper Entertainment, HarperCollins, New York, 2003.

Moen, Bruce, *Afterlife Knowledge Guidebook: A Manual for the Art of Retrieval and Afterlife Exploration,* Hampton Roads Publishing Company, Charlottesville, Va., 2005.

Moody, Raymond A., *Life After Life,* 1st HarperSanFrancisco ed., HarperSanFrancisco, San Francisco, Calif., 2001.

Roberts, Jane, (channeled by), notes by Robert F. Butts, *The Nature of Personal Reality: Specific, Practical Techniques for Solving Everyday Problems and Enriching the Life You Know,* Prentice-Hall, Englewood Cliffs, N.J., 1974.

———, (channeled by) notes by Robert F. Butts, *Seth Speaks: The Eternal Validity of the Soul,* New World Library, San Raphael, Calif., 1994.

Roman, Sanaya and Duane Packer, *Opening to Channel: How to Connect with Your Guide,* H. J. Kramer, Inc., Tiburon, Calif., 1987.

Schwartz, Gary E. and Linda Russek, G. S., *The Living Energy Universe: A Fundamental Discovery that Transforms Science and Medicine,* Hampton Roads Publishing Company, Charlottesville, Va., 1999.

Schwartz, Gary E. and William L. Simon, *The Afterlife Experiments: Breakthrough Scientific Evidence of Life After Death,* Pocket Books, New York, 2002.

———, *The Truth about Medium: Extraordinary Experiments with the Real Allison DuBois of NBC Medium and Other Remarkable Psychics,* Hampton Roads Publishing Company, Charlottesville, Va., 2005.

Consciousness

Baars, Bernard J., *In the Theater of Consciousness: The Workspace of the Mind,* Oxford University Press, New York, 1997.

Damasio, Antonio R., *The Feeling of What Happens: Body and Emotion in the Making of Consciousness,* Harcourt Brace, New York, 1999.

Grof, Stanislav, *The Adventure of Self-Discovery: Dimensions of Consciousness and New Perspectives in Psychotherapy and Inner Exploration,* State University of New York Press, Albany, N.Y., 1988.

Grof, Stanislav with Hal Zina Bennett, *The Holotropic Mind: The Three Levels of Human Consciousness and How They Shape Our Lives,* HarperSanFrancisco, San Francisco, Calif., 1993.

Johnson, George, *In the Palaces of Memory: How We Build the Worlds inside Our Heads,* Vintage Books, Random House, Inc., New York, 1991.

Jung, Carl, edited by Joseph Campbell, translated by R. F. C. Hull, *The Portable Jung,* Viking Press, New York, 1971.

Lipton, Bruce, *The Biology of Belief: Unleashing the Power of Consciousness, Matter, and Miracles,* Mountain of Love/Elite Books, Santa Rosa, Calif., 2005.

Sheldrake, Rupert; Terence McKenna, and Ralph Abraham, *Chaos, Creativity, and Cosmic Consciousness*, Park Street Press, Rochester, Vt., 1992, 2001.

Targ, Russell, *Limitless Mind: A Guide to Remote Viewing and Transformation of Consciousness*, New World Library, Novato, Calif., 2004.

Targ, Russell and Jane Katra, *Miracles of Mind: Exploring Nonlocal Consciousness and Spiritual Healing*, New World Library, Novato, Calif., 1998, 1999.

Varela, Francisco J., editor, *Sleeping, Dreaming, and Dying: An Exploration of Consciousness with The Dalai Lama*, Wisdom Publications, Boston, Mass., 1997.

Vasiliev, L. L., *Experiments in Mental Suggestion*, Hampton Roads Publishing Company, Charlottesville, Va., 2002.

Walker, Evan Harris, *The Physics of Consciousness: The Quantum Mind and the Meaning of Life*, Perseus Books, Cambridge, Mass., 2000.

Wilber, Ken, *Integral Psychology: Consciousness, Spirit, Psychology, Therapy*, Shambhala Publications, Inc., Boston, Mass., 2000.

―――, *The Spectrum of Consciousness*, 20th anniversary edition, Theosophical Publishing House, Wheaton, Ill., 1977, 1993.

Woolger, Roger J., *Other Lives, Other Selves: A Jungian Psychotherapist Discovers Past Lives*, Doubleday, New York, 1987.

Energy Work, Chakras, Kundalini, etc.

Bardon, Franz, translated by Gerhard Hanswille, and Franca Gallo, edited by Ken Johnson, *Initiation into Hermetics: The Path of the True Adept*, Merkur Publishing, Inc., Salt Lake City, Utah, 1956, 1962, 1971, and 1999.

Bartlett, Sarah, *Auras and How to Read Them*, Collins & Brown, Ltd., London, 2000.

Bruce, Robert, *Astral Dynamics: How to Travel out of Body*, Hampton Roads Publishing Company, Charlottesville, Va., 1999.

Gerber, Richard, *A Practical Guide to Vibrational Medicine: Energy Healing and Spiritual Transformation*, Quill, HarperCollins, New York, 2001.

Krishna, Gopi, *The Awakening of Kundalini*, The Institute for Consciousness Research and Kundalini Research Foundation, Ltd., Flesherton, Ontario, Canada, 1975.

Oschman, James L., *Energy Medicine: The Scientific Basis*, Churchill Livingstone, Elsevier Ltd., Edinburgh, Scotland, 2000.

Paulson, Genevieve Lewis, *Kundalini and the Chakras*, Llewellyn Publications, St. Paul, Minn., 2002.

Webster, Richard, *Aura Reading for Beginners: Develop Your Psychic Awareness for Health & Success*, Llewellyn Publications, St. Paul, Minn., 2002.

Healing

Childre, Doc and Howard Martin, with Donna Beech, *The Heartmath Solution*, HarperSanFrancisco, San Francisco, Calif., 1999.

Dale, Cyndi, *Advanced Chakra Healing: Energy Mapping on the Four Pathways*, Crossing Press, Ten Speed Press, Berkeley, Calif., 2005.

―――, *New Chakra Healing: Activate Your 32 Energy Centers*, Llewellyn Worldwide, St. Paul, Minn., 2005.

―――, *New Chakra Healing: The Revolutionary 32-Center Energy System*, Llewellyn Publications, St. Paul, Minn., 2002.

Gattuso, Joan, *A Course in Love: Powerful Teachings on Love, Sex, and Personal Fulfill-ment*, HarperSanFranciso, San Francisco, Calif., 1996.

Gerber, Richard, *Vibrational Medicine: The #1 Handbook of Subtle-Energy Therapies*, 3rd Edition, Bear & Company, Rochester, Vt., 2001.

———, *A Practical Guide to Vibrational Medicine: Energy Healing and Spiritual Trans-formation*, Quill, HarperCollins, New York, 2001.

Goldner, Diane, *Infinite Grace: Where the Worlds of Science and Spiritual Healing Meet*, Hampton Roads Publishing Company, Charlottesville, Va., 1999.

Gordon, Richard, *Quantum-Touch: The Power to Heal*, Revised Edition, North Atlan-tic Books, Berkeley, Calif., 2002.

Myss, Caroline, *Anatomy of the Spirit: The Seven Stages of Power and Healing*, Three Rivers Press, New York, 1997.

Oschman, James L., *Energy Medicine: The Scientific Basis*, Churchill Livingstone, Elsevier Ltd., Edinburgh, Scotland, 2000.

Pearsall, Paul, *The Heart's Code: Tapping the Wisdom and Power of Our Heart Energy*, Broadway Books, New York, 1998.

Pert, Candace B., *Molecules of Emotion: The Science behind Mind-Body Medicine*, Touchstone Books, Simon & Schuster, New York, 1997.

Hemi-Sync and The Monroe Institute

Atwater, F. Holmes, *Captain of My Ship, Master of My Soul: Living with Guidance*, Hampton Roads Publishing Company, Charlottesville, Va., 2001.

DeMarco, Frank, *Muddy Tracks: Exploring an Unsuspected Reality*, Hampton Roads Publishing Company, Charlottesville, Va., 2001.

McKnight, Rosalind A., *Cosmic Journey: My Out-of-Body Explorations with Robert A. Monroe*, Hampton Roads Publishing Company, Charlottesville, Va., 1999.

———, *Soul Journeys: My Guided Tours through the Afterlife*, Hampton Roads Publish-ing Company, Charlottesville, Va., 2005.

Monroe, Robert A., *Far Journeys*, Doubleday, Garden City, N.Y., 1985.

———, *Journeys Out of the Body*, Doubleday, Garden City, N.Y., 1971.

———, *Ultimate Journey*, Doubleday, New York, 1994.

Russell, Ronald, editor, *Focusing the Whole Brain: Transforming Your Life with Hemi-spheric Synchronization*, with enclosed audio CD, Hampton Roads Publishing Company, Charlottesville, Va., 2004.

Meditation

Bruce, Robert, *Astral Dynamics: How to Travel out of Body*, Hampton Roads Publish-ing Company, Charlottesville, Va., 1999.

———, *Practical Psychic Self-Defense: Understanding and Surviving Unseen Influences*, Hampton Roads Publishing Company, Charlottesville, Va., 2002.

Castaneda, Carlos, *The Teachings of Don Juan: A Yaqui Way of Knowledge*, (30th Anniversary Edition), University of California Press, Berkeley, Calif., 1968, 1998.

Edward, John, *Developing Your Own Psychic Powers*, audiobook—cassette and/or audio CD, Hay House, Carlsbad, Calif., 2000.

Gyatso, Geshe Kelsang, *The Meditation Handbook: A Step-by-Step Manual, Providing a Clear and Practical Guide to Buddhist Meditation,* Tharpa Publications, Glen Spey, N.Y., 1995, 2001.

Johnson, Robert A., *Inner Work: Using Dreams & Active Imagination for Personal Growth,* HarperSanFrancisco, San Francisco, Calif., 1986.

Liao, Wayson, translator and commentator, *T'ai Chi Classics,* Shambhala Publications, Inc., Boston, Mass., 1977, 1990.

Wong, Eva, *The Shambhala Guide to Taoism: A Complete Introduction to the History, Philosophy, and Practice of an Ancient Chinese Spiritual Tradition,* Shambhala Publications Inc., Boston, Mass., 1997.

Mysticism and Revelation

Barks, Coleman, translator and editor, *Rumi: The Book of Love: Poems of Ecstasy and Longing,* HarperSanFrancisco, and New York, 2003.

―――, translator, *The Essential Rumi,* New Expanded Edition, HarperSanFrancisco, San Francisco, Calif., 1995.

―――, translator, *The I Ching or Book of Changes,* Third Edition, Princeton University Press, Princeton, N.J., 1967.

Hall, Chloe, *Last Hope,* ImaJinn Books, Denver, Colo., 2000.

Housden, Roger, editor, *Risking Everything: 110 Poems of Love and Revelation,* Harmony Books, New York, 2003.

―――, editor, *Ten Poems to Change Your Life,* Harmony Books, New York, 2001.

―――, editor, *Ten Poems to Open Your Heart,* Harmony Books, New York, 2003.

Millay, Edna St. Vincent, *Collected Poems,* Harper and Row Publishers, New York, 1956.

Oliver, Mary, *New and Selected Poems, Volume One,* Beacon Press, Boston, Mass., 1992.

St. John of the Cross, edited by E. Allison Peers, *Dark Night of the Soul,* Doubleday, New York, 1959, 1990.

St. Teresa of Ávila, translated and edited by E. Allison Peers, *Interior Castle,* Doubleday, Garden City, N.Y., 1961.

Wilhelm, Helmut and Richard Wilhelm, *Understanding the I Ching: The Wilhelm Lectures on The Book of Changes,* Princeton University Press, Princeton, N.J., 1960, 1979, 1988, 1995.

Wilhelm, Richard, translator, *The Secret of the Golden Flower: A Chinese Book of Life,* Revised and augmented edition, Harcourt Brace & Company, San Diego, Calif., 1962.

Wing, R. L., *The I Ching Workbook,* Doubleday, Garden City, N.Y., 1979.

Out-of-Body Experiences

Bruce, Robert, *Astral Dynamics: How to Travel out of Body,* Hampton Roads Publishing Company, Charlottesville, Va., 1999.

―――, *Mastering Astral Projection,* Llewellyn Publications, St. Paul, Minn., 2004.

Maclaine, Shirley, *Out on a Limb,* Reissue edition, Bantam, New York, 1986.

McKnight, Rosalind A., *Cosmic Journey: My Out-of-Body Explorations with Robert A. Monroe,* Hampton Roads Publishing Company, Charlottesville, Va., 1999.

Monroe, Robert A., *Far Journeys,* Doubleday, Garden City, N.Y., 1985.

———, *Journeys Out of the Body*, Doubleday, Garden City, N.Y., 1971.

———, *Ultimate Journey*, Doubleday, New York, 1994.

Physics and Cosmology

Aczel, Amir D., *Entanglement: The Greatest Mystery in Physics*, Four Walls Eight Windows, New York, 2002.

Caudill, Maureen, *In Our Own Image*, Oxford University Press, New York, 1992.

Caudill, Maureen and Charles Butler, *Naturally Intelligent Systems*, MIT Press, Cambridge, Mass., 1989.

Goswami, Amit, *The Self-Aware Universe: How Consciousness Creates the Material World*, Jeremy P. Tarcher/Putnam, Penguin Putnam, Inc., New York, 1993.

Greene, Brian, *The Elegant Universe: Superstrings, Hidden Dimensions, and the Quest for the Ultimate Theory*, Vintage Books, New York, 2000, 2003.

———, *The Fabric of the Cosmos: Space, Time, and the Texture of Reality*, Borzoi Books, Alfred A. Knopf, New York, 2004.

Kaku, Michio, *Parallel Worlds: A Journey through Creation, Higher Dimensions, and the Future of the Cosmos*, Doubleday, New York, 2005.

Laszlo, Ervin, *Science and the Akashic Field: An Integral Theory of Everything*, Inner Traditions, Rochester, Vt., 2004.

———, *The Connectivity Hypothesis: Foundations of an Integral Science of Quantum, Cosmos, Life, and Consciousness*, State University of New York Press, Albany, N.Y., 2003.

McTaggart, Lynne, *The Field: The Quest for the Secret Force of the Universe*, HarperCollins Publishing, New York, 2002.

Radin, Dean, *The Conscious Universe: The Scientific Truth of Psychic Phenomena*, HarperCollins Publishers, New York, 1997.

Sheldrake, Rupert; Terence McKenna, and Ralph Abraham, *Chaos, Creativity, and Cosmic Consciousness*, Park Street Press, Rochester, Vt., 1992, 2001.

Talbot, Michael, *Mysticism and the New Physics*, revised edition, Arkana, London, 1981, 1993.

———, *The Holographic Universe: A Remarkable New Theory That Explains the Paranormal Abilities of the Mind, the Latest Frontiers of Physics, and the Unsolved Riddles of Brain and Body*, HarperCollins, New York, 1992.

Walker, Evan Harris, *The Physics of Consciousness: The Quantum Mind and the Meaning of Life*, Perseus Books, Cambridge, Mass., 2000.

Psychokinesis (Spoon-bending, etc.)

Mishlove, Jeffrey, *The PK Man: A True Story of Mind Over Matter*, Hampton Roads Publishing Company, Charlottesville, Va., 2000.

Radin, Dean, *The Conscious Universe: The Scientific Truth of Psychic Phenomena*, HarperCollins Publishers, New York, 1997.

Smith, Paul H., *Reading the Enemy's Mind: Inside Star Gate—America's Psychic Espionage Program*, Forge Books, Tom Doherty and Associates LLC, New York, 2005.

Psychology, Parapsychology, Creativity, and Relationships

Cameron, Julia, *The Artist's Way: A Spiritual Path to Higher Creativity: A Course in Discovering and Recovering Your Creative Self,* Tenth Anniversary Edition, Jeremy P. Tarcher/Putnam, Penguin Putnam Inc., New York, 1992, 2002.

Caudill, Maureen, *Never Say Goodbye,* Bantam Books, New York, 1997.

Gattuso, Joan, *A Course in Love: Powerful Teachings on Love, Sex, and Personal Fulfillment,* HarperSanFranciso, San Francisco, Calif., 1996.

Grof, Stanislav with Hal Zina Bennett, *The Holotropic Mind: The Three Levels of Human Consciousness and How They Shape Our Lives,* HarperSanFrancisco, San Francisco, Calif., 1993.

———, *The Adventure of Self-Discovery: Dimensions of Consciousness and New Perspectives in Psychotherapy and Inner Exploration,* State University of New York Press, Albany, N.Y., 1988.

Hall, Chloe, *Ariel's Dance,* Dorchester Books, New York, 1998.

———, *Last Hope,* ImaJinn Books, Denver, Colo., 2000.

Hall, Marissa, *Affair of Inconvenience,* Silhouette Books, New York, 2001.

James, William, *Writings 1878–1899: Psychology: Briefer Course; The Will to Believe and Other Essays in Popular Psychology; Talks to Teachers on Psychology and to Students on Some of Life's Ideals; Selected Essays,* The Library of America, Penguin Putnam, Inc., New York, 1992.

———, *Writings 1902–1910: The Varieties of Religious Experience; Pragmatism; A Pluralistic Universe; The Meaning of Truth; Some Problems of Philosophy; Essays,* selected and annotated by Bruce Kuklick, Literary Classics of the United States, Viking, New York, 1987.

Johnson, Robert A., *Inner Work: Using Dreams & Active Imagination for Personal Growth,* HarperSanFrancisco, San Francisco, Calif., 1986.

Jung, Carl, edited by Joseph Campbell, translated by R. F. C. Hull, *The Portable Jung,* Viking Press, New York, 1971.

Maclaine, Shirley, *The Camino: A Journey of the Spirit,* Pocket Books, New York, 2000.

Marion, Jim, *Putting on the Mind of Christ: the Inner Work of Christian Spirituality,* Hampton Roads Publishing Company, Charlottesville, Va., 2000.

Myss, Caroline, *Anatomy of the Spirit: The Seven Stages of Power and Healing,* Harmony Books, New York, 1996.

———, *Sacred Contracts: Awakening Your Divine Potential,* Harmony Books, New York, 2002.

Radin, Dean, *The Conscious Universe: The Scientific Truth of Psychic Phenomena,* HarperCollins Publishers, New York, 1997.

Ruiz, Don Miguel, *The Mastery of Love: A Practical Guide to the Art of Relationship,* Amber-Allen Publishing, San Rafael, Calif., 1999.

Ruiz, Don Miguel and Janet Mills, *The Voice of Knowledge: A Practical Guide to Inner Peace,* Amber-Allen Publishing, Berkeley, Calif., 2004.

Steiner, Rudolf, *Theosophy: An Introduction to the Spiritual Processes in Human Life and in the Cosmos,* translated by Catherine E. Creeger, Anthroposophic Press, Hudson, N.Y., 1994.

Tart, Charles T., *Body Mind Spirit: Exploring the Parapsychology of Spirituality*, Hampton Roads Publishing Company, Charlottesville, Va., 1997.

Webster, Richard, *Aura Reading for Beginners: Develop Your Psychic Awareness for Health & Success*, Llewellyn Publications, St. Paul, Minn., 2003.

Wilber, Ken, *Integral Psychology: Consciousness, Spirit, Psychology, Therapy*, Shambhala Publications, Inc. Boston, Mass., 2000.

Woolger, Roger J., *Other Lives, Other Selves: A Jungian Psychotherapist Discovers Past Lives*, Doubleday, New York, 1988.

Religion, Spirituality, and Philosophy

A Course in Miracles: Combined Volume, Foundation for Inner Peace, Glen Elen, Calif., 1992.

Beattie, Antonia and Bill Beattie, *I Ching: Navigate Life's Transitions Using Ancient Oracles of the I Ching*, Barnes and Noble Books, New York, 2004.

Castaneda, Carlos, *The Teachings of Don Juan: A Yaqui Way of Knowledge*, 30th Anniversary Edition, University of California Press, Berkeley, Calif., 1968, 1998.

Das, Lama Surya, *Awakening to the Sacred*, Broadway Books, New York, 1999.

Frost, Gavin and Yvonne Frost, *Tantric Yoga: The Royal Path to Raising Kundalini Power*, Weiser Books, York Beach, Me., 1989.

Gyatso, Geshe Kelsang, *The Meditation Handbook: A Practical Guide to Buddhist Meditation*, Tharpa Publications, Glen Spey, N.Y., 1995.

James, William, *Writings 1878–1899: Psychology: Briefer Course; The Will to Believe and Other Essays in Popular Psychology; Talks to Teachers on Psychology and to Students on Some of Life's Ideals; Selected Essays*, The Library of America, Penguin Putnam, Inc., New York, 1992.

———, *Writings 1902–1910: The Varieties of Religious Experience; Pragmatism; A Pluralistic Universe; The Meaning of Truth; Some Problems of Philosophy; Essays*, selected and annotated by Bruce Kuklick, Literary Classics of the United States, Viking, New York, 1987.

Jung, Carl, edited by Joseph Campbell, translated by R. F. C. Hull, *The Portable Jung*, Viking Press, New York, 1971.

Laszlo, Ervin, Stanislav Grof, and Peter Russell, *The Consciousness Revolution: A Transatlantic Dialogue*, Elf Rock Productions, Las Vegas, Nev., 1999, 2003.

Laszlo, Ervin, *Science and the Reenchantment of the Cosmos: The Rise of the Integral Vision of Reality*, Inner Traditions, Rochester, Vt., 2006.

Marion, Jim, *Putting on the Mind of Christ: the Inner Work of Christian Spirituality*, Hampton Roads Publishing Company, Charlottesville, Va., 2000.

Muller, Wayne, *How, Then, Shall We Live?: Four Simple Questions That Reveal the Beauty and Meaning of Our Lives*, Bantam Books, New York, 1996.

Powers, John, *Introduction to Tibetan Buddhism*, Snow Lion Publications, Ithaca, N.Y., 1995.

Renard, Gary R., *The Disappearance of the Universe: Straight Talk about Illusions, Past Lives, Religion, Sex, Politics, and the Miracles of Forgiveness*, Hay House, Carlsbad, Calif., 2004.

Sogyal, Rinpoche, edited by Patrick Gaffney, and Andrew Harvey, *The Tibetan Book of Living and Dying*, HarperSanFrancisco, San Francisco, Calif., 1992.

Suggested Reading List

Talbot, Michael, *Mysticism and the New Physics*, revised edition, Arkana, London, 1981, 1993.

Tart, Charles T., *Body Mind Spirit: Exploring the Parapsychology of Spirituality*, Hampton Roads Publishing Company, Charlottesville, Va., 1997.

Varela, Francisco J., editor, *Sleeping, Dreaming, and Dying: An Exploration of Consciousness with The Dalai Lama*, Wisdom Publications, Boston, Mass., 1997.

Vogler, Christopher, *The Writer's Journey: Mythic Structure for Writers*, 2nd Edition, Michael Wiese Productions, Studio City, Calif., 1998.

Wilber, Ken, *Integral Psychology: Consciousness, Spirit, Psychology, Therapy*, Shambhala Publications, Inc., Boston, Mass., 2000.

———, *One Taste: Daily Reflections on Integral Spirituality*, Shambhala Publications, Inc., Boston, Mass., 2000.

———, *Sex, Ecology, Spirituality: The Spirit of Evolution*, Second Edition, Revised, Shambhala Publications, Inc., Boston, Mass., 1995, 2000.

———, *The Simple Feeling of Being: Embracing Your True Nature*, Revised Edition, compiled and edited by Mark Palmer, Shambhala Publications, Inc., Boston, Mass., 2004.

———, *A Theory of Everything: An Integral Vision for Business, Politics, Science, and Spirituality*, Shambhala Publications, Inc., Boston, Mass., 2001.

———, *The Spectrum of Consciousness*, 20th anniversary edition, Theosophical Publishing House, Wheaton, Ill., 1977, 1993.

Wilhelm, Richard, translator, *The Secret of the Golden Flower: A Chinese Book of Life*, Revised and augmented edition, Harcourt Brace & Company, San Diego, Calif., 1962.

Wong, Eva, *The Shambhala Guide to Taoism: A Complete Introduction to the History, Philosophy, and Practice of an Ancient Chinese Spiritual Tradition*, Shambhala Publications, Inc., Boston, Mass., 1997.

Zukav, Gary, *The Seat of the Soul*, Simon & Schuster, New York, 1989.

Remote Viewing

Brown, Courtney, *Remote Viewing: The Science and Theory of Nonphysical Perception*, Farsight Press, Atlanta, Ga., 2005.

Buchanon, Lyn, *The Seventh Sense: The Secrets of Remote Viewing as Told by a "Psychic Spy" for the U.S. Military*, Paraview Pocket Books, New York, 2003.

McMoneagle, Joseph, *Remote Viewing Secrets: A Handbook*, Hampton Roads Publishing Company, Charlottesville, Va., 2000.

———, *Mind Trek: Exploring Consciousness, Time, and Space Through Remote Viewing*, Hampton Roads Publishing Company, Charlottesville, Va., 1993, 1997.

———, *The Stargate Chronicles: Memoirs of a Psychic Spy*, Hampton Roads Publishing Company, Charlottesville, Va., 2002.

———, *The Ultimate Time Machine*, Hampton Roads Publishing Company, Charlottesville, Va., 1998.

Smith, Paul H., *Reading the Enemy's Mind: Inside Star Gate—America's Psychic Espionage Program*, Forge Books, Tom Doherty and Associates LLC, New York, 2005.

Targ, Russell and Harold E. Puthoff, *Mind-Reach: Scientists Look at Psychic Abilities*, Hampton Roads Publishing Company, Charlottesville, Va., 2005.

Tart, Charles T., Harold E. Puthoff, and Russell Targ, editors, *Mind at Large: IEEE Symposia on the Nature of Extrasensory Perception*, Hampton Roads Publishing Company, Charlottesville, Va., 2002.

Spirit Guides and Guidance

Atwater, F. Holmes, *Captain of My Ship, Master of My Soul: Living with Guidance*, Hampton Roads Publishing Company, Charlottesville, Va., 2001.

DeMarco, Frank, *Muddy Tracks: Exploring an Unsuspected Reality*, Hampton Roads Publishing Company, Charlottesville, Va., 2001.

Hall, Chloe, *Last Hope*, ImaJinn Books, Denver, Colo., 2000.

Roberts, Jane, (channeled by), notes by Robert F. Butts, *The Nature of Personal Reality: Specific, Practical Techniques for Solving Everyday Problems and Enriching the Life You Know*, Prentice-Hall, Englewood Cliffs, N.J., 1974.

———, (channeled by), notes by Robert F. Butts, *Seth Speaks: The Eternal Validity of the Soul*, New World Library, San Raphael, Calif., 1994.

Wiemer, Liza M., *Extraordinary Guidance: How to Connect with Your Spiritual Guides*, Three Rivers Press, New York, 1997.

Index

About the Author

Maureen Caudill graduated *summa cum laude* in physics from the University of Connecticut, and received a master's degree from Cornell University. A former senior scientist for a major Department of Defense contractor specializing in artificial intelligence and neural networks, she holds three patents for concept-based search and retrieval technologies, ontological parsing technologies, and for clustering techniques in document analysis. She has written general science books and textbooks in the fields of neural networks and robotics for MIT Press and Oxford University Press. She also has published several romance novels for multiple publishers including Bantam Books. Several years ago she discovered her abilities as a psychic while attending a weeklong residential retreat at The Monroe Institute in Faber, Virginia. She is an accredited Outreach trainer for TMI, and a member of their Professional Division. She has personally experienced all the psychic phenomena discussed in the book and is now a practicing psychic, leading workshops in the U.S. and Canada on developing psychic talent and learning to access altered states of consciousness safely and reliably. She is an experienced public speaker, and has lectured internationally to wide acclaim.

Hampton Roads Publishing Company

. . . for the evolving human spirit

HAMPTON ROADS PUBLISHING COMPANY publishes books on a variety of subjects, including metaphysics, spirituality, health, visionary fiction, and other related topics.

For a copy of our latest trade catalog, call toll-free, 800-766-8009, or send your name and address to:

HAMPTON ROADS PUBLISHING COMPANY, INC.
1125 STONEY RIDGE ROAD • CHARLOTTESVILLE, VA 22902
e-mail: hrpc@hrpub.com • www.hrpub.com